AF572324

Books by Mark Adams

Glimpses of an American Century

Price and Price Policies
(as Associate of Walton Hamilton)

Portrait of a People's Senator
(with Creekmore Fath)

How to Read the Wall Street Journal
(with Franklin Jones, Sr., and Ann Adams)

How to Live with an Uneasy Conscience
(with Bernard Rapoport)

How to Write So People Will Know What You're Trying to Say

How to Tell If It's Art

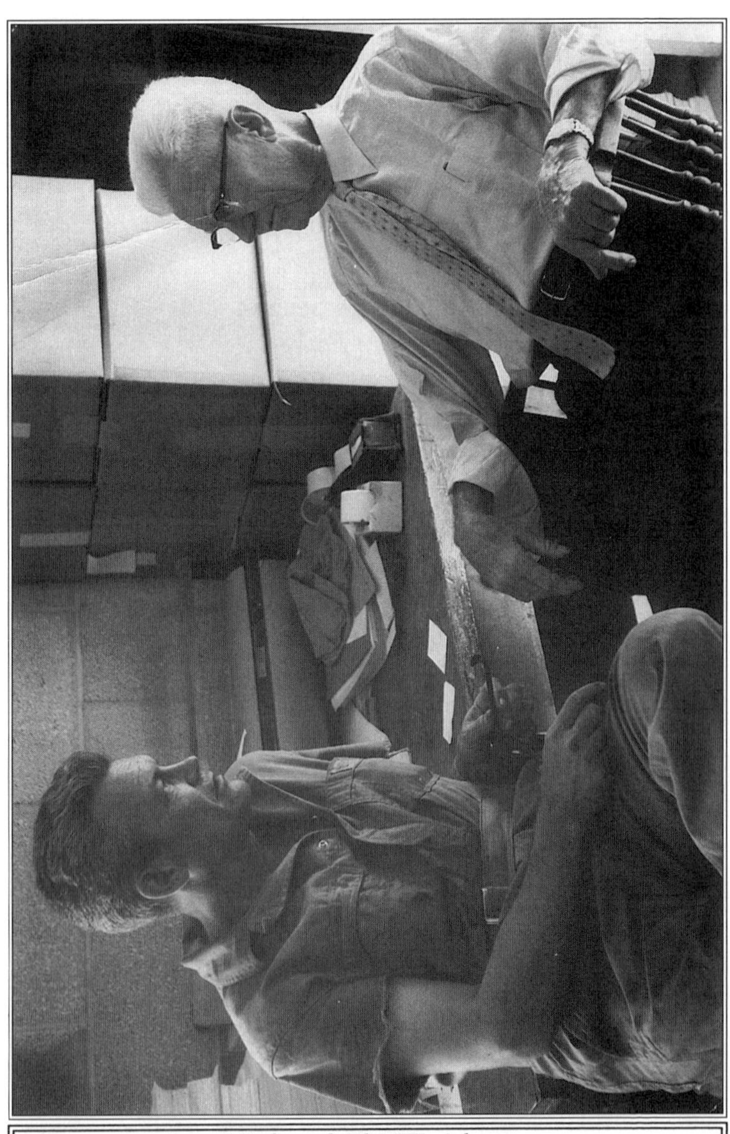

Mark and Silas W. Adams
Chaparral Press, Austin, Texas, ca. 1958
(Photograph by Russell Lee)

GLIMPSES

of an
AMERICAN CENTURY

by a mouse
in the halls
of the mighty

MARK ADAMS

PACKRAT PRESS
Oak Harbor, Washington

Library of Congress Cataloging-in-Publication Data

Adams, Mark, 1910-1997.
Glimpses of an American century: by a mouse in the halls of the mighty / Mark Adams. -- 1st ed.
p. ca.
Includes index
ISBN: 0-915433-19-2
1. United States--History--20th century. 2. Adams, Mark, 1910-1997. I. Title.
E741.A58 1997
973.9--dc21 97-23605
CIP

First edition.

Printed in the United States of America

Dedicated to my daughters, SASKIA and KATHLEEN, and my grandchildren, TERRAN, KELLY, BECKY, MITCH, JIMMY, WESLEY, and SAMANTHA -- and to their five billion human contemporaries sharing Earth.

ACKNOWLEDGMENTS

As I sat myself down to describe these *Glimpses* for our changing world, I realized how near totally I had relied on the help of others who had opened my eyes upon this earth and its people and their ways, thus helping me to understand and so to perceive the images I seek now to convey to you.

I want to acknowledge the contributions of these others. But due acknowledgment is difficult because my witting and unwitting aides in this effort have been so many that I despair of mentioning even a tiny fraction of them here. Nevertheless I would like to acknowledge the help of a few of them -- all important to me -- by name.

My initial and basic view of our world was shaped, quite naturally, by my parents, S.W. and Ora Adams. Both had been schoolteachers before I was born, so throughout my childhood they encouraged me to seek the guidance of a literally innumerable host of other thinkers and scientists and poets who have, through books and journals, severally and sequentially gifted me with still wider views of my world.

After I left home it was my good fortune to encounter more teachers adept at opening for me windows on a wider world, including, importantly for me, Carey Thompson and Bob Montgomery at the University of Texas and Walton Hamilton who taught at Yale and in New Deal Washington.

Beyond schoolrooms I learned through specific collaborations with Otto Mullinax, Herman Wright, Creekmore Fath, Franklin Jones, Sr., and Walter Prescott Webb. For newly opened windows on the world, I owe much to each of them.

And working in friendship in one role or another on one project or another with many other Texans and Americans through the years, I gained more and valued additional glimpses into features of my world -- the one I devise to you herein.

I mention only a few of them here, alphabetically by name. Nina Allen, Howe Bancroft, Bob Barton, Ann Beard, Hank Brown, Phil Brown, Cmdr. Colin Campbell-Horsfall (RN), Kathleen and Willena Casey, Al Chang, Carl Chelf, Clay

Cochran, Minnie Fisher Cunningham, Chris Dixie, Frank Dobie, Carl Duaine, Ronnie Dugger, Bob Eckhardt, Parke Engle, Glen Evans, John Fischer, Louis Franke, Daniel Garber, Henry Gonzalez, Web Hays, Elmo and Jennie Hegman, Russ and Jean Lee, Byron Lockhart, Val Lorwin, Henry McCarter, John McCully, Kenneth MacLeish, Maury Maverick, Sr., Maury Maverick, Jr., Gladys Montgomery, Pearl Morris, Sarah Payne, Bill Pool, Ed Pranger, H.Y. Price, John Provence, Al Ramirez, Barney Rapoport, Margaret Reading, Walter Richter, Jimmy Rodriguez, Fred Schmidt, John Simpson, Cmdr. Daniel Fletcher Smith (USN), J. Edwin Smith, Rhea Starnes, Chuck Stevenson, Coke Stevenson, Joe Storm, Roy Stryker, Tommy Sutherland, Irene Till, John Vachon, Dave Weichselbaum, Margaret Willis, Brown Woolley, Ralph Yarborough.

To each friend named in this patchwork sampling -- and to the numberless and nameless others who have contributed to provisions of this testament -- herewith my acknowledgments ... and my sincere thanks.

Mark Adams

Editor's Note

When Mark Adams died January 18, 1997, he had almost finished this book.

In finishing it after his death, I wrote some connective passages. I have put these in italics and in the third person so the reader can tell my words from Mark's.

Ann Adams
Oak Harbor
March 20, 1997

Mark Adams Chronology

1910	Born March 20 in Lindale, Texas, to Silas Walter and Ora Woolley Adams.
1924-1927	Worked with his father on a number of Texas weekly newspapers.
1927-28	Attended Texas A&M in College Station.
1928-29	Attended Pennsylvania Academy of Fine Arts in Philadelphia.
1929-34	Attended the University of Texas intermittently, while working with his father on the *Gladewater Journal*, a weekly newspaper in the Texas oil fields.
1931	Displeased the Governor of Texas for opposing him in print. He and his father were threatened with prison for libel.
1934	Worked in Austin as aide to Texas House Speaker Coke Stevenson while the legislature was in session.
1934-35	Member of the Progressive Democrats at the University of Texas.
1935	Married Willena Casey January 18 in Austin, Texas.
1935-1937	Worked in Washington, D.C., as an economist on the Cabinet Committee on Price Policy.

1937	Birth of Saskia, his first child, March 23, in Washington, D.C.
1938-40	Worked as Information Specialist for Farm Security Administration in Washington, D.C.
1940	Returned to Texas to work with his father on the weekly *Jefferson Jimplecute.*
1941	Worked as Information Specialist for Farm Security, March to October. Worked for Office of Strategic Services October to December.
1942	After Pearl Harbor was assigned to the staff of the U.S. Senate Committee on Patents.
July 1942- Oct. 1945	Served in the U.S. Navy on aircraft carriers in both oceans.
1948	Birth of Kathleen, his second child, in Austin, Texas, October 6.
1945-1977	Worked in Austin as a printer and political writer in the liberal movement in Texas. Printed books in his own shops.
1959-1971	Worked as technical writer at the Bureau of Reclamation in Austin (second job).
1977	After retirement, left Texas, heading west with his mobile print shop.
1977-78	Lived in Albuquerque, N.M., doing odd jobs and printing his own writing.

1978-82	Lived in Everett, Washington, doing odd jobs and printing his own writing.
1979	Married Ann Price in Everett.
1982-97	Settled in Oak Harbor, Whidbey Island, Washington. Built Packrat Press and published books there.
1997	Died January 18 in Coupeville, Whidbey Island, Washington.

CONTENTS

ILLUSTRATIONS

GLIMPSES
OF AN AMERICAN CENTURY

INTRODUCTION

A Map of My World

Now, in my 87th year, and drawing largely on recollections of my own experiences, I am writing a history of my people during my century.

I propose a history of the American people through this twentieth century -- which saw their dream of personal prosperity as citizens of a political democracy approach fulfillment near mid-century and then, within a generation, plunge into a decline ... which continues.

Of course I have misgivings about my worthiness to undertake a history of such broad concern and grave import. I am a common man. I have no academic credentials to attest learning; I am not even a college graduate, much less a claimant to honors in History. I have no place among leaders and achievers of note -- I have never been rich; I have never been powerful; I am no sort of a hero; I have never molded public opinion in a way to suggest I was a policy maker. And I am no such egomaniac as to be blind to these limitations.

But here I go.

(1) I rationalize.

I ask myself a rhetorical question: Who better to tell the story of our common people than a common man? What better criterion for judging reality than common sense? And who better to write of the twentieth century than an octogenarian who has lived through most of it -- certainly through the eras I think most critical (except for the current unresolved crises).

(2) I evade.

I point out that I do not propose a *definitive* history of the American people through this century; so if I fall short of reaching that goal for my handful of readers, they can fall back on any number of other books from among the two or three million new titles informed sources tell me are published in a single year -- for instance John Kenneth Galbraith's magnificent

Journey Through Economic Time and Barnet and Cavanagh's perceptive and sweeping *Global Dreams,* both of which appeared in 1994.

(3) I disavow responsibility to readers en masse.

I cannot imagine mass readership for this book. Instead I reach for justification by association -- claiming a kinship of motivation with old Bernal Diaz.

Bernal was a soldier with Cortez in the conquest of Mexico from Day One to triumph. Growing old in the service, he finally retired to a hacienda in backwater Guatemala. There, in his eighties, he got peed off at the grandiloquent -- and somewhat slanted -- histories of the conquest written by prestigious historians of the day (guided by a cultivated awareness of the politics of attracting royal favor, not by knowledge of the blood and sweat of actual events). So Bernal sat himself down and wrote a *Historia Verdadera* based on his own recollections. He provided copies to a few friends in Mexico City, but the book was not published until 1632, a half century later. Nevertheless his *Historia* has become the most important source on the era for modern historians. But that's neither here nor there for me -- I am not claiming achievement by association, just kinship of motivation. Like old Bernal I am not motivated by hope of publishing success; I am having my say for my own reasons.

And lo, my intended book is now in your hands.

This book attempts to outline the American people's adjustment to their world through this century. In doing so it draws heavily on my personal recollections, but it is not an autobiography. Intended focus is always on the relationship of our people to their environment and their times, not the personal adventures of this spectator.

I attempt to tell this story of adjustments by presenting a series of significant tableaux which convey, in total, a panoramic view of our people and the world in which we all live -- as I have seen it. Shall we say a montage of snapshots? And naturally, if the snapshots are to convey an overall view, they must be placed in relation to one another in a fairly coherent pattern -- must be joined together in such a way as to indicate where each image fits into the whole picture. Herein the autobiographical bits are used simply as an organizing framework for displaying the montage.

Creating the montage seems to me analogous to the work of a land surveyor -- with transit angles and linear distances measured from a basic datum (a known location) plotted to yield, in sum, a useful map. I have used the chronology of my life to identify roughly the basic datums -- the knowable locations -- from which I read the transit angles and made chain measurements. But I think of myself only as a sanely self-aware -- and fallible but honest -- surveyor attempting to make a map that may be of use to others trying to make their way upon terrain I have mapped. This book is in no sense a biography of a historically important person.

I have called the five sections of the book "datums" because they describe the eras and turning points in my life from which I swung my transit and measured distances for a time.

In Datum I, I describe family sources which shaped my perception of my people and my times when I was a boy in small-town East Texas.

Datum II describes my education as a journeyman printer, my schooling beyond the home, and my first experience with official power that undermines democracy in the early tumultuous years of the Great Depression.

Datum III describes the widening and hardening of my perceptions during the New Deal, when I spent some years in Washington, D.C., as a junior brain truster in the Roosevelt Administration.

Datum IV describes the sharpened (and somewhat embittered) perceptions accompanying my service in the U.S. Navy during World War II, and the generation or so of struggle which followed the war, up to my retirement.

Datum V covers my final perceptions arising from events (not many) and influences (some horrifying) that modified my views (increasingly obstinate) during my "golden years."

Most of the materials in this book are taken from letters and other oddments written to friends long ago in which I discussed in other contexts events which concern me now. These are interlarded with introductory and connective passages and things written just for this book, to give it shape and continuity.

I have kept editing of the older manuscripts to a minimum, thinking that to rewrite now, to make the material fit present purposes, would distort what I was thinking then.

I hope the reader will find both the content and style of succeeding chapters more lighthearted than this laborious introduction might lead them to expect.

MARK ADAMS
Oak Harbor, Washington
January 1997

DATUM I

Coordinates of a Natal Homeland and Familial Hearth

Chapter 1

Swimming in the Gene Pool

I was born human March 20, 1910, in Lindale, Texas, USA, Latitude 36° 31' 40" North, Longitude 95° 24' 38" West, and have lived for 86 years. That makes me absolutely unique, of course; of no other organism in the many billion year history of the world can this be said.

However, reluctant as I may be to admit it, my uniqueness was, is, and forever must remain a matter of elegant inconsequence in the history of humanity's survival on this globe. At the time I was born, the human race had already adjusted and survived for a million years or so -- depends on at what point in its evolution you may choose to identify the evolving organism as a distinct species. And in 1910 the global population of the species had already reached about 1.7 billion. And certainly Lindale, Texas, would have been hard to find on even the most detailed map of the western segment of the northern hemisphere of this globe. So my 86 years made me witness to only a negligible fraction of human history to be seen from the narrow corner of the world within my ken.

On the other hand, the very facts that rob my life of consequence from the standpoint of its uniqueness lend back significance as an *example* -- a case history -- indicating the way mankind has adjusted and survived over long epochs on all the lands of this earth.

So let us understand the processes of adjustment before we examine the nitty-gritty of their functioning -- as I have seen it.

My understanding of these processes I described a few years ago in a [Last Will and] *Testament* addressed to my children and grandchildren. I do not think I could explain it more clearly or fully now; so I include here that description written earlier.

"

Dear Young Ones:

Scientists tell us that somewhere back in the dimness of earth time -- several billion years ago -- an atmosphere formed around earth and the sun's energy started the great water cycle, evaporating water from the seas and forming clouds, which were struck through with lightning (just as all clouds are now). The lightning catalyzed some chemical reactions among the oxygen, carbon dioxide, nitrogen, and water vapors of the atmosphere -- simple carbon-hydrogen-oxygen-nitrogen compounds we call organic because they are the stuff of which organisms are made.

In the water solution, reactions among these compounds continued until very complex compounds we call nucleic acids were formed, and these in turn interacted until somehow still more complex chains of nucleic acids we call RNA molecules formed.

The thing about an RNA molecule is that it has the power to take loose ions from the solutions around it and make another molecule like itself, in whole or in part.

You have read in life science texts about replication of RNA. We do not understand exactly how these first steps took place, although some scientists working with Dr. Harold Urey and another group working with Dr. Carl Sagan have been able to take an earth-model laboratory shot through with artificial lightning and duplicate the process as far as an amino acid stage.

But certainly a time came when a community of these replicating RNA molecules, in some microscopic part of the waters, evolved into a DNA molecule and under its leadership built a wall around the community which thus set itself apart from the rest of the sea full of solutions and made itself a living cell -- which in turn was capable of creating other completely walled communities -- living cells -- like itself.

Thus life began.

And notice something very important. That giant step which was the beginning of life was not a matter of a beginning for new chemical processes but a beginning for a form of *organiza-*

tion of those processes.

And notice also that air and water's usefulness -- as source and solvent for chemical processes -- made them vital elements in the very beginning of life.

And notice again that from its very beginning the energy for the processes of life came from our sun -- starting with the initial evaporation, clouds, and lightning and including photosynthesis in early cells.

Evolution: Millions of Years of Solitude

After more millions of years some living cells began to gather in communities which walled themselves into cooperating groups and thus became multicell creatures.

Note again the basic change was in the form of organization -- with *specialization* of members of the group.

And after that came still more complex creatures with nervous systems, and then creatures with backbones called vertebrates -- creatures like modern fish.

All this was in an environment of waters. But finally some plant lifted partly out of the water into the air (where the carbon-dioxide-sunlight mix was richer) while it kept roots in the water (where the mineral mix was richer). And thus combining richer resources above and below the water line, this plant outgrew all previous plants.

And shortly afterward some fish which had long used its fins to crawl along the bottom of the lake or sea as it browsed for food tied up a package of sea water inside its skin (things dissolved in our plasma and in sea water have about the same concentration even now) and crawled ashore with it (where the food grazing and oxygen supply were richer). We call such creatures amphibians.

The amphibian had to return to the water to lay its eggs for hatching. But later some amphibian learned to package its eggs in waterproof shells also, so even the hatching could occur on land. Thus it became a reptile. And these reptiles could stay on the food-and-oxygen-rich land all their lives, just replenishing the water supply for the solutions inside their skins from time to time by drinking from streams or pools.

The reptiles, including such dramatic examples as the dinosaurs, ruled the earth for millions of years. The system of packaging and replenishing their water supply served well enough. The processes of change -- mutation -- and competition for survival hinged on other, less basic, factors.

Finally some animals developed which not only maintained their internal water solutions at proper concentrations through replenishment -- drinking -- but maintained those solutions at the best temperature for life's chemical reactions with built-in thermostats; we call them warm-blooded animals. (This increased the need for water because warm-blooded animals use an evaporative cooling system to avoid internal overheat.)

And then some of these animals developed a system of hatching eggs not only kept moist but also kept warm and protected inside themselves until the embryos were highly developed -- and then feeding the newborn with milk. We call them mammals.

And finally man became the most successful mammal.

Mind-Mutations: Millennia of Survivals

With the appearance of man, substituting mind-adaptations which can take place in a few days or years for bodily adaptations which take millennia, the processes of change (mutation) and of competition for survival sped up.

Instead of growing a longer arm, man learned to lengthen his reach by picking up a club; and instead of growing stronger and sharper claws, man learned to put sharp stones on the end of the club. And then he lengthened his reach still farther by learning to throw the club, which thereupon became a spear. And then again he lengthened his reach by strengthening his throwing arm with special tools -- first an atl-atl (spear-throwing stick) and then a bow which threw smaller spears we call arrows, but threw them farther.

All these things just made man more successful as the hunter and food gatherer he had been for about 900,000 years. They increased his sphere of control, his power, in the competition for survival in his natural environment -- which included millions of other species of plants and animals and also other mind-groups (families, tribes, sometimes called pseudo-species) of bodily identical humans who were making similar but distinct mind-mutations.

With a bow and arrow man could reach more food animals by reaching farther. Then he made another great advance by learning to reach still more food animals and reach them more reliably by bringing them closer, domesticating them. And in parallel with this he learned to gather more edible seeds, fruits, nuts, and roots by domesticating them also -- planting and cultivating, and irrigating them from nearby rivers.

And still the processes of mutation, competition, and survival went on. With his new efficiency, man's organization into mind-groups (pseudo-species) broadened from tribal to city-state size. And there was division of labor among specialists (herdsmen, farmers, builders, traders) and even specialists in a competitive role (soldiers). And this specialization led in turn to specialists in a coordinating role for a given mind-group -- rulers. Mind-groups thus became complex organisms.

And then another great advance was made -- the invention of writing as a language form. Writing, by extending the mind's reach, and preserving mind-mutations from generation to generation via written records and education, again vastly broadened the size of mind-groups. City-states became nations, even empires. And still the processes of mutation and competition for survival went on in the same vein.

So it has gone through the millennia.

The Story of Your Life

The life scientists have come up with a fact that ties it all together and provides a sort of key-to-the-keys for understanding that complex, highly adapted and very adaptable, many-faceted creature which is yourself.

They note this fact in a rattle of big words: "Ontogeny recapitulates phylogeny." What they mean is that your individual life will retell the whole history of the race of which you are at this point the final, climactic example. Your own personal experience will repeat the whole history of the human race on this earth from its beginning right on up to its pinnacle in yourself.

Truly the beginning of life on earth was the appearance of a one-celled creature. And just so you began.

And then you were a multicelled creature, with a specialization of cells developing. And then a notochord and then a backbone developed. And for a while, as an embryo, you had gills like a fish. And so it has gone, and so, up until you are fully matured as a physical specimen of our species and also fully matured as a member of our mind-group, it will continue to be.

As you grow, your own body and mind will make all the mutations (changes) that our species and our culture (mind-groups, pseudo-species) have made during the past two billion years.

The scientists can help you recognize these mutations in yourself, and by knowing what they are and what they signify and the reach and limitations of their contribution to your own survival, you take a giant stride in understanding yourself and a giant step toward coping with the changes in yourself -- your needs, your moods, your jobs, your goals (including the basic goal of survival) -- and your whole relationship to your environment, the earth, Texas, your neighborhood.

Ancestral Memories

Your own, individual life, of course, retells the first two billion years only in synopsis form. As an embryo you were fishlike -- with gills -- for about a week. In the history of the race, that period covers about eighty-five million years.

For that brief period in your life you were, indeed, a fish, and memories of that time will always lurk in the back of your mind to affect your impulses. So to understand yourself it will help if you understand that you are still a little bit a fish in some respects -- as well as that you have changed hopelessly far beyond fishdom in other respects.

In all human beings there persists in the back of the mind

a memory of this time when the race -- and the individual -- were fish. This memory is below the level of consciousness; there is no specific recall; but still our literature is filled with recitals of the "mystical" fascination with bodies of water -- such as the sea -- which hits even inland dwellers when they encounter them. The "ancestral memory" is latent in us all.

The process is something like a process of reminiscence. In a way you have memories of all the long history of the human race lurking in the back of your mind alongside -- and akin to -- memories of your early childhood.

A human being aboard a ship or walking on a beach looks out at the waters and "mystically" senses their relatedness; he senses both promise and terror lurking in the deeps. In English literature, Masefield and Conrad have described this eloquently.

There is even a phenomenon referred to among scuba-divers as "the rapture of the deep" in which this "ancestral memory" gets out of hand and becomes deadly. A diver breathing air from his tanks under pressure of the depths experiences an emotional high -- and forgets that he is artificially surviving in an alien environment. Then when air supply nears depletion, instead of returning to the surface he swims deeper -- beyond point of safe return.

It is a verifiable fact that all mankind seems to favor vacation spots at the seaside or by a lake or near a stream -- even if swimming or boating is no part of the vacation agenda. Horseback riding along paths which border lake or stream (or the sea) is preferred -- for some vague reason having nothing to do with riding the horse.

And you, for sure, like to go swimming and boating and fishing. In surf, lake, or pool, you relive a long past era and a bit of your embryonic experience, and you enjoy reliving the early days of the race just as your grandfather enjoys going back to the scenes of his boyhood and reliving his own early days.

Not surprisingly the influence of these "ancestral memories" on our behavior shows up most dramatically in the activities we refer to as "recreation" -- which are chosen and pursued in freedom.

The word "recreation" quite logically points to this fact. If we let an arm dangle helplessly at our side, its muscles wither away. If we exercise the arm, it stays strong -- it regenerates itself. And just so it is with the part of us that is fish-impulse. We call swimming and boating and fishing "recreation" because they re-create a part of us, just as exercising the arm re-creates the arm.

The fish-gill phase was a relatively brief phase of the history of the race and of ourselves, so water recreation must be supplemented with other activities if regeneration is to be complete and life full and enjoyable and a human being whole. You are a little bit fish, but *only* a little bit fish -- those gills disappeared under a succession of subsequent mutations long ago; so now if you forget and try to breathe under water, for instance, it is disastrous.

Your memory of the history of the race even after man became *homo sapiens* lurks in the back of your mind in much the same way as the water-memory. It also has persisted despite mutations.

There was a long period of a million years or so when man lived in the wilds and was hunter and food-gatherer. Memory of this era stays with us. So we find re-creation -- a fuller, more wholesome joy in life -- in periodic returns to the wilderness and in a rekindling of the hunting impulses. We even enjoy rekindling the food-gathering impulses -- going berrypicking in the woods was fun when I was a boy, just as going fishing and hunting was fun -- because the activity helped me relive a part of the history of the race.

Of course we all know that berries, fish, and meat can be acquired more quickly, more easily -- and even more cheaply -- by a trip to the supermarket. But we still enjoy camping out, hiking through forests or over prairies, hunting, wild berry picking, "living off the country" a bit, as recreation.

Cultural Memories

The history of the race after mind-groups developed to the point where cultural mutations were important ones persists in your memory and is retold in your life.

I don't know how much of this persistence of cultural memories is inborn and how much is the product of education and communication around the breakfast table or at school. Some experiments with planaria which indicate it is easier for a young one to learn something the parent had learned than it was for the parent to learn it in the first place seem to qualify somewhat our earlier and easier assumption that cultural inheritance is all pure education. The persistence of cultural memories as well as the continuous, slight mutation of cultural patterns is unquestionable.

Perhaps the evolution into their present forms of survive-or-perish competition modes -- between species and within a species -- will help us understand our own retelling of the history of the race with respect to these cultural memories.

The scientists tell us that even primitive hunting and gathering animals such as wolves, aside from killing and eating animals of other species, also compete among themselves.

A wolf will claim for himself a territory in the wilderness which is almost as sharply defined as if it were fenced. Within this territory, the wolf hunts and eats. If another wolf invades his territory, thus threatening his food supply, the settled wolf will forget about his hunting and even his hunger and fight the invading wolf until one of them is dead or runs away.

The winner of this fight survives. The loser wolf either dies right there or, if he runs away and finds no unoccupied territory, dies of starvation. He is an instance of overpopulation. Thus competition within this hunting species is as rough as the competition between species.

However, there are provisos in this inflexible wolf-versus-wolf competition. A she-wolf and her cubs are accepted within the territory. As a matter of fact the wolf will fight just as hard to protect his family -- his mind-group -- as to protect himself or his territory.

And sometimes, when winter makes food scarce, a group of neighboring wolves will band together to hunt -- because hunting in packs is more efficient than hunting as individuals --

and then the pack hunts over the combined territories.

The competition between wolf and wolf is merciless -- except when they are members of the same mind-group -- the same family or pack. Within the family or pack, peace is maintained by a leader who metes out punishments that stop short of killing if possible.

Piecing together evidence from remains found in caves, plus studies of surviving primitive societies, scientists find that man, the primitive hunter, began almost exactly where the wolf left off. He had territories where he hunted. He killed human invaders of this territory excepting members of his own mind-group (family, clan, tribe).

This pattern has persisted into the present day. But there have been continuing slight mutations in the direction of size and complexity of organization for the past million years.

In the present day we have a complex system of "territories" with boundaries that overlap in complex patterns. Personal properties -- the smallest type of territory -- are lumped together in larger mind-groups (partnerships, corporations), which in turn are combined into cities, counties, states, nations, alliances, or treaty organizations, and even "worlds" separated by iron curtains. We fight mercilessly -- even recklessly -- with other human invaders of these territories.

Within our own mind-groups we maintain peace by an elaborate system of justice designed to settle quarrels and disturbances by means which stop short of killing if possible -- thus permitting the greater efficiencies of cooperation and avoiding the "drop-everything-and-fight" losses and inefficiencies of wolf-like man-vs.-man competition. That we can forget our own hungers when we feel challenged -- like the challenged wolf -- is obvious in modern Russia, which has pursued armament production to the point of wholesale food and other shortages, and the United States, which supports awesome military budgets while leaving millions of its own people homeless, underfed, and untaught. The goal is still survival -- life. The goal of "a life worth living" is a second priority for individuals and mind-groups of humans, just as it is for the somewhat more primitive wolves.

The mutations in size and complexity of mind-groups -- from families, to tribes, to city-states, to empires, to half-worlds, to (hopefully soon and finally) one world have been slow, a matter of about a million years. But the pace of change has had a steady acceleration throughout that period of time.

Getting from Neanderthal cave-groups to the Sumerian city-states took about 100,000 years; from the Sumerian city-states to the Roman Empire about 10,000 years; from decadent Rome to the New World and colonial empires about 1,000 years; and thence to world trade and an embryonic Union of Nations about 100 years.

The scale of competition in territorial disputes has had similar escalation. From individual combat to tribal wars and still bigger wars of nations and finally all-out world wars of alliances, the pace has increased and the casualties have increased.

Nuclear technology may have brought us to a major mutation here. Since the atom bomb there has been evidence of a general awareness among world populations that among us moderns all-out war may be as self-defeating as breathing under water has been since we grew out of our gills.

And similarly the methods of settling disputes and keeping the peace within mind-groups have undergone a slow refinement -- without change of pattern -- as those mind-groups increased in size. Settling of disputes within mind-groups by punishments administered by rulers has mutated into a rule of law as writing became widespread (notably under the Roman Empire).

And settling of territorial disputes among smaller mind-groups within larger mind-groups has also been brought under the rule of law through slow mutation.

England's Wars of the Roses -- a territorial-type conflict between English families -- so exhausted England that Spain got a century's head start in colonizing the New World. Nowadays two corporations within a nation (each may represent more people and property than either Spain or England could boast in 1500) can settle such quarrels in a court of law instead of through wars. And this can be done without death or bloodshed, even on the part of participants in the dispute (though legal fees may run high enough to impoverish both sides).

As the size of our mind-groups has grown, the organizations for cooperation -- for hunting in packs -- have become almost unbelievably complex, and the roles of individuals have become more specialized and compartmented until, for instance, a farmer and a worker in a farm tractor factory may belong to different mind-groups which will fight each other unless their disputes are settled in the name of some larger, inclusive mind-group such as a nation.

When we speak of two men "fighting like small boys," we mean like cave-dwelling Neanderthalers of different clans who confronted one another (without being able to define exactly what territorial issues were at stake) as well as like the small boys retelling the 75,000-year-old Neanderthaler experience just yesterday (again without being able to define exactly what territorial issues were at stake).

And the later tribal wars and city-state wars of history somehow seem to have been repeated in our own boyhood, at least, in the rivalry between the Green Dragons (who lived mostly on Elm Street) and the Black Pirates (who lived across the little creek). The way we raided their tree house in retaliation for their stealing our secret codes from the barn was epic -- and a pretty fair analogue of the ancient wars of Ninevah and Babylon.

In recent football wars of the Jonestown High Yellowjackets versus the Smithville Tigers we have entered a more modern world. We have referees and we talk of sportsmanship and we have never actually killed anybody or enslaved anybody from Smithville, even when we won the game.

Toward Self-Knowledge and Self-Rule Tomorrow

From these analogies, perhaps you can learn how to handle some other ancestral memories affecting current events -- and handle them rationally.

Notice that to exercise the old reaction patterns -- to swim, to hunt, to camp out in the wilds, to fight for the alma mater -- are all wholesome things to do. They exercise parts of us, retell part of the racial history and our own life history, and thus make us alive and whole. Exercising the primitive impulses is healthy and beneficial -- as long as we remember that nowadays primitive behaviors are only a game, so when we swim we do not try to breathe under water, and when we camp out we do not forget to plan the trip or take along supplies, and when we leap to our feet in the grandstand and shout "Kill the Smithville Tigers," we do not actually intend to do so.

The big point I set out to make is that with the aid of science and history we have clues to understanding you, and you have clues to understanding yourself, that reach back two billion years and can be projected into the future for sixty years with reasonable accuracy.

Within this context (of your life retelling the history of the race) suddenly we realize that *all* science, *all* history, *all* literature are part of *your* autobiography -- and full of meanings based on our experiences which are modified only slightly by events in your day-to-day life.

When an ancient fish swam in the primordial sea, when the first tiny mammal fled from a dinosaur, when Cro-Magnon hunted reindeer, when a caveman made friends with a wolf-like dog, when the Sumerians harnessed two river systems, when Magellan sailed around the globe, when men fought to the death, asking no quarter, at the Alamo, in effect *you* were there.

And also when we killed off an entire sub-race of our own human species, the Tasmanians, and when we mined the soil and left wastelands like the Sahara, and when the attacking commander ordered the *"deguello"* (no mercy) at the Alamo, *you* were there, too. (Remember we are trying to understand you, not flatter you; science can tell you some bad things as well as some good things about yourself.)

It is all part of your life story. And books of science, history, and literature help you, in effect, to refresh your memories.

And then, with memory refreshed -- with understanding of

yourself -- you are ready at last to slide into the driver's seat of this, your world, and steer it toward a future of your choice.

"

Chapter 2

The Family Heritage

Lest some reader be misled by the above chapter title, let me hasten to say this book will have nothing to offer genealogists. The writer is, for instance, no kin to *the* Adams family; they were all natives of Massachusetts, and the earliest ancestor in the patronymic line I ever heard of was my great-grandfather (whose given name I do not know), and he was a native of South Carolina who had apparently never been farther north of the family plantation than it was necessary to go in following his foxhounds.

This chapter is concerned with the way my particular family -- unique, of course, but undistinguished and hence typical -- adjusted to their environment and the events of their times and passed along to me by oral transmission around the family hearth perceptions and ideas which colored my view of my own environments and the events of my own times -- 1910-1997.

The Civil War

Great-grandfather's world was his own plantation, extended superficially by an occasional visit to Charleston (site of Fort Sumter). Grandfather Archie Adams was indulged in wider travels -- apparently in his youth he visited at least as far north as Pennsylvania and once, I seem to have heard, had voyaged to England -- to which the staple products of South Carolina (including scions) were conventionally shipped for final processing. And he had read books that acquainted him with even wider horizons.

For both Great-grandfather Adams and Grandfather Archie Adams, the big event of their times was, of course, the Civil War.

Of their adjustment to this event, I wrote some years ago in a letter to the late Griffith D. Lambdin (copy to J. Edwin

Smith, "Smitty"). Here I quote from that letter, unedited, with the thought that to edit now in light of current interests would distort more than it clarified.

"

August 24, 1986

Mark Adams to Griffith Lambdin
Galveston, Texas

I nominate myself as moderator of the discussions on the Civil War and its consequences which may impend between Smitty and yourself.

On grounds that I would be almost totally impartial.

It seems obvious to me that Smitty would be biased on the subject of the Civil War by thoughts of his ancestors who fought with the 1860s version of a claymore for the Confederacy. And you just might be biased by thoughts of your paternal grandfather's missing arm -- thanks to some Rebel Smith or other.

But *my* ancestors ...

True, when Fort Sumter brought the topic under discussion, my great-grandfather proclaimed (a) that slavery was recognized in the Bible and (b) that "One Southerner could lick a dozen Yankees with a cornstalk." However, my grandfather, who had read widely and traveled some, respectfully disagreed with both statements. He wasn't directly contradictory, but he argued (1) that regardless of what the Bible said, slavery as a legal device for dominance and exploitation was *passé* -- no other nation of the dominant North European community of nations accepted slavery -- and (2) that Great-grandfather (who apparently had never been farther from his own plantation than Charleston and didn't read much) underestimated the Yankees.

Quite aside from his dark suspicion that the Yankees wouldn't fight with cornstalks, my grandfather had met some Yankees face-to-face and seen some of their steel mills and factories. He did not think they would be pushovers. In fact he announced before the echoes of Sumter died away that the South would lose the war.

Then, his arguments having fallen on deaf ears, he set off to enlist in a Confederate Army.

Grandfather Adams was a tall, skinny drink of water, and the surgeons at the induction centers of Virginia, South Carolina, Tennessee, and Mississippi all opined that he either had tuberculosis or would immediately contract it amid the rigors of military service. They rejected him. He wound up in the Florida militia and spent the war in the garrison of the old (but redoubtable) fort Spaniards had built at St. Augustine. There he occupied off-duty hours reading things like Victor Hugo's *Les Misérables* -- meanwhile writing letters home urging his father to sell the slaves and put the money into Georgia land or something else he could hang onto after the war ... and otherwise wasting his time.

So I insist that from Grandpa Adams my heritage of impartiality is on a firm foundation.

His service in a Confederate Army unit doesn't taint this impartiality. The only time he ever heard a Yankee gun fired in his direction was one day when an army buddy and he rowed out from the fort's inlet into the open sea bent on fishing, and a Yankee gunboat anchored offshore (inshore waters were too shallow to allow a sea-going vessel to maneuver) put a whaleboat over the side. The whaleboat rowed toward them until it was within range and a (damn poor) marksman with a rifle fired in Grandpa's direction. Thereupon Grandpa and his buddy rowed back toward the inlet and the protection of the fort's guns as fast as they could.

Grandpa and his buddy won the boat race -- they had a head start and were highly motivated -- so the Yankee whaleboat broke away before a rifle ball landed anywhere close. The only issue at stake in that combat situation was whether the best escape from boredom was fishing or hunting, and even that issue remained unresolved. So Grandpa's account was not one steeped in bitter memories. And no derivative bias devolved upon his descendants.

And if my claim to impartiality inherited from my Grandpa Adams is substantial, it pales beside my inheritance of impartiality through my maternal Grandfather Woolley. Grandfather Woolley fought on both sides in the Civil War.

A youngster big for his age, Grandpa Woolley ran away from home and joined a Mississippi regiment at age fourteen. He was captured in battle and interned in a Yankee prison camp shortly afterward. When Yankee brainwashers appeared at the camp offering enlistment in Union forces to the repentant, Grandpa Woolley decided to outfox the Yanks by joining up and then deserting first time he was within walking distance of a Confederate detachment.

It didn't work out. The Yankees put him on a Naval vessel aboard which he served as cook's assistant (or should I say galley-slave?). Thereafter he did not set foot on terra firma nearer a Confederate unit than Vera Cruz until after Appomattox.

Grandpa Woolley apparently never talked about The War at home. I can remember my mother's astonishment when she first heard of his military service record from visiting Granduncle "Ren" Woolley -- I was a high school graduate and she was well along in middle age at the time.

At any rate, both my grandfathers avoided Confederate reunions for the rest of their lives -- the one because he thought they were a waste of time and the other because he was afraid somebody would show up who would know about his divided allegiances and upbraid him about it.

So you see I come by my impartiality honestly -- from grandfathers on both sides of the family.

My grandmothers both had traumatic experiences in consequence of "the inevitable conflict," but not in a manner to bequeath me bias about the issues of it.

My Grandmother Cora Cobb Woolley's father was wounded while serving in the Confederate Army and sent to his home in Northern Mississippi (believe it or not, such a region exists) to recuperate. Some draft-dodgers hiding out in the area thought he had come to spy on them. They surrounded the house and demanded he surrender to them. He refused. They set a fire against the house on one side. My grandmother and her sister went out and extinguished the fire with a few buckets of water. My great-grandfather pleaded with the little mob, offering to come out and surrender if they would leave his daughters unharmed. They agreed; he rode off among them as prisoner. An hour or so later, the two young women followed down the road he had taken and cut him down from the tree limb from which he hung. Following this incident, all Great-grandfather's slaves took out for parts unknown except one partially crippled aging black man who stayed and helped the girls farm until after the war.

Grandmother Woolley did not (could not) blame the Yankees for her traumatic experience; and the example of compassion (unforced in any way) of the aging black man left a grateful memory; if she had a race prejudice it was in the form of a "noble black man" view.

So, again, from Grandmother Woolley, my heritage of impartiality is confirmed.

The suffering of my Grandmother Anna Harrison Adams came by a subtler route but was also war-related and ultimately, perhaps, more traumatic. Her brother (the chum accompanying my grandfather on the fishing sortie) came home to Georgia cracker country on leave from duty at St. Augustine during the later stages of the war bringing along his buddy -- who fell for her like a ton of bricks. First thing you know, they were married.

And there she was, hitched for life to an ignorant and footless husband. My grandmother was a well-educated woman; she could cook, sew, card wool and cotton, spin and weave and knit, cure meats and preserve vegetables, etc. -- all summa cum laude. (She never learned to read and write; I have heard my father reminisce about happy evenings when my grandfather read aloud to her and the children by the cabin hearth on the lonely Texas frontier to which he took her after The War.) But my grandfather's ignorance was crippling. In his youth everything from tying his shoes to baiting his fishhooks had been left to a body slave a year or so older than he; so when he came to build a cabin in the Texas wilderness, he started nailing the shakes on the roof starting at the top.

However, my Grandmother Adams never blamed her misfortunes on the army which had sent her brother on leave. So my heritage of impartiality includes no tarnish from that quarter.

Moreover, I am inclined to regard the sort of issues you fellows talk about -- such as the saving of the Union and the freeing of the blacks -- as peripheral to discussion of the realities of the Civil War or any other war. Freeing of Great-grandfather Cobb's slaves, you will have noted above, was not the result of any Emancipation Proclamation; it was the unplanned result of a counter-intelligence operation by a band of rebels against the Rebels. Fortuitous results are the bulk of war's realities.

My Grandfather Adams once remarked, "I don't see how the Union victory did much for the blacks -- they are poor, untaught and oppressed now as they were then. But it was the salvation of the poor whites of the South." He cited incidents illustrating the way the young bloods of his native South Carolina had sported with powerless poor whites of the area by ordering black slaves to insult them publicly, and to vandalize their wagons, etc. (The bloods owned the law, and it would be attempts at reprisal which would land a culprit in jail.)

And my own lifetime of observation inclines me to think he was right. The Civil War's effect in bringing the South into more modern times seems to me minor. The Fourteenth Amendment, words on paper, did little for the Negro, though it did much for the corporations who got themselves declared persons (by the judiciary) -- and whose way of life was intimately involved with shaping of words on paper.

The Negro's lot advanced substantially only a hundred years after Appomattox when black men and some sympathetic whites walked to work in Montgomery and braved cattle prods and savage dogs throughout the South to demand a better lot.

I don't even think the South was effectively brought into the Union economically until Arnall's freight rate case and the New Deal (and World War II) mobilized the powers of the area into an (unstable, I fear) coalition of minorities which became a (non-military) national force.

So I claim impartiality even about the issues you and Smitty discuss, because they are issues as defined by words on paper, and I can regard them with detachment tantamount to impartiality because I am unswerving in my conviction that such verbally defined ideas, except as they are validated by (possibly unrelated) events, are essentially meaningless. Words on paper and events do not necessarily correspond closely.

So let me desist before I say something solemn or meaningful. You two partisan panelists have at it. I'll moderate because I ain't biased like youall.

”

Adjusting to the Reshaped World

So much for a view of the way the Civil War reshaped their world for my grandparents -- which view was passed along to me by my parents through talk around the family hearth. Of more immediate interest for my present purposes is the way my grandparents adjusted individually to that reshaped world into which the war had plunged them.

I wonder how much the views of my Grandfather Archie Adams may have been shaped by his reading -- rather than by his personal experiences. He had been born a feudal princeling on a fairly prosperous plantation; yet his view of the Civil War and its aftermath seems, from beginning to end, to reflect a certain detachment as of distance and perspective -- to have been singularly free of the self-righteous indignation and refusal to accept the new realities which were, understandably, more common among his natal peers. So I wonder if reading Hugo's *Les Misérables* at that fort in St. Augustine had endowed him with an empathy with Jean Valjean? Did that shape his thinking? I cannot know.

Perhaps his reading shaped his thought to some degree. But after all he had told his respected father the South would lose the war before he enlisted for service at St. Augustine or read Hugo. And I recall that a natally more prestigious prince, Leo

Tolstoy, seems to have arrived at attitudes deviant from those of his peers -- without obvious literary persuasion and in less critical circumstances. Who knows? I just wonder.

My father passed along to me many anecdotes told him by Grandfather Archie which explain how he adjusted, but not why.

Grandfather told of his first vote after the war. To reach the ballot box he had to walk between two lines of black Union soldiers. A few paces along he heard a voice saying, "Howdy, Mistah Archie." He glanced up and saw his boyhood chum -- and body slave -- in uniform, rifle at parade rest. He responded, "Howdy, Tom." (My father told me that Grandpa Archie's voice indicated unfeigned warmth in recollection of the incident.) But there was no occasion for anything more. Added fraternizing would have made either man suspect among his own associates. The two never saw one another again -- and if they had, what more would there have been to say? Events had changed their world.

And that was that.

Apparently Archie accepted wholesale change matter of factly -- without ideological twistings of any sort. In that vein he seems also to have avoided most of the conflicts and the confusions of ambiguous adjustment attending Reconstruction in his native society -- at least partly because after the war he had not returned to the area or the society in which he grew up.

Immediately after the war he joined his new wife in Georgia. Her people and her native community had never been slave owners. Back in his native South Carolina region they might have been proscribed as "poor whites," but in the atmosphere of seamless equality in the ranks of the St. Augustine garrison, he had chosen her brother as best friend and it seems obvious that he adored her. So after the war he faced the problems inescapable anywhere post-war. But problems of reconstruction were not formidable in that area where there had been no vital structure to be destroyed by war in the first place. Psychologically he apparently was simply a young man getting married and leaving his parents' household to establish a new household of his own -- a conventional change rooted in no particular social crisis.

The homefolks of his wife and buddy welcomed him. A community log-rolling built a log cabin for the newlyweds, and they settled in and tried to tend a little farm as their neighbors did. But their neighbors were established in that way of life. And they were adapted to it by training and by habit, while Archie was neither. I imagine that made him a bit of an outsider, though I never heard any hint of antagonism either way in the relationship.

On the other hand there is little evidence that Archie was a success in his new lifestyle either. Family legends passed down to me include an anecdote about Archie's going to a town on the coast (Savannah?) hoping to earn a little cash money. No entree and no special skills; the job he found was stevedoring. He was set to forcing bales of cotton into place between decks of a ship with a two-man screw jack. His partner on the job was a Negro, and Archie strove to hold up his end of the load as they worked together amicably. But by the end of the day Archie's right hand was blistered, and by the end of the week, bandages on the hand were removed to yield a glimpse of bone. In his first experience with racial equality of opportunity, the Negro had proven qualified and he had not.

And that was that.

He returned home with a hand that healed but that remained partially crippled for the rest of his life -- and perhaps with a bit more wisdom about the nature of reality.

Starting Over Out West

At any rate, after a few years in Georgia, Grandfather Archie apparently found prospects something less than hopeful. And like many thousands of his American contemporaries, north and south, he opted to start over in a new world out west. On that western frontier, he thought, a man might find new hope -- recapture the American dream.

Accordingly, less than a decade after Appomattox, his little family -- wife and two toddlers -- embarked for Galveston and thence traveled inland via the Houston and Great Northern Railroad to Lovelady, Texas -- which was about as far as their money would take them.

The world Archie found was no land of milk and honey, but its newness was real. To invite settlement the state had granted Great Northern twenty square miles of public land for each mile of road built; the railroaders translated land into construction money by selling it in large blocks to individual buyers (for an average seventy cents an acre); and these owners, in turn, conveyed to settlers through *ad hoc* negotiations. Lovelady had been laid out by the area's owner immediately upon arrival of the rails (in 1872) in theretofore undeveloped wilderness.

By the time settler Archie arrived, Lovelady already had a general store, several related facilities -- smithy, livery stable, etc. -- and a growing number of farms under cultivation roundabout. But it was ten years later when the village could claim a population of 300.

Archie arrived in Lovelady with negligible resources beyond his determination. So initially he rented "on the halves" -- with the landlord providing teams and tools and receiving half of the cotton and corn -- and he bought supplies on credit at the general store (which also was owned by the landlord).

Archie had always thought of debt as an imagined horror. (He had read of Jean Valjean.) Now facing the realities of debt, his fear hardened. He understood that unless the crop he made that first year paid the rent, *plus* the charges at the general store, *plus* enough to carry him through another year without added charges at the store (which for others it did not), *plus* something more for future capital, he would be frozen into place -- little, if any, better off than the black slaves his father had owned. Yet he had no vocation but farming -- and that more by association than by training -- so he had no choice. He rented a farm "on the halves" and bought supplies on credit at the general store.

There followed a year or so of hard work and harsh frugality. Happily, the hard work on fertile new ground with timely rains resulted in a couple of good harvests. And the harsh frugality -- Anna gardened, stored foods, spun and wove, knit socks, etc. -- kept the charges at the store minimal. So at harvest their half of the cash crops enabled them to pay off debts at the general store, and there was enough left over to buy some livestock, tools, and supplies.

Hence in the following years he rented "on the third and fourths" -- a third of the cotton and a fourth of the corn going to the landowner. With continuing emphasis on the subsistence aspects of their farming -- enhanced by Anna's numerous skills and her surprising endurance -- and with minimal purchases at the general store (for tools and factory-made items), the two began to feel more and more self-reliant -- and hopeful.

It remained a life of extreme hardship -- and isolation -- for the young couple. The isolation was particularly bitter for Anna. Archie had changed worlds several times before -- when he left the plantation for the wander years of his youth, and when he joined the army, and when he left the army for Georgia, and when he left Georgia for Texas. But she had left behind home and kin and a familiar society for the first time in her life when she had come with Archie to this raw Texas wilderness. And the loneliness and insecurity of life in this strange land among strangers was a trial over and above the stresses attendant on the frontier and poverty. There were times of emotional crisis when one of their little boys came running to Archie out in the fields, and he would leave his plowing and return to the house to hover solicitously -- though ineffectually -- until she regained enough composure to send him back to his work.

Owning the Land He Lived On

After the better part of a decade of renting, Archie planned to own his own farm. When harvest was in during the fall of 1878, he rode beyond the fringes of settlement exploring. He decided on a plot a few miles to the west of the cultivated areas and approached its owner with his head full of dreams.

The owner -- the storekeeper -- listened to his proposal to purchase: six bales of cotton and a wagonload of corn, to be paid the following autumn after Archie had cleared fields, built a cabin, and made a crop. The storekeeper agreed; it was a fair price for an unimproved quarter section beyond established roads.

That fall Archie worked furiously clearing a field on his promised land for cultivation the next year. When a new tenant appeared in midwinter to claim the farm he had rented the previous year, Archie threw together a lean-to to shelter Anna and the small boys while he built a log cabin close at hand on the new farm. He kept a fire going before the lean-to's open side to break the chill for them until the cabin could be occupied.

He had learned a bit about building a cabin from neighbors participating in the log rolling for his and Anna's Georgia home. By early April the cabin was nearing completion and he was carrying shakes up a ladder to the roof one morning when three horsemen rode up. They said they were hunting for deer and swapped a few casual words with him.

The horsemen could see he was tense with anxiety to get the roof on the cabin. They could see the dark clouds on the far northern horizon which boded a blizzard by nightfall. They could see the kids huddled in the lean-to beside their mother, who was obviously growing heavy with another child. They rode away a short distance and paused to chat with each other for a few minutes, then rode back and without another word tethered their horses and pitched in to help him with the roofing.

They worked all day as hard as Archie -- and probably more effectively. As dusk came on they helped him move his family into the cabin, and then, dismissing his thanks with a murmur and a smile, rode off into the night.

He never knew their names other than the given names with which they addressed each other as they worked. He never saw or heard of any of them again.

And that was that.

On the frontier -- beyond civilization, as we say -- things mandated neither by conventions nor by paperwork sometimes happened.

A few days later, my father was born -- truly in a log cabin, as old-time politicians once liked to claim. But as a matter of fact, that log cabin represented a step up in status for his parents at the time of his birth.

Crops on the new land were good that year, and in September Archie, having delivered his six bales of cotton, drove into town with a heaping wagonload of corn -- his final payment for the land.

It was late morning when he drove into Lovelady and asked the merchant where he should deliver the corn. The merchant said he wanted it in a crib behind his house, and since it was dinnertime he would ride to the house beside Archie and point out the crib. On the way he eyed the wagonload of corn and stipulated that it should be shucked before it was placed in the crib. This was unusual since it was customary to store corn in the shucks until it was fed or readied for the mill. But Archie did not demur. While the merchant ate his dinner and returned to his work, Archie shucked the wagonload of corn and put it in the crib, then followed the merchant back to town, left team and wagon at the livery stable, and went over to the store and asked for a deed to the land he had paid for.

The merchant replied that he had talked to his wife over lunch and they had decided not to sell that land but to keep it as part of the estate their children would someday inherit.

Archie was stunned. He insisted that they had made a deal a year earlier -- before he spent a year clearing fields, building a cabin and sheds, making a farm out of wilderness. The merchant was adamant, offering to accept the cotton and corn as payment in full for the year's rent and to toss in a reasonable amount of goods from the store as pre-paid.

Archie did not react violently but insisted over and over that the merchant had made a deal without consulting his wife in the first place and that he should close the deal on the terms they had agreed the year before. When more talk neither provoked Archie to violence (with which Archie suspected the storekeeper was prepared to cope) nor saw Archie budge from his position, the storekeeper said he needed to attend to customers and walked away.

Archie simply stood where he was and waited for the

storekeeper to return for further discussion. All afternoon he waited and all afternoon the merchant avoided the part of the store where Archie stood. At closing time the merchant spoke to him again, announcing that it was time to lock up. Archie walked out the door and stood beside it as the merchant locked up, then fell into step beside him as he walked home and up the steps of his porch.

The merchant's wife opened the front door and seemed surprised to see Archie but greeted him cordially and invited him to join them for supper. (Obviously she had not been clued in.) Archie said he wasn't hungry and walked on into the parlor and sat in a comfortable chair. His reluctant hosts went on back to the kitchen for supper.

As it grew dark, the wife came into the parlor and lit a lamp. Archie thanked her.

For several hours he just sat.

Toward midnight the merchant came down from their upstairs bedroom and said that he and his wife had talked it over and decided to sell the land after all, adding that he would execute a deed before a notary next morning.

Archie thanked him. He asked where Archie was going to sleep. Archie said, "This will do just fine; it is a very comfortable chair."

Next morning early the two went to a notary who filled out a proper deed and notarized the signature. By noon Archie was back on the farm he owned -- and with a deed in hand to prove it.

A dozen years later my father, having heard again the saga of that crucial twenty-four hours, asked his father Archie what he would have done if the merchant hadn't relented. Archie said he didn't know. But at any rate he had made his point. The merchant-landowner didn't know either -- and apparently was queasy about gathering further information the hard way.

And that was that.

The rest of his life Archie owned the land he lived on and farmed. In that narrow corner of the world, he was master of his own destiny. And as a matter of historical fact the outside world did not thereafter intrude on him from beyond the boundary lines of his 160-acre farmstead except upon his invitation and with his consent. In the round, he managed an acceptable lifestyle.

This is not to suggest that in achieving total control of his own life, Archie withdrew from the society of the area. In those days when nobody filed for county commissioner, his neighbors elected him twice; when a third election loomed, Archie actively campaigned against himself, and his neighbors acceded to his wishes. He was always a member of the school board.

But there remained deep in Archie's mind a great fear of debt -- and a grim scorn for and resentment of grasping lenders. And that became a basic part of the heritage of attitudes he passed along to my father (and through him, to me).

Chapter 3

The World Before Grandpa

Archie's experiences following Appomattox had compressed two centuries of American history -- 1670 (date of settlement in South Carolina) to 1776 (Declaration of Independence) to 1875 (Archie's settlement in Texas) -- into a few excruciating years of personal history. Nevertheless by 1879 (date of his getting deed to his own land) he had reached adjustment to his world with some sense of stability and achievement -- self-reliance and self-respect.

Those two centuries of the broader American experience -- Archie's own heritage -- were basis of what was passed along to me. My sense of that still-living heritage I try now to put into words.

Of course the core of Archie's heritage -- conceptions of the world and attitudes toward it and modes of adjustment to it -- can be traced even farther back into the mists of time. Twelve of the thirteen American Colonies which were to form a Union of States were established during the 1600s as extensions of English society at that time -- linguistic, governmental, legal, social, commercial, economic, technological -- you name it. In every way the Colonies were English. But this is not to suggest uniformity.

Britain itself encompassed great variety. England, Scotland, Wales, Ireland were not exactly ethnically homogenized or politically unified then -- or since.

And the English Isles were in a ferment, lurching from feudalism toward newer forms of organization through rapid changes -- developments distinctly and uniquely English. After all, Cromwell's rule which included formal and explicit rejection of feudal ideology (with a regicide) also happened in the 1600s -- the same century in which the thirteen Colonies were established.

Feudalism

Feudal society in England and throughout Europe was a pyramidal power structure resting on a largely agricultural -- hence land-based -- productive economy. A king, through the favor of God (as evidenced by the king's military prowess), held title to all the land in the kingdom (with two-legged livestock annexed). Accordingly all the people on the land owed him service -- in person or in payments of rents and taxes.

As a practical matter, having to do with the pace and perils of feasible military operations over extended distances, much of his kingdom was administered by subordinate barons who held varying portions of the land in kinglike fashion -- but only as tenants owing service and payments to the king. The barons in turn sublet lands and left supervision of production to manorial lords (knights) -- who channeled a portion of services and payments skimmed from the productive efforts of common servants and plowmen up to the barons and thence to the king.

Land titles were passed father to son, and thus families of title holders -- the God-favored "nobility" -- came to be thought a distinct breed of humans genetically endowed with special abilities at governing which the low-born could not have. The class structure of feudal societies was thus frozen.

Since the economy was agricultural -- land based and technologically rather stagnant -- the obvious way a feudal king or baron could increase his wealth was by acquiring more land. Consequently there was continual warfare among the kings and barons of medieval Europe for ownership of the land.

The Church

Woven into this social structure based on realities of power and wealth was another, overlapping, social structure, the church, which aimed at helping humans of all classes and conditions adjust to other aspects of their destiny. (The church explicitly denigrated the importance of both power and wealth, though churchmen often succumbed to appetites for both.)

The church operations spread its influence through writings (*clerk* and *cleric* are variants of the same word), which overleapt the geographic boundaries of kingdoms. Since writings could be preserved for years and generations, the march of Christian ideologies across Europe was continuous through many centuries. And given a common language for writings -- Latin, which had been introduced among all the illiterate tribes of northern Europe by Roman conquerors -- the church overleapt the ethnic as well as geographic boundaries which defined the kingdoms' political boundaries.

One church held sway throughout feudal Europe's many kingdoms.

The interweaving of the two overlapping social structures -- of church and state -- varied from one kingdom to another and one time to another.

Conflicts there were, of course, when church operations impinged on the power or wealth of the political kingdoms -- that is, when the church intervened in conflicts among feudal hierarchies to favor the more amenable, or when it set up monasteries to engage in agricultural production, or held lands in fee after the fashion of the more ordinary manors. But where there was conflict between church and state over policy, the state usually won because the state controlled the military. The church at best was an influence, not a prime mover, in the overall social structure.

At the time of the Conquest, the Conqueror's authority was so complete that he took over control of English church personnel, implicitly displacing the theretofore superior authority of the Pope in Rome.

Conquest -- With Problem Built In

The Norman Conquest in 1066 crystallized feudalism in Britain. The Conquest was like a modern corporate takeover with a new and able CEO installing a complete new cadre of middle managers; but it did not change the basically feudal social structure at all.

However, for all their organizational skill, the Normans brought with them a big problem which was never quite solved -- that of simultaneously holding onto the continental lands from which they had come. For several succeeding centuries Britain was drained of men and money to defend royal holdings on the continent. And that drainage eroded the social structure of England dramatically.

Immediately after the takeover, Normans reorganized and tightened tax collections -- essentially land rents -- throughout England. (The famous Domesday Book was a census of the newly acquired land and human livestock for use in levying taxes.) But the increased yield from that fiscal efficiency was scarcely enough to subsidize defense of royal holdings on the continent from such aggressive neighbors as were typical of all feudal Europe. So in return for "loans" to supplement royal income further, Norman kings gave north German merchant combines ("hanses," which later formed the powerful Hanseatic League) special access to English town fairs (markets). That helped the king in the short run -- and coincidentally stunted growth of English mercantile enterprises.

Nevertheless, better tax collecting and royal borrowing notwithstanding, there were recurrent crises calling for special new tax levies in England to bail out royal trans-channel operations. So finally, about a century and a half after the Conquest (in 1215), vital elements of rent-tax paying middle management got together and forced a theoretically absolute Norman monarch to sign a Magna Carta which gave their parliament (talk-fest) a say in money -- and related -- matters. That cracked the feudal structure of trickle-down power wide open.

And still yet the problem of bailing out those continental operations remained. In 1337 a Hundred Years War with rival French monarchs began -- and was finally, and definitively, lost in 1453.

England and its society were left impoverished and restive.

In 1455 bubonic plague broke out; one-third of the English people died of it. As if this weren't enough, in that same year rivalry between two English families claimant to the throne developed into the (civil) Wars of the Roses, which went on for another thirty years (with aftershocks continuing a century or so after that).

In light of all this, it is hardly surprising to note that geographically expansionist activities were largely neglected by neo-feudal English rulers throughout the fifteenth century. When Columbus set sail in 1492, it was only five years after the Wars of the Roses had been officially concluded. By the time England's rulers got back on their feet and were looking toward geographic expansion again, Spain already had extensive colonies in the Americas and the Pacific.

Cash Crops and Trade Displace Feudalism

Meanwhile, the domestic power structure of England was changing rapidly from feudal, primarily subsistence, agriculture toward more modern, cash-crop agriculture, and therewith toward a more fully monetized economy and a new emphasis on trade with distant (overseas) markets.

These developments toward modernization of English society were not planned. They just happened.

The claimant who managed to get himself crowned as sovereign of England and thus bring the Wars of the Roses to a close -- as Henry VII, first of the Tudors -- seems in the history books oddly reminiscent of William the Conqueror, first of the Norman kings.

Henry's claim to the throne, like William's, was dubious. If it had been tested before jurists instead of on the battlefields, it would probably have been thrown out of court. Nevertheless it was validated decisively in the jurisdiction of events.

Henry's primary problems, once he was crowned, were the same as those of the Conqueror -- an emptied purse, inadequate revenues, and the near certainty that his title would be challenged in the same jurisdiction by other claimants.

Facing these problems, Henry (like the Conqueror, ambitious, unscrupulous, and ruthless) proved (also like the Conqueror) an able administrator and intelligent pragmatist.

Like the Conqueror's, Henry's first step was to reorganize and tighten his tax-rent collecting system. Within months of his victory at Bosworth and formal crowning, he got his parliament to adopt an act restoring huge segments of the original royal ("public") domain which had been parceled out to supporters by one or another incumbent during the Wars of the Roses. Enforcement of this act doubled income from the royal estates -- from £6,471 to £13,633 -- within a year.

In following years he developed his household treasury into a royal ("federal") bureaucracy handling most fiscal affairs -- including collateral judicial and administrative affairs -- for the nation. He personally went over the books with his chief auditors every day. Within five years he had become solvent -- no longer a borrower, sometimes even a lender, and even able to reduce special tax levies to meet emergencies -- thereby consolidating general public support.

This development, relying on his personally selected councillors rather than on a parliament chosen by and representing lesser powers, simply bypassed parliamentary participation in much day-to-day government. In the last twelve years of Henry VII's reign, a parliament was convened only once. This process automatically subordinated baronial intermediaries such as had, in parliament, forced Magna Carta from an English king three centuries earlier. In terms comprehensible to modern Americans, it was as if a president (chief executive) turned government affairs over to his cabinet, dismissing Congress.

Low-Born Clerks Displace Scions

A side effect of this shifting of administrative functions from baronial (genetically ordained) personnel to bureaucratic (monarchically chosen) personnel resulted, oddly, in a democratizing of the overall English social structure.

There was an increase in status for individuals functioning in the bureaucracy -- "clerks" of various origins selected on the basis of training and performance with minimal reference to status in the feudal family (hence local) hierarchies.

And there were subtler consequences. Reorganizations in the judiciary similar to those in fiscal administration served commoner interests. Literate judges with minimal local interests displaced locally interested courts (which more easily coerced or corrupted locally summoned juries). This change revitalized the common law, which was rooted in traditionally accepted custom, some of it crystallized in Magna Carta; and reinvigorated the jury system, which was rooted in customs of Teutonic tribes which had migrated into northern Europe millennia earlier.

Thus a monarch restored protections of the common people (democracy) not because he was a bleeding heart sympathetic to victims of injustice, but because fines and forfeitures decreed by his courts were paid into his own royal treasury and because his expenses in maintaining civil order -- combatting lawlessness or rebellion -- were substantially reduced.

Henry VII seems to have been hampered by none of the ethnic, class-hereditary, or religious ideologies common in his era; he seems to have had no convictions about "what's right," only about "what will work." So his solutions to his problems -- self-serving, autocratic and centripetal ("federal government") -- proved as important in developing the distinctive and increasingly democratic qualities of English social organization as did the more communal, democratic, and centrifugal ("states' rights") forces that produced Magna Carta.

Losing a War Proves Way to Go

Concurrently, Henry VII's foreign policies were also aimed at tightening his grip on domestic administration. His objective was not to acquire foreign land holdings but to negotiate alliances (non-aggression pacts, sometimes sealed by arranging marriages in conventional fashion between his offspring and scions of other royal families).

Thus he protected his grip on his own land against rival claimants who might plot against him from abroad under the protection of some antagonistic neighboring king.

Significantly, when a French monarch attacked a ruler (in Brittany) firmly allied to England a few years after Henry VII came to the throne, Henry countered by negotiating alliances with antagonists of the French monarch (notably Spain and rulers of the Netherlands). When that did not suffice, and the necessity of saving his credibility forced him to send troops to fight French aggressors over on the mainland, he shipped a token force across the channel -- and within a month had negotiated a peace, which, although it truly enough accepted French control of Brittany, also involved payment to him of a £159,000 indemnity. For the first time in four hundred years, royal operations on the continent showed a net profit for Britain!

Like much else in Henry VII's reign, his foreign policies appear ideologically ambiguous -- and pragmatically triumphant.

He seems to have internalized the dictum widely held by feudal royalty: "What's good for the king is good for the country," in an importantly variant form, to-wit: "What's good for the country is good for the king." The result of this variant attitude in reshaping the history -- and social structures -- of England was profound.

Free Trade Abroad, Protectionism at Home

The aspect of Henry VII's reign which did most to shape the later English colonization in America was his understanding of the importance of manufacture and commerce in the economy which underpinned his current social structures -- while feudal (land-based) social structures obsolesced. He promoted trade aggressively and vigorously throughout his quarter-century on the throne.

Earlier, at the time of the Norman Conquest, merchants operating under the aegis of the Hanseatic League had prospered in trade -- by sea, hence continent-wide -- enough to buy (from a conqueror-king needing money) special access to markets in English towns.

By the time Henry VII took the throne, local (English) Merchant Adventurers had grown more powerful. They were exporting to overseas markets, and were even challenging Hanseatic merchants by concurrently importing other goods to sell retail in English markets.

Overseas trade, of course, was feasible only in relatively

compact commodities which would not perish en route. Initially the commodity produced by England's basically agricultural economy which best met these criteria was wool, and early English traders prospered primarily in the wool trade.

This specialization was modified by a side effect of the Hundred Years War. Flemish weavers, pillaged alternately by French and English forces marching and countermarching over their homeland, fled to England for refuge -- and continued to employ their skills. So by the time of Henry VII, most of the wool sent to market was already woven into textiles and hence more profitable for the traders.

At any rate Britain enjoyed a growing balance-of-trade surplus.

Conquests Behind Portable Borders

Accordingly, seeking to enlarge his own piece of the action, Henry negotiated treaties widening access to markets for English merchants abroad -- from the Baltic to the Mediterranean -- giving them advantages in competition with longer established Hanseatic, Netherlands, and even Venetian traders.

He even tried to restrict Hanseatic traders still operating in English towns to wholesale trade only, leaving all retail sales to English merchants. (He didn't succeed, but he tried.) He embargoed export of precious metals (money) lest some of the balance of trade surplus be bargained away from England by English or other (Hanseatic, for instance) traders in an international money market.

He even chartered a group of Bristol Merchant Adventurers who sent Cabot in search of a westward route to China (which would bypass the Mediterranean routes dominated by Venetians) in 1497 -- just five years after Columbus embarked on the same quest. When Cabot's quest was frustrated by his encounter with the North American continent, more immediate problems diverted the English Adventurers from follow-up voyages, and the English did not settle in the newly found lands for another century.

Britannia Goes to Sea

With trade expansion (predominantly in wool and woolen textiles) came the need for more seagoing ships. Henry VII subsidized ship-building directly. He levied special export taxes on wool leaving English shores in foreign ships and import taxes on several classes of goods arriving in foreign ships. The number and quality of English ships multiplied rapidly.

Whether by calculation or coincidence, this emphasis on shipping proved an effective replacement for wars of conquest aimed at wider geographical borders -- which had preoccupied feudal royalty throughout Europe for previous centuries. The flag of a British ship on the open seas was in effect a portable boundary line which marked off a thing under Britain's sovereignty, so building more ships enhanced royal revenues in the same way conquest of more land once had.

There was as yet little specialization of marine architectures such as later set naval combat ships conspicuously apart from commercial vessels. Ships on the open seas (like cowboys on the open range in recent times) went always armed to counter pirates (rustlers).

And Englishmen Look for Land

This growth in trade had repercussions in other sectors, of course. As wool production for a cash income became more profitable, manorial and other large landholders enclosed for sheep pastures lands which had once been small cultivated plots, along with commons on which the lowly had customarily grazed their livestock for no additional fee. The small plots and commons had once provided subsistence to a large population. Sheep on the enclosed pastures were tended by a few retainers only.

The population thus evicted and left unemployed drifted about in vagrant bands -- troublesome to the established and still employed. Henry VII tried to slow the displacement of subsistence farming populations by decreeing limits on enclosures but couldn't enforce the limits against antagonistic feudal lords and estate owners. Meanwhile he assigned new functions to justices of the peace aimed at coping with vagrancies. But though obviously aware of this upheaval of the national economy and accepting some responsibility for it, he left it to his granddaughter Elizabeth to cope more fully -- about a hundred years later.

And certainly the lowlier populations thus divorced from the land in England later responded eagerly to the prospect of settling on new lands in American colonies where they could again find subsistence -- and a hope for something more.

Genetics and Disaster

By the end of Henry VII's quarter-century reign, he had solved all of the major problems he had faced at the beginning. Britain's prosperity and prestige had reached new and impressive levels. Unprecedented surpluses had accumulated in the royal treasury -- and the political structure of the kingdom was stable in commensurate degree.

But his son and successor, Henry VIII, blew it all -- in the process plunging the country into a ferment of change and counterchange, progress and reaction, which, in the course of the next century, revamped the whole social structure of England.

It does not appear that Henry VIII was any less ambitious, unscrupulous, ruthless, self-seeking -- or even intelligent -- than his father. But his father had initially faced fundamental uncertainties -- which could be instructive, even humbling, to absolute monarchs -- while the son was born to security. Ergo the son was less informed, less realistic, less pragmatic in all his judgments -- at least until it was too late for his blunders to be avoided.

Henry VIII inherited his crown at age nineteen -- proof enough that his initial qualifications for the role of ruler were solely genetic. He appears to have believed that genetic qualification was all-sufficient; he strove throughout his life to provide a male heir to the English throne -- to the delight of the gossip-columnist element among later historians. (Though it was two of his publicly spurned daughters who ruled for sixty years after his death.)

He enjoyed and cherished the satisfactions of being a king, being always center of attention, leader of every parade, general of every military expedition. But he despised the sweaty tedium of organizing a parade or a war -- or a government -- and left those things to lesser mortals.

Between his vanity, his lack of information and judgment in spheres basic to his job (governing), and his innocence of any personal grounding in what might be called a work ethic, he was ill-equipped for success. And truly enough, a history of his long reign is replete with blunders and resulting disasters.

Like Father, Lost Son

Henry VIII's crown came to him unchallenged because his father had carefully insulated the crown against challenges by (1) avoiding foreign wars whenever possible -- negotiating non-aggression pacts instead; and (2) building up the royal treasury at home -- personally recruiting and supervising a bureaucracy to strengthen that treasury.

The son seems to have understood none of this. Within a few years he had destroyed both of these foundations of the power structure his father had crafted over a quarter of a century.

First to go was the foundation of the royal treasury's surplus -- apparently without the young king's even noticing, much less understanding, what was going on.

Henry VIII's accession to the throne had been hailed with relief by court circles -- the entire society he knew and understood. The court consisted of holders of hereditary wealth and power in the kingdom, as well as notable ideologues such as Erasmus, all of whom had been subordinated to his father's single-minded and hard-nosed governance. Naturally the wealthy and powerful were the big taxpayers from whom the "clerks" of his father's bureaucracy were collecting augmented royal revenues; and naturally there was no love lost between most courtiers and the relatively low-born clerks.

As long as Henry VII was going over the books with his

bureaucrats daily, the clerks had been protected by royal authority. But Henry VIII would not bother with details such as monitoring bookkeepers, so protections of the clerks melted away.

Within months of his coronation two key bureaucrats, Dudley and Empson (lawyers charged with identifying and collecting from tax dodgers and hence about as popular as the I.R.S. in modern America) were arrested and executed for "constructive treason." Thereupon fiscal affairs drifted into the care of less abrasive agents.

Courtiers hailed a new era.

Thus the first major initiative of Henry VIII's reign was a tax break for his crowd of wealthy cronies -- the courtiers who surrounded him -- which incidentally destroyed one pillar of his father's stabilizing policies.

His second major initiative, a glory-seeking war against the French on the European mainland -- which soon also pitted him against a French ally, the monarch of Scotland -- incidentally destroyed the other pillar supporting his father's stable government.

Within three years Henry VIII had spent his father's lifetime savings and was bogged down in deficits that forestalled further war efforts. A special levy intended to raise £160,000 actually yielded only £48,000. (By that time Dudley and Empson were long dead.)

Making the best of his swiftly acquired penury, Henry VIII made peace with France and relied on his marriage to Catherine of Aragon to pacify Spain. And in following years he coasted along on his position as a bystander courted by both sides in the continuing wars on the mainland -- even without England's active participation.

Toward the end of the first decade of his reign (in 1520) -- during this fortuitous interlude of being consequential without added defense expenditures -- Henry VIII and the King of France met for a goodwill conference near Calais at a site still famous as the Field of Cloth of Gold. The fame of the Field of Cloth of Gold event, of course, rests solely on the lavish (and expensive) on-site setting the two monarchs provided themselves for the meeting. Henry's tent palace covered 12,000 square yards; it included an audience hall "larger than Whitehall," an enormous chapel, and impressive appointments -- including fountains which ran streams of claret, hippocras (a spiced wine), and water.

Diplomatically the meeting was meaningless. Two months later at a meeting in Kent, Henry was plotting with the same French king's arch-rival on the continent to destroy France. But as a memorably impressive display, the Field of Cloth of Gold remained unrivalled until four centuries later when, at a spot a hundred miles up the coast from its site near Calais -- at Omaha Beach -- American President Ronald Reagan stood before a chorus line of European heads of state (all recruited at considerable expense to the U.S. Treasury through foreign aid) to star in the photo-op of the twentieth century -- which was also, in terms of diplomatic effect, utterly meaningless.

(If Henry VII's rule was reminiscent of William the Conqueror four centuries earlier, his son's reign is oddly suggestive of Ronald Reagan's administration four centuries later. There is the same love of prominence; the same distaste for hard work and grubby details; the same early initiatives -- a tax break for obsequious cronies; dreams of glorious victory in worlds overseas -- and the same plunge into debt for defense expenditures that spelled fiscal disaster for future generations of Americans to cope with. But of that, more later.)

The Details of Disaster

The immediate problems which troubled Henry VIII at the time of the Field of Cloth of Gold and Kent conferences were (1) an empty purse, and (2) the fact that he had not enlarged his power on the continent in the feudal mode by territorial acquisitions there.

In his basic ignorance of realities, he did not understand that both these problems which troubled him were aspects of a single reality -- a reality painfully learned and then forgotten by English rulers through previous centuries following the

Conquest: The island kingdom simply did not have the resources to support military operations across the channel against powers already entrenched there, specifically France.

Ironically, the problems which troubled Henry VIII were identical with the solutions his father had achieved after his first war with France -- that is, an end to defense expenditures which automatically left his treasury with a surplus. Certainly Henry VIII did not realize that fate had provided him with solutions his father had sought by diligence and cunning; he still dreamed of glory.

At that conference in Kent following immediately after the Field of Cloth of Gold, Henry VIII had joined forces with Charles Hapsburg, who had recently inherited from one grandfather (Maximilian) the title of Emperor of the Holy Roman Empire, and from another grandfather (Ferdinand) the crown of Spain. With the active support of the Pope, Charles was embarking on a lifelong war with the French monarch aimed at uniting all Europe, with himself as emperor.

Henry thought he was joining a winner in Charles and hoped to profit with a piece of the action for himself -- maybe all or part of a shattered France. And Henry's chief bureaucrat (and mentor), Cardinal Wolsey, thought that Charles could and would support him in a bid for the papacy. Both king and councillor counted on winning that one lottery.

Within a year Henry VIII was at war with France -- as ally of Charles and the Pope. His effort was wholehearted. He published a tract attacking the Lutherans, and the Pope rewarded him with the title of Protector of the Faith -- which was flattering though not otherwise remunerative. He affianced his daughter Mary (a toddler at the time, and through her mother, Catherine of Aragon, a second cousin of Charles) to Charles himself, hoping thus to include Tudors in the projected pan-European league of genetically empowered monarchies.

For a couple of years Henry VIII made war on borrowed money -- but his already strapped treasury made the best he could do in that line rather puny. And shortly it became apparent that Charles and the Pope were not, by themselves, going to make short work of France. A nearly continent-wide war dragged on for several years with nothing more conclusive than previous centuries had witnessed. And Henry got a painful lesson in the techniques of European diplomacy -- still typically a game of cross and double-cross.

Charles jilted his juvenile fiancee to marry a princess of Portugal -- whose fortune was still intact (and growing because of Portuguese colonizations and expanded markets in the New World and Africa). And the Pope, by that time held hostage by his ally, Charles, did not dare to approve a divorce so Henry could pursue his other objective -- a male heir for the English throne. (His queen, Catherine of Aragon, had reached menopause with only the one daughter surviving.)

Twenty years into his reign, Henry VIII was back at his starting point -- except that he was flat broke. His rule had proven a series of fiascoes.

Beneficent Side Effects of Fiasco

Henry VIII's fundamental fiascoes nevertheless led to some beneficent side effects of profound consequence. These side effects of his ineptitude appeared in the form of changes in (1) the power structure (government) of English society, and (2) the relations between church and state.

Neither change was planned. Both developed in the course of efforts to cope with immediate problems -- that is, problems seen as such by the glory-hungry young king -- with little if any realistic thought given to possible residual effects.

Henry VIII's twenty years of bootless adventuring in wars across the channel had forced him to turn repeatedly to parliament for supplementary revenues -- a situation precisely analogous to that which had forced King John to sign Magna Carta three centuries earlier. And parliament, finding a theoretically absolute monarch appearing before it as supplicant, assumed a more and more important role, not just in fiscal affairs but in matters of national policy only distantly related.

And concurrent with this increase in the role of parliament itself there was new emphasis on the importance of the House of Commons in parliament. The House of Lords could more readily be coerced by a king genetically placed in the establishment hierarchy (like themselves), so it was the more democratically chosen Commons -- wealthy burghers and landowners (businessmen) without noble pedigree -- who tended to legislate independently.

No single enactment like Magna Carta emerged, but in sum the legislating in Henry's reign raised the power of parliament permanently to new levels -- enough to eclipse the significance of the earlier document. Government by king-in-parliament began to replace government by absolute monarch restrained only by time-honored customs (articulated in the common law and such documents as Magna Carta).

And at the same time, since (1) micromanagement of a bureaucracy grown large and unwieldy by a parliament was impractical (because parliament was itself multiple and diverse) and (2) micromanagement by a monarch was impractical because government had become too extensive and complex for any human to tend it in detail, a semi-independent bureaucracy to handle day-to-day affairs had an increased role. A distinction between the privy council and the wider conciliar bureaucracies (functionally equivalent to the distinction between the cabinet and the department bureaucracies in modern America) was being defined.

The relations between church and state were changed even more dramatically.

In medieval times the feudal power structure and the religious organization were separate but seldom if ever in conflict. Rulers and prelates were joined in informal but effective arrangements serving mutual interests -- a king's support could determine the church's selection of a bishop; bishops rather uniformly supported policies of the king.

The interweaving of interests was particularly strong when it embraced joint plans for expansion -- conquests for the power structure, conversions for the church. The Church of England confirmed closer ties between the English government and the English church.

DATUM II

Boyhood and the Great Depression

Chapter 4

Education of a Journeyman Printer

I was born in Texas, lived there most of my life, and have always regarded the Texas scene as a basic element of my self.

My father was a country editor. I worked in the associated print shops and by age fifteen was a journeyman printer.

A turning point for me was reading Felix Shay's *Elbert Hubbard of East Aurora,* which opened my eyes to printing. I was fifteen at the time and working after school helping produce our weekly paper strictly as a chore akin to splitting kindling and bringing in stovewood and mowing the lawn. Shay's book made me aware that it could be something more than a chore -- even aside from its symbiosis with writing. In high school I chose printers as role models: Elbert Hubbard with his Roycroft Press and *his* role model William Morris with Kelmscott Press, and Dard Hunter. Add a touch of William Blake, plus T.E. Lawrence and Joshua Slocum, and there you have it. These youthful enthusiasms crystallized in a resolve that someday I would write, illustrate, print, and bind a book with my own hands -- recapitulating the feat of Dard Hunter except omitting his paper, ink, and type manufacturing and with a little more emphasis on the writing and a lot more emphasis on the illustration elements. The *relevance* of this early bent is that fifty years later as my life neared full circle through retirement, I returned to the interests and dreams of my youth -- which were little changed from what they had been at age sixteen.

Books That Shaped My View of the World

Of these books which have shaped the way I see the world, I suppose the earliest-experienced were the most influential.

The first book I remember having held me in thrall was Jack London's *Call of the Wild.* I was nine or ten when I first read it. Nearly seventy years later I think it to be The Great American Novel. It is not a dog story; it is an allegory about a boy leaving home and finding his place in our world -- social and environmental. I think other books I read since which have seemed profoundly true to me did so by adding on to that core reading experience.

In *Call of the Wild* the protagonist is taken from a comfortable home -- forcibly, not by choice, all unplanned in every circumstance. Out in the world, the first thing he learns is to respect a man with a club -- not as a man but as the bearer of a club. Then rapidly he picks up street smarts -- be it in a slum street in Brooklyn, or Main Street, or Wall Street, or the Rue de la Paix, street smarts are much the same. And then he learns to work, and to aspire, and to identify with wise and loving fellow creatures -- and thus to survive. London's *Burning Daylight* -- far less allegorical and allusive, more specific, but on the same theme -- I found less convincing.

Later additions to the novitiate as a reader included, importantly, Anatole France's *Penguin Island* and other summary comments on the human condition, such as Samuel Butler's *Erewhon,* Aldous Huxley's *Brave New World,* Ruskin's *Gnomes* series, Gibbon's *Decline and Fall,* and Frazer's *Golden Bough.* (These last mentioned multi-volume works, I cannot remember reading entire; I dipped into them here and there until I had convinced myself I had the idea; nevertheless ideas so derived, however fragmentary, somehow stuck.) And of course, there was *Gulliver's Travels,* read at several different ages with additional meanings found with each reading.

Along with these were hosts of books that I found more immediately and specifically helpful as I tried to feel out shape and texture of my particular world, such as Mark Twain's *Huckleberry Finn* and *Life on the Mississippi,* Willa Cather's *Youth and the Bright Medusa,* Mencken's *The American Language,* Lincoln Steffens' *Autobiography,* Tolstoy's *Ivan the Fool,* Kipling's *Puck of Pook's Hill* and *Jungle Books,* Conrad's *Nigger of the Narcissus* and *Heart of Darkness,* Curwood's *Valley of Silent Men,* Kent Curtis' *The Blushing Camel,* and the Lynds' *Middletown.*

The world is wide and varied; so also are books that depict

it -- in endless streams and giving infinite detail.

Of special interest to me as a Texan: For the Southern element in Texas society, Margaret Mitchell's *Gone with the Wind,* Faulkner's *Sanctuary,* Erskine Caldwell's *Tobacco Road,* Howard Odum's *Southern Regions.* For the Western element, Gene Rhodes' *Stepsons of Light* and *The Little Eohippus,* J. Frank Dobie's *Coronado's Children.* For the Spanish element, Gruening's *History of Mexico,* Bancroft's *History of Texas and Northern Mexico,* Bernal Diaz's *History of the Conquest,* Garcilaso Vega's *The Incas,* Willa Cather's *Death Comes for the Archbishop,* Paul Horgan's *The Rio Grande,* Carl Duaine's *With All Arms.* And on the American Indian aspects, Schultz's *Seizer of Eagles* and Texan John Graves' *Goodbye to a River.*

Marquis Childs' *The Raven* (a biography of Sam Houston) gave an insight into the Tennessee element of Texans who arrived overland and were quite different from the planters who arrived with their slaves mostly by sea along the Gulf Coast.

On our environment: *Two Little Savages* and *Wild Animals I Have Known* by Ernest Thompson Seton, *America* by geographer J. Russell Smith; *Storm* by Stewart, *The Great Plains* by Walter Prescott Webb, *Silent Spring* by Rachel Carson, *Kon-Tiki* by Thor Heyerdahl.

I should also include the *Report on Strategic Materials* prepared by the National Resources Planning Board for Harry Truman in 1950, with its beautiful quantifying of problems.

Shaping my concepts of science: Sinclair Lewis's *Arrowsmith,* Paul de Kruif's *Microbe Hunters,* James Watson's *The Double Helix.*

Of histories tying into our European heritage, I liked Churchill's *History of the English Speaking Peoples* and Tuchman's *March of Folly.* Spengler and Toynbee I found tendentious frauds.

Economics bedrock books were R.H. Montgomery's *Brimstone Game,* Walton Hamilton's *Patterns of Industry,* Walter Webb's *Divided We Stand,* Thurman Arnold's *Folklore of Capitalism.*

About government, Charles Beard's *The American Leviathan,*

Maury Maverick's *In Blood and Ink,* a book on the Constitution, *The Letters of Thomas Jefferson,* T.E. Lawrence's *Oriental Assembly,* Trotsky's *My Life.* I was fascinated by a biography of Kemal Ataturk, but I cannot remember the name of either book or author. And I have been fascinated by the history of China since the Boxer Rebellion, but on reflection I find I cannot associate a book with this; nearly all of what I know came from conversations with a personal friend, Alfred Z. Chang, son of one of Sun Yat-sen's lieutenants and in World War II, Maj. Gen. Chang-tse on the staff of Chiang Kai-shek. Al, after the retreat to Formosa, came to America, won citizenship and an MA degree from Colorado U., and was a colleague of mine in the Bureau of Reclamation.[1] Which offers an opening for a comment which belongs in any discussion of the roles of books: Always, always, books and experiences supplement and reinforce each other -- else both are rather meaningless.

About war: *Men at War,* an anthology edited by Ernest Hemingway, *Revolt in the Desert* by T.E. Lawrence, *The Art of Modern Warfare* by Wilhelm Foertsch, *Genghis Kahn* by Harold Lamb, and *Wind, Sand, and Stars* by Antoine Saint-Exupéry.

On art: *On the Name and Nature of Poetry* by A.E. Housman, and Max Eastman's *On the Enjoyment of Poetry* and other related essays.

Philosophy: *The Story of Philosophy* by the Durants, *The Territorial Imperative* by Ardrey, *Theory of the Leisure Class* by Thorstein Veblen.

---

[1]See Chapter 14.

Chapter 5

School Away from Home

After high school I entered the nearest college -- which happened to be Texas A&M -- with intention of learning more about writing and illustrating. (I was already a journeyman printer.) At the end of my first semester my instructors in both English composition and drawing took me aside and said, "Here we teach high school classes for kids who didn't have a chance at a decent high school back home. You are wasting your time here. Why don't you go someplace else?" As far as I know there was no collusion about this, and I was too egotistical to believe each burned with some wish to be rid of me. So I went someplace else.

I asked the English teacher where he would suggest, and he equivocated about suggesting anything more specific than the Great Beyond. The drawing teacher indicated three schools, adding that the last named -- the Pennsylvania Academy of Fine Arts -- was his alma mater. Accordingly, I packed a couple of hundred books into a big box and spent the next semester holed up on the snowbound western slope of the Colorado Rockies, reading. And the following autumn I entered the Academy in Philadelphia. There all went well until, as the end of the first term approached, in mid-winter, my mother wrote that my father's health was failing and I should come home and take over the shop of our weekly newspaper.

When I got home, my father said he was in perfect health and had a good printer to help in the shop. He obviously didn't know that rumors to the contrary were afloat. He asked what I intended to do during the rest of the school year. I told him I'd think about it. And I did. I understood from further remarks from my mother that she figured that if I returned to Philadelphia, I would fall into the impractical -- and probably immoral -- ways of *la vie Bohème* and general damnation. So I told my father I had decided to enter the University of Texas at Austin and put my ideas about art on hold -- where, sixty-odd years later, they remain. (My father died at age ninety-three never knowing how I came to change my plans; I understood my mother intervened because she loved me and wanted a happier life for me -- and that my father would never have forgiven the intervention -- so I accepted a path for my life including a detour which as it turned out involved a change of destination.)

At UT, beginning my sophomore year in September 1929, I idly elected a course in economics taught by Carey Thompson. And I recall that in late October, Carey came into the class one morning and asked if anybody had noticed what had happened in the stock market the previous day. I hadn't; what greasy Babbitt type cared what happened in the stock market?

Encountering Americans of Other Cultures

In a letter to Al Ramirez, publisher of New Santander Press in Edinburg, Texas, Mark tells the story of first encountering a person of another American culture with whom he was compatible.

"

Jan. 20, 1988

Mark Adams to Al Ramirez
Edinburg, Texas

I was startled because you seemed surprised to find yourself mentioned on the acknowledgment pages of *Texas Testament.* I wondered if I could explain why your name was there. Then I wondered if I could explain to anybody, including myself, why any of those particular names were there.

I absolved myself from the suspicion this might have been an exercise in name-dropping. A few of the people mentioned were prestigious -- celebrities -- but most of them were not. Some I had known for a generation or so; some I had known only relatively briefly -- Al Ramirez, for instance. All of them had added breadth and depth to my experience of our world. But how to explain in what way or why your name had popped into my mind while thousands of others I had talked with much more extensively did not.

As I was casting about for explanatory analogy, my eye fell on the name of Dave Weichselbaum in the list.

Dave was a classmate and friend in my early days at the University of Texas. In retrospect it must appear that ours was a strange friendship. I was a product of that narrow corner of the world called East Texas -- typical of a culture by no means cosmopolitan in its viewpoints, practices, or politics. My insularity was only lightly tainted by a taste for literature. Dave was born and raised in an equally narrow corner of the world called Brooklyn and -- not atypically -- he was a Jew, very poor, and a member of the Young Communist League. He was, perhaps, even more heavily tainted by a taste for literature. It was probably by a sharing of those literary cultural taints that we became friends. And through the friendship I got some glimpses of his world which opened my eyes a bit to situations and events and ideas totally unlike any I had known on my native heath.

Dave was brilliant and earnest and open. But he never offered me any coherent descriptions of that different world from which he came. On the other hand, his casual conversation helped me understand aspects of his different world in vivid ways I would never have gathered from a description or a book.

About being Jewish, for instance. In East Texas there were so few Jews that being Jewish we regarded as an individual trait, like wearing a beard or being a carpenter -- a matter of significance only to the individual person. In Brooklyn there were many Jews -- identifiable and identified as a group -- a minority group. And being Jewish took on a significance bare facts and figures would never have made intelligible to me.

I remember Dave telling me of youngsters in the prize ring -- fighting under names like Shawn Flaherty or Paddy O'Shannon to win support of boxing fans who were predominantly Irish -- youngsters who nevertheless when they returned to their corners before coming out to fight, glanced down fleetingly at that six-pointed star sewn on the hem of their trunks. That little image helped me understand about what it was like to be Jewish in this world -- more clearly and vividly than volumes of ideology or statistics.

It was the Prohibition era. And I had read news stories about gang wars in New York. Gangster movies portraying characters totally unlike the bootleggers of East Texas were the rage. But people in Brooklyn saw them the same way Texans saw cowboy movies. And I understood that subculture of his world much more clearly because Dave helped me see how, for his bit of Brooklyn, to be "hard" -- remorseless -- was a consciously sought virtue. Another time he mentioned to me that Jewish gangs in Brooklyn routinely mutilated the victims of their gang killings so the police would suspect the Mafia (which had over centuries developed some exotic rituals for their terror-killings).

There was much more, of course.

After that first year, Dave did not return to UT -- he had come there initially because it was cheaper than matriculating at Columbia or even CCNY. And after that one year he had been unable to afford another. The only time I saw him afterward was when, in the late thirties -- on a trip required by my job in New Deal Washington -- I took a subway over to Brooklyn from Manhattan and hunted him up at his previous address. He was away from home -- he worked at the post office -- but I left word and he met me for dinner that evening. He had changed little; but he added an image to the picture. He told of meeting with the Central Committee of the U.S. Communist Party and urging that its Jewish leaders withdraw from the party on grounds that the Jewish temperament, modes of thought, and accents -- however blameless and well meant -- would hopelessly alienate the masses of Middle America. I was not surprised by his thesis. Us Young Turks of New Deal Washington tended to refer to the Communist Party as "The Little Red Church," equating it with sects of religious fundamentalist ideologues like the Mormons or Primitive Baptists.

He got nowhere with the Central Committee, of course, as I would have expected. But I was not surprised that Dave had risked ostracism from his own groups. That was Dave. True to his ideals, he sensed the force of some of the irrational, often tragic, undercurrents of history and urged adaptation.

In the upshot I realized that Dave had taught me -- about Brooklyn, about Jews, about a world unlike the one into which I was born, about some generalities concerning distinguishable and bulldozed minorities and their modes of surviving.

And Al Ramirez?

From the word go, I found him quick-witted and clear-eyed with a sense of humor that bespoke sanity and realism. And from the word go, sans hint of any classroom atmosphere or procedure, Al taught me -- about the Rio Grande Valley, and about Spanish-speaking peoples (there were none in the East Texas of my boyhood) -- and in general provided glimpses of his world not to be had from facts and figures.

I had long known some facts about the Valley, of course. About the time I knew Dave I had a job one summer in a ratlike printshop, upstairs, back, on Fannin Avenue in Houston. The owner, I speculated, was a big bootlegger because the shop would not have made sense except as income laundering. Also because seventeen-year-old Mark Adams was sole employee, and because there was little work aside from printing three-color labels for bottles of "Pete's Good Ole Panther Piss."

The owner was seldom around, but one day he waxed very talkative about having lived in the Valley and boasted about the way irrigation districts had been created and ruinous taxes immediately levied so Anglos could get title to the best lands cheap through sheriff's sales -- an appropriate length of time before irrigation actually appeared, of course. So I understood something about the conquest of the Valley by Anglo marauders -- but that was a glimpse of marauders like to those I had known from boyhood. About the Valley and its peoples and their attitudes and modes of adapting I had only such clues as Carl Duaine's histories foretold.

But your story about the token Mexicano on the Edinburg City Council -- the one who voted "Ai!" when kicked on the shin -- and the fact that majorities thought it funny -- gave me a glimpse of something currently valid.

And the *tripas* journalism added another glimpse at how people who are like me under the skin but speak with accents derived from a different culture and language have adapted -- and transcended and survived rather nicely.

There was much more, of course. I am only trying to hint at why my brief list of people who widened and deepened my understanding of our world included Al Ramirez.

Thank you.

"

Chapter 6

Displeasing the Governor

All my college training was a matter of sporadic single semesters sandwiched between eight- to eighteen-month periods of working with my father for funds. As I turned twenty-one and was back from school for another period of working, my father had a little weekly in Gladewater, Texas -- in the depths of the Depression, with the newly discovered surrounding oil field booming madly -- when Governor Ross Sterling sent the National Guard to shut down the huge oil field until the Texas Company could finish its pipeline to the major company refineries on the Gulf Coast. (Gov. Sterling had entered politics from his post as CEO of Humble Oil Company -- now Exxon -- which was the Trojan horse through which Standard Oil of New Jersey got back into the Texas oil business after a state anti-trust action had exiled it from the state. The troops were under the command of Gen. Jacob Wolters, counsel and Austin lobbyist for the Texas Company.)

My father immediately denounced the military occupation of our area as unconstitutional -- a view later affirmed by a federal appeals tribunal. He added derogatory remarks about Gov. Sterling ("The only difference between Ross Sterling and his militia and Al Capone and his mob is that Sterling's gunmen wear uniforms") and General Wolters ("Jelly-belly Jake").

I remember the night we put that ultimate unequivocal and unsparing issue to bed in the wee hours of a Friday morning. My father anticipated efforts at retribution by the civil or military establishment or the economic establishment behind them both -- prison? inspired vandalism or arson? maybe even a little dry-gulch marksmanship? -- and discussed them with me. I agreed prospects were grim, but agreed also that we had no choice but to print the truth as we saw it. About 2 A.M. I climbed up to the feed board and started the press. By daylight I was out with the delivery boys scattering copies all over the area.

The Governor's response met our expectations. Shortly we learned (contra the rules, from a grand juror) that the Gregg County district attorney had made a trial-summation-type speech to the grand jury urging them to indict us for criminal libel. When they asked to hear other witnesses, he stalked out of the room. They did not indict. (We did not think the DA dreamed up the idea on his own. In all the years we ran that paper we never lost a local election in which we took an interest, and local politicians tended to approach us with circumspection, if only because most of our readers trusted and even liked us.)

A few weeks later the Governor provided a job in Austin for that DA who had failed and appointed from another district an interim DA who had a reputation for getting indictments almost infallibly and instructed him that his first duty was to see us indicted.

Same song, second verse. The grand jurors were local and we always had a friend on the panel.

Then the Governor provided a job as a major company legal counsel for the District Judge and appointed a new judge for Gregg County, outlining to him the judge's duty to indict and convict S.W. and Mark Adams.

That new judge empaneled a new grand jury and publicly, formally, from the rostrum of his courtroom, *directed* them to indict us for criminal libels we *had* committed. The new DA did his stuff as before, but this time the foreman of the grand jury insisted that they should hear my father before acting. So next morning my father appeared before them, law books on libel under his arm.

My father heard the polite welcome extended him by the jury foreman (he had not been subpoenaed, only invited) as sincerely respectful, but he felt most of the jury were wary to the point of antagonism. And of course the new DA was openly hostile. My father immediately accused the DA of being a corrupt cat's paw for a major-company Governor's malice -- seeking to force them (the grand jury) to indict without evidence. The DA did not argue the point -- knowing that it was the truth and fearing, perhaps, that my father had evidence to support that particular charge. At any rate, he stormed out of the room in loud but essentially inarticulate indignation.

(My father did not, incidentally, have any such evidence; it was only his interpretation of events. After the Governor's defeat in the following election, State Senator Holloway representing that district, who had been present to acknowledge appointment of an out-of-district man to a post in Holloway's district, told us of the Governor's instructions to the new DA and judge, which were specific, including names.)

The grand jurors seemed as astonished as my father was at the DA's abrupt departure. Perhaps they listened with added respect as my father read a few passages from his law books and outlined his views on what was going on in the oil field -- and in this matter of the Governor's trying to force their action. Some of the jurors started asking questions, and my father talked on for about two hours -- he had been a schoolteacher for a decade before he turned to journalism.

At noon the foreman of the grand jury told my father they felt they had no reason to inquire further about the libel matter, which was baseless, but they wished to hear more about developments in the oil fields and asked if he would return for their afternoon session. He assented and went out to lunch with several of them. He returned that afternoon for another two-hour session, at the close of which they thanked him and he came home to tell me about it. Anybody who is surprised that I am a believer in the jury system to the point of fanaticism may find in this snippet of history some of the reasons why.

No bill; and that was that. But we wondered what was next. We doubted the Governor was mollified; we said nothing conciliatory in the paper.

A few weeks later an imposing Texas Ranger called "Red" Burton (six feet three or four, 240 pounds, with two pearl-handled 45s swung low from his belt and strapped to his thighs) walked into our print shop office and started telling my father (rather loudly -- I had no trouble hearing him distinctly from the back of the shop) that we "better stop printing all those lies about the Governor."

My father stood about five feet six, weighed about 130 pounds, and did not own a firearm. But he had the Ranger outgunned -- two of the coldest grey eyes in Christendom. In the middle of the Ranger's second sentence, he pointed to the door through which Burton had entered and said, in savage, imperious tones I can still hear sixty years later, "There is the door. Hit it!"

Burton stammered for a few incoherent syllables (I doubt he had been trained or practiced in public speaking) and then took a deep breath preparatory to beginning again when my father repeated himself more savagely, more imperiously -- and louder -- and still pointing, "There's the door. Goddamn you, hit it!"

I picked up a crescent wrench from the stone where I had been working and started toward the two facing each other when Burton hesitated, hands poised over gun butts, and then started backing out the door, across the street (a seldom traveled one), and a few steps toward the town's business district, never taking his eyes off us or his hands away from the pistols. Then he turned and walked on away, glancing back over his shoulder. We followed him only as far as the door, but watched him out of sight.

So that was that. And what next?

In retrospect I can name two things which followed:

1. From the Governor, nothing. We anticipated further melodrama -- the subsequent uneventful months were eerie for us.

2. My plans and priorities underwent a sea change which reshaped my life for the subsequent half-century.

Let me explain:

1. We had expected that the Governor's next step after the grand jury failures would be beyond the encumbrances of legal procedures -- attacks or vandalism by one or several Humble or Texaco employees acting in the guise of outraged citizens or mobs -- in short, that the distinction between Al Capone and the Governor would disappear. So when a "genuwine" Texas Ranger appeared, we had been surprised in more ways than one.

And since we didn't understand why a Ranger had been sent, it made guessing about what was to follow even more difficult; we awaited the next step with apprehensions enhanced by that all-too-human tendency to fear the unknown irrationally.

After Sterling's defeat later that year, one of a company of Texas Rangers stationed in Gladewater to supplement martial law at the time of Burton's visit had stopped by and told me his view of the incident -- he wanted to keep his job as a Ranger, and we had become people worth knowing to anyone with such hopes. We were assumed to be close to the new Governor.

That Ranger told me the Governor had phoned the Ranger office in Gladewater and told them that our paper was inciting to riot, and to prevent insurrection in the oil fields it was necessary to quiet us down -- arrest us for resisting arrest to be released only after posting impossible peace bond, or beat us up, or whatever was necessary to change our attitude and behavior.

He said the Rangers were ill at ease with the Governor's order. Traditionally a Ranger was sent in as backup for local peace officers and to deal with desperate men already defined as outlaw by being fugitive and/or violently defiant from behind some barricade. So to take the initiative against newspapermen who were neither hiding, fleeing, nor embattled in defiance seemed out of character for Rangers. Moreover, under the classic "one Ranger-one riot" disposition of forces, to assign a company of Rangers (eight men) to one incitement seemed also badly out of proportion.

On the other hand, Ross Sterling had actively sponsored an expanded Ranger force; his brother was a Ranger -- and after all, he was the Governor. So the Ranger company talked it over and sent Burton -- who looked the part of a traditional Ranger.

He said that on Burton's return they had talked it over and called back to the Governor, telling him that to silence us they would have to kill us -- and that if they killed us, there would be real riot in the oil fields. (Their estimate of necessary measures may have been accurate -- who can ever know how he would behave under torture or a hostage situation until after the event? But the second possibility, equally unprovable, was supported by evidence I know: At one time or another numbers of individual drillers and roughnecks stopped one of us on the street or came to the shop to mutter variants on "I've got a 30-30 in the trunk of my car. If it comes to trouble, let me know." We always expunged our memory and other records of their names and assured them such aid would never be needed. But if we had been killed, I do not know what would have happened any better than the Rangers.)

That Ranger's story jibed with all facts I knew; I never tried to check it further -- by that time it was, if not true history, at least ancient history and irrelevant. And somehow I was pleased to revert to my youthful respect for Rangers as resolute paladins of frontier justice. I could not fault them for their level-headed refusal to flout their own traditions when the chips were down.

Still, after the Burton incident, we were expecting further events -- some escalation of aggression -- and when nothing further from the Governor appeared, it left us with an eerie feeling.

Nevertheless, nothing further occurred that could be identified as gubernatorial aggression. To our surprise: Nothing! We learned *why* only months later -- as sidelight of another development.

There was never any indication the Governor had changed his mind. But certainly he had been distracted by events which changed *his* priorities.

In 1932 the Great Depression was hitting rock bottom and the Governor's bank in Houston faced bankruptcy on terms that would obliterate his personal fortune and political stature. And in his scramble to save himself, he found no time to tend to obstreperous country editors. We had been reprieved by the Depression.

Incidents in Governor Sterling's financial scrambling included a melodramatic session in an office high up in a Houston skyscraper in which he demanded bailout money from other Houston financial powers, alleging that he had in his coat pocket documents that would take them all down with him and that if they didn't ante up, he would open a window and jump, thus putting the documents in the public domain via the coroner's office. He also sent a wire to Walter Teagle, CEO of Standard Oil of New Jersey, demanding -- and getting -- a half-million-dollar contribution from him.

A court reporter had been hired to record the session and agreements reached in the course of it.

The Governor's novel idea of publication methods was never tested. The court reporter did his job faithfully and well -- and sold at least one transcript to a non-participant in the session. (I seem to recall mention of a price of $20,000 -- more than $200,000 in today's dollars -- certainly enough at that time to cover the cost of extra carbon paper.)

Back in Gladewater we knew no details of the Governor's financial problems until a friend of ours -- a leading independent refinery owner, Judge Rhea Starnes -- told us about the transcript. Starnes had been a county judge in Eastland during "Farmer Jim" Ferguson's first term -- hence the title "Judge" simply as an honorific. He had been a supporter of Ferguson ever since.

When Starnes told my father about the transcript, he no doubt knew my father would react like a caged lion shown a chunk of raw meat. In a rented Waco biplane he flew my father down to Austin where the transcript reposed in the sanctum of Ferguson's *Forum.* I suspect Starnes figured that if the information was printed in the *Forum,* its effect would be blunted by charges of opportunistic smearing and the whole matter would be thrown into court immediately by civil suits for libel -- in which case Ferguson had much to lose, including the coming election. On the other hand, we could not be branded as opportunistic for continuing in the same vein as our attacks in previous years. For us the only change would be having proof of the facts *before* printing the story.

Moreover, Ferguson wouldn't -- possibly couldn't -- get the story written with the courageous and eloquent candor characteristic of my father -- which Starnes had seen to be politically effective. And certainly the three of us had no more to lose than John Hancock when he stepped up to become first signer of the Declaration of Independence. (British authorities had already set a price on Hancock's head before the Declaration was written.)

At any rate, my father studied that transcript, stressing the tie-ins between the Governor, Standard Oil, and martial law in East Texas, and wrote a story to appear on Page One under a screamer headline: "The Shameful Record of a Crooked Governor." We filled the rest of a four-page special edition with clips from our papers of previous years and took it down to a fast press in Temple which produced an even million copies -- at which point the Ferguson organization took over and arranged distribution statewide.

Sterling lost the following election. "Ma" was Governor. Starnes treated my father to a tour in Austin covering the new legislature, and I stayed in the still turbulent oil fields, running our paper and thumbing my nose at the National Guard and the business establishment of the oil industry -- and the oil field. (The local business establishment tended to resent my cavalier coverage of Chamber of Commerce functions, but the roughnecks and drillers still loved us -- a grocery merchant who transferred his ad to the opposition paper saw his sales drop by $500 to $1,000 the following Saturday.) So the paper stayed in the black, and life went on as before -- except that I was newly Senior Officer Present and alone in an atmosphere likely to reinforce my previous leaning toward introspective inner-direction in determining my plans -- and priorities.

About my change in plans and priorities: I did not abandon my interest in *belle lettres* or art or the printing crafts. But those interests were long range: "*Some day* I will ..." And I had always assumed that achieving my personal goals would be about as important to the rest of my world as Joshua Slocum's lone circumnavigation of the globe was to world maritime commerce. *No sense of social responsibility was involved in these long-range plans.* And they had no deadline.

In the meantime, political events -- with social and family responsibilities explicit -- were demanding all the time, energy, attention, and even skills that I could command. And these wider social responsibilities were omnipresent, *here and now,* impossible to avoid without real betrayal of all the principles of my society -- my family, clan, culture ... the bony structure of my self.

I recall that during a later semester at the University of Texas, I came upon role model William Morris's opening stanza of *The Earthly Paradise:*

Of heaven and hell I have no power to sing.
I cannot ease the burden of your fears
Or make quick-coming death a little thing
Or bring again the pleasures of past years.
Nor shall you hope again for aught that I may say,
Idle singer of an empty day.

And I recall that, smiling with grim humor, I reflected that destiny had assigned me the themes of heaven and hell, but that I nevertheless could identify with role model Morris, lock step, right up to that last line which suggested that he, personally, had lived in a comfort zone -- which I envied.

Chapter 7

The Progressive Democrats

In 1934, Mark was living at Little Campus at the University of Texas, monitoring some courses, waiting for the legislature to reopen, where he was going to work as an aide to Speaker of the House Coke Stevenson.

One day a couple of young fellows, Clay Cochran and Herman Wright, visited me and said they were newly entering the University of Texas after two years at Amarillo Junior College. They said a favorite professor of theirs in Amarillo, Carey Thompson, had urged them to get to know me and Dr. Bob Montgomery.

Herman and Clay became the nucleus of the UT Progressive Democrats, whose development I later watched from off-campus with the fond casual attention appropriate to a doting uncle with a nephew burning up the track in academe.

In 1987, Otto Mullinax asked me to send Ronnie Dugger a copy of the PDs Constitution and a brief history of the organization.

"

November 1987

Mark Adams to Ronnie Dugger
Washington, D.C.

At the request of Otto Mullinax I send herewith a copy of the Constitution of the University of Texas campus Progressive Democrats and a brief note on the PDs who drafted it.

The UT Progressive Democrats of Great Depression I

The UT campus Progressive Democrats -- the individuals and the group -- reflected their time and place (the early 1930s and the University of Texas -- that is, within the orbit of R.H. Montgomery).

The way the individual students became a viable social organism is too complex to be explained either briefly or accurately. The best I can do is offer a few hints.

Human societies have a way of reproducing themselves very similar to the way humans do -- thus permitting the parent to survive individual mortality. And it seems to me that at that time, in the thirties, American democracy, failing a rebirth, was on the brink of extinction. The oligarchic tissues of American society had become cancerous -- that is, the cells were multiplying so rapidly as to debilitate and ultimately destroy the host organism.

The Individuals

The process by which the individual PDs became an embryo organization began, I think, at Amarillo Junior College where Carey Thompson (who had taken his PhD under Montgomery) was fondly fostering the development of two brilliant students -- Clay Cochran and Herman Wright. When Clay and Herman completed their courses at the junior college, he sent them along to Austin, enjoining them there to get in touch with Montgomery -- and me, though this was inconsequent -- and he wrote Montgomery commending the two to his special attention.

Encouraged by Montgomery -- his benign teachings, his charm, and his generosity -- the two became a nucleus which drew together the group of kindred spirits that became the PD organization. Clay was energetic and particularly outgoing by nature, as well as bright and thoughtful. I suspect it was primarily he who became the intellectual and emotional core personality that drew and held the group together.

Through debating societies and campus politics other individuals of like democratic cultural heritage came to know Clay and Herman and one another, and ultimately came to organize themselves as the Progressive Democrats.

These individuals -- including Otto Mullinax, Chris Dixie,

Creekmore Fath, Bob Eckhardt, Barney Rapoport, Carson Glass, and Paul Crume -- had varied and disparate cultural heritages that had shaped them admirably for the role of paladins of democracy. And individually and collectively they were remarkable for their ability and their steadfastness in devotion to their cause through thick and thin. Since their devotion was to democracy, it was mostly thin, of course, but their abilities were such that they all survived -- reasonably well financially and exceedingly well in esteem.

Perhaps it will help to convey an idea of how varied these heritages were if I cite here a more detailed history of a single one.

(

[From the "Afterword" to Otto Mullinax, *Thus Spake Idion*, Packrat Press, 1984.]

The writer who signed the essays in this book with the pen name Idion II lives outside these pages under the name of Otto B. Mullinax and in the role of a lawyer in Dallas. If you want additional formalities of identification, you can look him up in *Who's Who* (the 1980 edition will do). On the other hand, if you want to understand where the author of these essays is coming from -- as a man and as a writer and commentator -- *Who's Who* may not be much help. Hence these notes from his publisher who also happens to be an old friend.

Geographically, where Otto is coming from is East Texas. Sociologically, he comes from a tribe that left Europe as individuals and in family groups and, here, holding true to individual and family precepts, survived for a subsequent 250 to 300 years. In the process, this kind of people did two rather remarkable things: they conquered a continent, and they developed a self-reliant nation from colonial status.

Now, anybody who can point to such remarkable achievements is an important person. So Otto Mullinax is an important person. Not, of course, because he or his family were what you would recognize right off as empire builders. He wasn't and they weren't -- in fact, as a matter of historical record, he and they have shown little tolerance for emperors, large or small, at any point in the last 300 years. Rather because, although Otto and the Mullinaxes and some millions of other people holding true to like precepts were not empire builders in the conventional mold, they actually built an empire -- one of the greatest ever known -- called the United States. That, also, is a matter of historical record.

The events by which Otto was confirmed in his individual faith in the precepts of his fathers, like his importance as a person and as a writer, are relevant to an understanding of this book, not so much because they show how a unique character was shaped as because they typify events that shaped the thinking of like-minded people of his generation in America.

Born in 1912, Otto grew up in Winnsboro, Wood County, Texas, the son of Claxton and Essie Mullinax. There, around the family hearth, he soaked up the Mullinax family legends through many evenings for many years.

The Mullinaxes were a close-knit family with an enduring sense of family ties. One of the legends Otto heard recited around the fireside was about the time, three years before Otto was born, when his grandfather, John J. Mullinax, then a man in his mid-fifties, upon learning that his father (Otto's great-grandfather) was dying in Arkansas, left his home near Good Hope, in Franklin County, Texas, swam Cypress Creek, which was at flood stage, and made his way to Mount Vernon, there to catch a train which would get him to Arkansas in time to pay his last respects at the graveside. Mullinaxes were like that; and the boy, listening by the fireside, understood beyond question that he was a Mullinax.

There were older and mistier legends. Colonial Mullinaxes had actively disliked exploitation -- or even well-intentioned interference -- from agents of a distant king; they wanted to govern themselves. They gave the King's agents a lot of trouble in colonial days in a variety of remembered instances. And during the Revolutionary War they scrapped up and down the Atlantic seaboard and inland to the frontiers of those days --

wherever they were -- until the King's agents fled and thirteen Colonies in America became the United States. Okay, Mullinaxes were like that, too. And he was a Mullinax.

Experiences of the wider world settled into place as strata overlying this basement rock of Otto's heritage.

Neighbors in Winnsboro were of a similar background, but with variations; and seeing and accepting those numerous individual variations, the youngster added a first layer of wider experience upon the bedrock of his own family heritage.

Winnsboro had a public library -- a large room with shelves and shelves of books around the walls. Discovering it, young Otto was shocked to find out that there were so many different books in this world. He was also delighted. He determined that he was going to read every book in that library, which he did. This reading, together with school, added another layer of experience of a wider world upon the basement rock of his heritage. But it did not erode or replace any part of that bedrock.

And that's how it was the rest of his life.

Otto went down to the University of Texas just at the time the Great Depression was sharpening everybody's awareness that something was going bad wrong in the whole world -- including Winnsboro and without Winnsboro's consent.

At the University Otto met a great teacher -- a brilliant and diligent scholar and an eloquent and appealingly effervescent raconteur, Dr. R.H. "Bob" Montgomery. Otto, along with a lot of fellow students, listened raptly as Dr. Bob taught them volumes of facts about the wider world and how it came to be what it was, and explained those facts so the whole structure of facts and ideas fit neatly on the bedrock heritage Otto had taken with him to kindergarten.

"Texas is the richest colony of Wall Street," Dr. Bob laughed in one of his summaries. The idea sank in on Otto Mullinax of Winnsboro, straight on down to bedrock. It does not seem to have occurred to him that in this circumstance he might better himself by becoming first Mullinax in recorded history to be a docile colonial -- or even an agent of one or more imperial powers with capitals in New York. (The idea of winning power and wealth by becoming agents of distant imperial interests occurred to a number of Otto's contemporaries, including some who were listening closely to the same lectures from Dr. Bob that Otto heard. It just didn't seem to occur to Otto.)

Dr. Bob cited evidence to support that summary statement about the colonial status of Texas and Texans, of course. But after all it was just words, and like all evidence that is just verbal, it cut only cerebrum deep. But Otto had not long to wait for emotionally vivid personal experience that was indelibly convincing.

In a book titled *The Brimstone Game,* Dr. Bob had written an economic study of the multinational sulphur cartel which set world prices on sulphur (mined largely in Texas). Cartel directors found the book an accurate picture of their operations, including aspects they wanted kept secret. Painfully accurate. They responded by buying up all copies of the book not already out of the publisher's hands to reviewers and booksellers -- somehow in the process persuading the publisher not to print any more copies. And they set their Texas lobbyist, whose job theretofore had been to keep sulphur taxes for support of Texas institutions at token levels by judicious distribution of campaign contributions and bribes, the somewhat more complicated job of having Dr. Bob dismissed from the University of Texas faculty -- pronto! now! 1936!

Next thing he knew, Otto, as a leading student admirer of Dr. Montgomery, found himself subpoenaed to appear before a legislative committee set up "to investigate subversive teaching and student activity at the University of Texas." He was grilled for long hours by legislators coached and funded by the sulphur cartel lobbyist and operating under rules of procedure which empowered them to fill the roles of both prosecutor and presiding judge and to put witnesses on trial as the accused.

Otto, who knew he had done nothing more heinous than pay attention in class to a professor he had admired -- and was going to continue to admire -- grew resentful and angry under the browbeating tirades of that officially constituted lynch mob.

And he held his ground as stubbornly as had Mullinaxes back in earlier colonial days.

In the upshot the "investigation" was a fiasco for the investigators.

From the multi-national cartel's standpoint, it was ill-timed. James V. Allred, at that time governor of Texas (and a popular one), was openly sympathetic to both the students and Dr. Montgomery. Franklin D. Roosevelt, then President (and a popular one), though called "communist" and "traitor" by groups he categorized as "economic royalists" (*sic*), was being re-elected by landslide votes in every state in the union except Maine and Vermont. At that time, resentful colonials were making their defiance felt. So, laughed at by the governor, scoffed at in the press, hooted at from the galleries, and speedily disowned by fellow legislators through a recall resolution, the investigations and the investigators, for all their imperial backing, sank quickly back into the shadows.

But Otto's character -- shaped from the cradle -- had been tempered and hardened in the fire of personal experience. He had been thrust into that fire by an agent of an imperial power; he could name the agent and he could name the alien empire. They had shown him that in 1936 and in Texas they could bludgeon him for being friend of a Texan they wanted destroyed. But he, a Mullinax from Winnsboro -- one of the breed that had been actively resenting that sort of thing for 300 years since landing on this continent -- was only confirmed in the precepts and made stubborn about the activities that had characterized his ancestors and his heritage. Far from changing, he emerged from the ordeal life-long stubborn about continuing to be what he had been from childhood -- open-eyed and open-minded but totally unlikely to become a Tory, however changeful his context or his times.

Since that graduation ceremony, Otto has done a lot of post-graduate work on the subject of what his world is like. After UT law school, he toured Europe at government expense with the 14th Armored Division and then, after VE Day, spent a year with War Crimes. Since 1946 he has practiced law in Dallas, which by this time is a rather cosmopolitan city where agents of numerous imperial powers -- and would-be agents of imperial power -- congregate in droves ... and where even greater numbers of reluctantly colonial (exploited, badgered) people -- his kind of people -- work for their living in wage-subordinate or unaligned roles. Most often in court and as a citizen Otto has represented his own kind -- as individuals or in groups. And he has learned a lot from and about them and the world in which they survive.

Times have changed since Otto's undergraduate days. While he was overseas with the 14th Armored, Jimmy Allred retired to a federal judgeship, Roosevelt died, and dollar-a-year men from dozens of empires used war powers delegated them by our government to solidify the positions of their various imperiums until they were virtually impregnable. Governors of Texas -- most of our politicos -- were what World War II had taught us to categorize as Quislings -- native sons placed in power over their own people to serve the purposes of distant empires. Hunting down and destroying teachers with views incompatible with rule by an interlock of empires -- governmental, economic, and social -- has been commonplace.

Times have changed since Otto's student days. So for a couple of generations past it has often been rough going for people following the precepts which were Otto's heritage. But Otto has held stubborn. I suppose the necessary nutrient of stubbornness is hope -- a sort of faith. And truly if times change, tides change too; so maybe hope is realistic.

At any rate, Otto has never wavered, never changed in all the years since he sat and listened by the family fireside. I say this who knew him when he lived in Winnsboro and know him now. His view of the world has filled in with detail over the years, but its outlines have held steady. Witness the essays you have read herein, which he wrote in the late seventies and early eighties. Witness also, if you will, how Otto, in an introduction to this book coming out in 1984 and writing in his persona as Idion II, datelines it, not from Dallas -- cosmopolitan "Big D" -- where he has practiced law with distinction from 1946 to date, but from Athens, in East Texas.

The Chamber of Commerce of Athens, Texas, boasts it is "The Black-eyed Pea Capital of the World."

MARK ADAMS
Packrat Press
Oak Harbor, WA

❩

Otto was not unique in never wavering, never changing.

At some more conspicuous points in their careers Clay was Washington lobbyist for Patton at REA and later for Walter Reuther at CIO. Herman was a successful labor and plaintiffs' lawyer in Houston. Otto founded a law firm in Dallas -- advocates for labor and other liberal causes -- that managed in that hotbed of conservatism to spawn political figures like Oscar Mauzy and Ann Richards. Chris, who was an early law clerk for Justice Hugo Black, established a law firm in Houston -- a successful civil practice with labor law and liberalism a continuing thread; the last time I saw him, Sissy Farenthold had a law office adjoining his and was using his library as a base for fund-raising in liberal causes. Creek Fath, operating behind the scenes in political actions, performed prodigies -- managed campaigns for Yarborough and Farenthold. Bob Eckhardt was a liberal leader in legislature and Congress. Barney Rapoport's role you know better than I do. Carson was a junior law partner of Clark Clifford. Paul Crume, who seemed to have no ambitions beyond the literary aspects of journalism, was a longtime and leavening columnist of the *Dallas Morning News.* Etc., etc.

The Original Purpose

The PDs first organized as the campus chapter of the Young Democrats -- affiliated with the Democratic Party -- intending to fight in causes of the New Deal. But immediately they found themselves restrained by conservatives perfunctorily installed as officials of a paper organization by an equally conservative state Democratic Party administration. The greying bald heads and paunches of these state Young Democrat officials who sought to discipline them seem to have been particularly galling to the campus Young Democrats -- not reflecting their own idea of youth.

The campus group was flattered but not persuaded when Jack Garner, the Vice President, wrote them a letter chastising them and demanding that they shut up and behave.

The campus group withdrew from under the authority of the Young Democratic organization and took the name of Progressive Democrats.

About this time two things happened which served to crystallize their own image of themselves for all time to come.

First, since they had crawled out from under the umbrella of announced policies and principles of the Democratic Party -- which at least partially reflected Roosevelt's embryo New Deal -- they decided they should set out a statement of principles and policies of their own. The result was the PD Constitution which, verbatim, concludes these notes.

I find this remarkable. It is a truism that humanity habitually backs into the future -- eyes focused on the horror it backs away from but with little thought of where it's going. But these youngsters -- the PDs -- looked very carefully back over their shoulders with firm intent to plan, to pick a better path.

It is to be noted that there is nothing radical whatever in their Constitution. Basically its principles might more accurately be termed reactionary -- it reflects a yearning for return to the local self-reliance, freedom, and independence they identified with their forefathers and the days of an American frontier. Their most radical specific proposals were (1) an increased tax on sulphur, which was the most air-tight and profitable monopoly exploiting Texas resources (Jefferson had urged an unequivocal prohibition of monopolies in the Bill of Rights). And (2) a law regulating public utilities and establishing a commission to enforce it. (They knew such regulation was rooted in the English common law governing millers -- dating back approximately to the reign of Richard the Lion-Hearted.)

A second crystallizing event occurred about the same time. The PDs were given their baptism of fire.

The Baptism of Fire

The lobbyist for Texas Gulf Sulphur, noting with approval the activities of Martin Dies and his Un-American Committee, got a resolution through the legislature to set up a similar committee "to investigate communist activities at the University of Texas."

The resolution, of course, was aimed at driving Dr. Bob Montgomery off the University faculty. The sulphur lobbyist thought Dr. Bob the root of all evil -- Bob had written a book about the sulphur monopoly and urged a steep state severance tax on sulphur, and besides he taught the course on public utilities in the Economics Department. So Bob's admiring students on campus -- specifically the PDs -- were directly in the line of fire.

The rationale of that lobbyist's Dies-McCarthy gambit, of course, is also rooted in the venerable past. I seem to remember that James I -- regarding Sir Walter Raleigh as a political threat -- accused Sir Walter of conspiring with the Spanish against England. That was an outlandishly improbable idea, but it was established to the satisfaction of King James on the basis of no evidence as yet known to historians. And thus having found Sir Walter guilty of treason, King James had him drawn and quartered -- that is, executed by the most cruel and inhuman method possible.

Happily the assault on Dr. Bob by the lobbyist's legislative lynch mob was abortive. It was a fiasco. (I speak of it at length in the Afterword I wrote for Otto's *Thus Spake Idion,* which you have just read.)

But before Bob got to the stand to answer the committee's questions with simple, direct answers that revealed the committee members to all eyes as the venal boobs they were, and an embarrassed legislature withdrew the committee's authorization, the student PDs had been put on the stand, browbeaten by the committee members in accusatory speeches based on nothing at all, and grilled at length about passages taken out of context from PD correspondence files (which the lobbyist had quite literally hired a thief to steal before the hearings were authorized).

It was a baptism of fire for the PDs, and they emerged from it as a cadre of blooded troops for armies of the democratic cause.

A blooded trooper knows two facts an untried trooper cannot feel positive about. And the knowledge is oddly strengthening. Fact 1: He knows he can be hit and hurt if he ever finds himself in battle. Fact 2: He knows for sure that from somewhere inside himself he can find the courage to face Fact 1, and such knowledge, once gained, is good for a lifetime.

Looking back over the half-century that has elapsed since the PDs graduated and left campus along their separate paths, I cannot think of a single one of the 1934 PDs who has not held true to the principles they drafted for themselves so long, so very long ago.

The Constitution

‘

We hold these truths to be self-evident for a modern democratic society:

1. That the function of our industrial order is to produce the most generous quantities of goods and services feasible, and to distribute them to the largest possible number of people.

2. That the individual's share in these goods and services should be determined by his efforts in producing them, unless he is physically or mentally unable to do productive work, or unless he is specifically exempted from such work by the group.

3. That the greatest political good is liberty -- that is, the right of the individual to make a free choice in the fundamentals of life, *e.g.*, in his job, his home, his religion, his politics and in goods and services which he will consume.

4. That private monopoly is against the public interest, and in the production or distribution of any important good or service cannot be tolerated in a democracy.

5. That equality of opportunity in securing the essentials of life, health, education, and economic advancement must be provided for all.

6. That the allocation of functions between various governmental units should recognize two basic propositions: (1) in a democracy, governmental powers should be as close to the citizen as is practicable; (2) governmental functions should be performed by the agency -- local, state, or national -- which can best perform each function.

7. That the people should perform through governmental agencies those functions that can be performed in that way more satisfactorily than through private business units.

’

I commend the examples of the PDs of Great Depression I to the (as yet unknown) PDs of Great Depression II, which is currently entering its darker phases.

”

DATUM III

The New Deal

Chapter 8

A Country Boy in Washington

Things quieted down when Gov. Ross Sterling was defeated for a second term in 1932. But shortly thereafter the great National Recovery Act campaign -- led by a drill sergeant with the rank (and authority) of a general -- was in full swing. To my father and myself this looked uncomfortably like wholesale martial law as in Mussolini's Italy and Hitler's new Germany, and again we cried unconstitutional and blasted.

This time retribution was more effective; we were enjoined from displaying a Blue Eagle, and our advertisers were persuaded that if their ads appeared in our paper -- sans Blue Eagle -- dire things would happen to them. Since some of the things being done under the NRA aegis were a little more ambiguous than we allowed anyhow, we sold the paper in disgust. For a while this "stormy petrel" (so I was introduced by the emcee at a meeting of the Texas Press Association shortly afterward) settled back quietly and looked around for a new foothold.

The New Foothold

Up to that point my career as a liberal writer-political activist had followed a remarkably straight line. My father had been raised on a frontier farm -- literally, he was born in a log cabin which my grandfather had built to shelter his wife and some older children and finished just barely in time to shelter the birth of my father. The teacher who had interested me in the academic aspects of economics, Carey Thompson at the University of Texas, picked up where my father's words and example had left off. And Carey passed me along to classes and office bull sessions at UT with Dr. Bob Montgomery -- under whom Carey had taken his PhD.

Dr. Bob commended me to Walton Hamilton, who hired me in 1935 to join his Cabinet Committee on Price Policy staff in early New Deal Washington -- Hammy was the man under whom Dr. Bob had taken his PhD. You might say my mind was the result of academic line breeding. Hammy was mining the massive seams of priceless information left in the files of the defunct NRA to make studies of sundry industries -- sort of a forensic post-mortem. My next six years were spent largely in New Deal Washington.

A Reception at the White House

"

December 7,[1] 1989

Mark Adams to Griffith D. Lambdin
Galveston, Texas

You cannot imagine how pleased I was to find in the margin of one of your letters to Gregg [Griff's son] about bowling and his prowess thereat an invitation to me to join in "the family reminiscences."

I was reminded of my similar elation when, in 1937, I received an engraved invitation to a White House reception, "on the evening of ... R.S.V.P." and all that. Unfortunately, I was also reminded of the dismay which followed on that occasion when I was overtaken by second thoughts -- the dismay having to do with a certain element of fraud in the background of my claim to the invitation and some ensuing procedural problems.

You understand, of course, I was never even an apprentice dervish in the Washington social whirl. I didn't read the stories or even look at the pictures in the society section of the newspapers. If I had met Alice Longworth or Evelyn Walsh McLean on the street, I wouldn't have recognized them -- would have been annoyed at the interruption if I had been introduced.

I had laughed heartily when told the story of Rex Tugwell's

---

[1]I hope the date of this letter is not, for some occult reason, significant.

reaction on the occasion of his pro forma inspection of the McLean mansion which his ballooning Resettlement Administration had leased for temporary office space. Rex took a look at the swank entrance leading to a foyer dominated by a statue of an abandoned and nude Diana tiptoe in a fountain and announced: "I will take a drink but I won't go upstairs."

The reception was specifically for the Washington Press Corps, and I was at the time listed as a member of the Senate Press Gallery, but alas, this listing represents a backfire in the engine of social structuring.

Earlier I had been unemployed for a couple of months after the Cabinet Committee on Price Policy had filed its report and disbanded and before I went to work as chief of the Editorial Section of Farm Security. During this period, after a couple of years writing reports, magazine articles and press releases for government agencies, I decided it would be interesting and instructive to glimpse the process of information distribution from the other end, so I got a couple of friends who were editors of small Texas dailies to attest that I was their Washington correspondent, and thus I gained accreditation to the Senate Press Gallery -- and therewith admission to any and all White House and executive branch press conferences, which I attended and found interesting and informative as anticipated. But that's another story.

The point here is that when the White House invitation arrived, I had already gone back to work for the government and had simply forgotten to cancel my fraudulently obtained press credentials. This is one reason I was dismayed on second thought.

It occurred to me that if I showed and encountered some of my friends who were real, genuine Washington correspondents, they could challenge my credentials and have me thrown out. But this passing thought I immediately dismissed -- what matters a little fraud among friends, anyhow?

Other second thoughts were more consequential.

It's all very well to get an invitation to a White House reception. But then what?

I inquired among friends at the Press Club -- of which I was a genuine member in good standing -- as to what one does if invited to a White House reception. They assured me formal dress was not *de rigeur* -- a tux would be all right -- and cocktails, dancing, and generally milling around would be the program.

Ulp. I could manage a cocktail if proffered one, but I had never learned to dance, and as for a tux, I had never owned one and quailed at the thought of renting one, as was suggested. Not only was I innocent of tux ownership, I had never worn one or even seen one except in a movie. I decided not to go.

However, my wife pointed to that "RSVP" on the invitation and translated it into English. It became obvious that not going also presented problems. We called the society editor of the *Washington Post* and asked how to respond to a White House invitation indicating that it was declined. The soc editor put us on hold while she consulted her staff; when she came back on the line, she said, "One never 'regrets' [*i.e.*, declines] an invitation to the White House. One accepts. If you don't go, you can only hope that nobody notices. It's a large reception, so your chances are probably good."

But how good? The only sure way off the hook was to show up and hand in our invitation at the door.

Further chat with friend Parke Engle (correspondent for the *Dallas News*) revealed that in previous years a number of correspondents had attended Press Corps receptions in plain business suits and escaped from the melee with whole skins -- the Press Corps was known to be representative of the great unwashed, so they were indulged by the White House as an aspect of intercultural diplomacy.

So we went.

All I remember of the occasion is my renewed amazement and amusement at the unobtrusive diligence of the Secret Service agents cloaked as butlers' assistants, waiters, etc., who visually frisked all guests at the entrance while the dean of correspondents verified that he recognized the person bearing the invitation and then kept an eye on us throughout the evening -- a replay of my observations of the approach to press conferences in the Oval Office when this grimly necessary but nevertheless ridiculous-seeming irrelevance always surrounding an American President was repeated. I didn't have a good time.

But to get back to your invitation. As I was saying, I was delighted to be invited to join in reminiscences with you and Gregg as I had been to get an invite to the White House -- and also was dismayed on second thought.

The dismaying second thoughts have to do with the fact that my appearance in company with you and Gregg, reminiscing in an atmosphere of *mens sana, corpore sana* must also be predicated on fraud.

Not that I plead any particular illness of mind or body -- it's just that development of relevant skills in a socially accepted context were retarded by the environment of my youth.

So far in my eightieth year, for instance, I have never learned to roller-skate. I was in high school before I ever lived in a town with paved streets, much less paved sidewalks. And muddy footpaths never seemed to suggest skates.

Similarly, although I can empathize with your devotion to your pool cue, I have no background reminiscences of exploits around the pool table to swap. I never saw a pool table close enough to touch until, at age twenty-five, I discovered one in the game room of the National Press Club, where, out of curiosity, I sank a few balls, not all of them cue balls and a few of them in the intended pocket. And though I remember playing a few games with Val Lorwin and Paul Ward (Washington correspondent for the *Nation* at that time), I was never any good at it. Paul or Val won five out of six games -- and they were no sharks.

And as for anecdotes about a deviated septum from football? Forget it.

I was fifteen, stood about five feet two, and weighed ninety-two pounds when I graduated from high school (I grew eventually to five-eleven and 180 pounds, but that took an additional fifteen years); I had never seemed to impress the coach as team material. It was a very small high school (Hull-

Daisetta in 1925 -- fourteen graduates), and in my last year the coach hesitated to see a senior included out altogether, so he designated me business manager for the team. This meant it was my job to sell tickets (absolutely nothing more), including at the field, which was a grassburr patch in a barbed-wire enclosed pasture. And if I'd been really gung-ho about my duties, I might have ended up with a deviated septum anyway. But ...

Passing oilfield workers often noticed the game in progress and climbed the fence to come over and watch. And I dutifully walked over and asked them if they wanted to buy a ticket. But if they said no, or pretended not to hear me, or stared at me with an expression like they were having difficulty focusing their eyes, I just let the matter drop. No effort to throw them out. No deviated septum either.

And as for counterparts of the fallen angel Emmeline: Fact is, all the girls in my class looked down on me. I mean literally.

All of them were eighteen-year-olds of normal-to-large size, and all of them could examine the top of my head without standing on tiptoe. Moreover, I had the distinct impression that this physical fact generated a certain psychological increment. So I was never surprised when Emmeline showed up at the dance with somebody else. Aside from the fact that I hadn't asked her, there was the additional consideration that I didn't go myself -- somehow enthusiastically nubile couples never seemed to welcome kid brother hanging around.

In sum: I am delighted by the invitation to join in with you and Gregg on the "family reminiscences." But on what pretext respond?

I thought long about this. I toyed with the idea of mentioning that in the Navy I had been awarded a medal for being an Expert Marksman with pistols. But I was daunted by the fact that even this indication of coordination of hand and eye was rooted in fraud.

When in 1943 Fighting Squadron 18 got to the place in the training syllabus calling for instruction in pistol shooting, I, the senior kiwi officer, was delegated to shepherd a crowd of young airplane drivers out to the target range and take part in the practice. (Although skill with a pistol was about as likely to be useful for the pilots as for me, it was thought good for their morale because it suggested that if forced down in enemy territory they would (a) survive, and (b) still feel contentious -- both were possible but also both were highly improbable.)

On the range I listened to the instructor -- a petty officer with a voice and manner appropriate to his rating (equivalent to drill sergeant) and dutifully emptied a 45 automatic and then a 38 Smith & Wesson at targets. But not earnestly. I was woozy with cat fever (flu) and trembling so bad I was slow getting sights and target lined up in the same neighborhood. And on rapid-fire all I was trying to do was empty the pistol without hitting anybody behind me with stray bullets.

Consequently I was surprised next morning when the squadron skipper called me over and handed me a medal for having qualified as an Expert Marksman the day before. What with my surprise added to the fact that I still had the flu, you could have knocked me over with a softball bat.

However, I reflected further, I had been a fan of James Fenimore Cooper's *Deerslayer* and Chingachgook as well as an avid reader of Ernest Thompson Seton and the *Boy Scout Handbook* (though I never lived in a town big enough to have a Boy Scout troop) throughout my boyhood. And I had spent most of my leisure hours through early adolescence roaming the forests and prairies and palmetto swamps of southeast Texas -- almost always alone and hence invariably with gun in hand. (The gun was defensive weaponry; I was not much of a hunter, but I respected some of the fauna of the area -- water moccasins, alligators, wild pigs, the occasional wolf or wildcat that roamed the Big Thicket where I roamed -- and I suspected them to be of aggressive intent. Hence the military response.) Nevertheless ... well, accidents do happen. What if I had actually hit ...

It was nearly a quarter-century later when a fellow printer from San Angelo joined the black gang at the *American* in Austin. He was a burly, loud-voiced type; and something about him seemed familiar. Finally I asked about his war record -- and sure 'nuff he had been pistol instructor at San Diego. After swapping a few lines of "small world" and "been there" talk, I mentioned to him my surprise at having won an Expert Marksman award under the instant circumstances. He nodded and asked, "Were you the senior officer with that group?" I said I was.

"You see," he explained, "every time an instructor qualified somebody as Expert, we were given liberty for the evening. So it may be you got that award because I had a date in town that night. It was less likely to raise questions if the award was to a senior officer."

Truth crushed to earth had just lain there for twenty-five years. But according to prophecy, it had risen again! I laughed till I was out of breath.

So! This final, tangential, harebrained pretext for muscling in on your and Gregg's reminiscences is tainted with fraud similar to that tainting my White House invitation. Not my fraud, but fraud nevertheless.

Hence, reluctantly, with real regrets, I decline the invitation.

"

Chapter 9

Report on Economic Conditions of the South

"

May 9, 1960

Mark Adams to Dr. Walter Prescott Webb
Austin, Texas

At last this long-promised memo on the genesis of the National Emergency Council's *Report on Economic Conditions of the South* [published in 1938 when I was working as Information Specialist in the Farm Security Administration in Washington, D.C.].

Since this memo is aimed primarily at some young historian of the future who may be digging back into the files to try to find out how things happened in an earlier day so he may, perhaps, understand the events of his own day a little better, I will try to set down everything I can remember which seems to me pertinent, though it will assuredly make this document lengthy enough to daunt anyone but a scholar.

I consider this the only safe course. Since I do *not* know what that scholar will be looking for, it would be wrong for me to act as if I did know his questions in advance and hence could make this a concise answer to those questions alone.

I will set down everything I can remember which seems pertinent, explicitly disavowing in behalf of myself and all other members of the human race any ability, much less intention, to be objective, and let that future young historian winnow out his own facts and evaluations from the raw ore -- even if his evaluation be that this ore assays only one featherweight of useful information per ton of ore.

I will begin with a synopsis of the aspects I will talk about in the following lengthy screed, and then plunge into an exercise in total recall.

(

Memo on the Genesis of the National Emergency Council's *Report on Economic Conditions of the South*

Synopsis

1. The *Report* was an outgrowth of developments in political ideas, attitudes, and groupings which had grown over the previous decade -- there is hardly a concept, phrase, or sentence of it which sprang into being for the first time in the course of its production.

2. As a consequence of this, the historical facts of who, what, when, where, and how are of negligible importance. The important thing is why and how the political developments of a decade led to, and dictated the nature of, the *Report.*

3. The *Report* was a public relations effort, not a work of scholarship. This is important because (1) the public relations man aims not at truth but at credibility, which isn't necessarily the same thing; and (2) the public relations man's primary intention is not to say something but to do something ... (The classic PR man's confession is "I have forgotten what words mean; I only know what they will do.")

4. What the *Report* was intended to do was to support some outsize appropriations from the Federal treasury to finance improvements in the South -- by "proving" that it was in the interest of the rest of the nation to make such appropriations, and that the need was urgent.

5. Despite the million copies of the *Report* distributed, the approrpriations Congress made afterward were in only negligible degree a result of the effect of the *Report* on public opinion. These appropriations were part of the industrial expansion accompanying World War II, and I have no way of knowing whether the share the South got was larger than it would have been if the *Report* had not been written.

****

I. The South of the 1930's in Washington

"The South" was a fad in Washington, D.C., of the 1930's. The South got much attention in the thinking of most of the nation because "The South" was a sub-heading under the category, "The Great Depression" -- and the Great Depression was in the forefront of every mind. The Depression had planted a germ of fear -- specifically fear of poverty, wholesale poverty -- in the mind of an entire generation including Northerners. And this somehow begot a feeling among them of kinship with the people of the South -- who had known wholesale poverty for three-quarters of a century.

In the earlier days, the misfortunes of the South were attributed to personal shortcomings and derelictions on the part of Southerners, and hence were occasion for recrimination if not punishment -- if Simon Legree lived in relative poverty, it was no more than he deserved and a proper if not divine punishment for him.

But in the thirties, one and all felt they were perilously close to sharing Simon's poverty; each individual felt this was through no fault of his own; and into this frame of mind crept the idea that poverty and backwardness might be the result of something besides evil and improvident ways willfully adopted by the poor and backward. The South got not only attention but sympathetic attention. In the eyes of the nation, the South began to graduate from the status of a culprit to that of a problem.

In the earlier days when the South was regarded by the North as a sort of regional criminal class, the Southern spokesmen had been wont to retort with defenses which were the obverse of the accusations and just as imaginary -- gallantry, gentility, *noblesse oblige*, and magnolia blossoms.

As the nation's attitude changed, so did the tenor of Southern leadership, and similarly in the direction of something a little closer to reality.

Since the existence of the problems of the South could at last be confessed without admission of evil intentions, some

Southern leaders began to discuss the nature of the area's problems realistically. Instead of denying that the area was in reality poor and behind the times, they began to discuss what could be done about it.

This discussion of the problems of the South in realistic terms was not, of course, a new thing. Some Southern scholars -- and Southern political leaders -- had long outgrown the *Uncle Tom's Cabin* vs. Magnolia Blossom Legend contentions and given much serious thought and study to the realities of the region's situation. The new thing was the sudden appearance of a vast and receptive national audience for such thought and studies during the thirties. The new audience spurred additional effort among those long at home with such problems; and it brought additional thought and study to focus on Southern problems.

I am not trying to suggest that scholars and newer-type leaders of the South had suddenly been presented with the support of an informed electorate. In the early thirties the nation understood the problems of the South no better than before -- they had simply become more willing to learn. In the White House, Congress, and the nation there were attentive students, not informed scholars.

The attention given the South took myriad forms and in sum illustrates democracy's glorious capacity for the amorphous and inconclusive -- which slows democracy's progression into maximum clarity and achievement as well as into fatal error and disaster.

There was, for instance, the incredible run of *Tobacco Road* on Broadway. That marathon performance would have been impossible without the slow dawning of the idea among New York theatergoers that creatures such as those described by Erskine Caldwell might on second thought actually be people -- instead of the animals which at first glance they appeared to be. I suspect that in the early twenties, Caldwell's play would have run about as long and to about as large an audience as a flea circus. But by the thirties, a whole segment of the egg-head population was ready to give Erskine Caldwell's version of the sharecropper the same solemnly serious consideration which they gave D.H. Lawrence's version of sex. (Personally, I react to both Caldwell and Lawrence only by laughing like a hyena, but I do not try to laugh off the whole segment of the population who not only take them seriously but usually have the leisure to express their concerns in political and propaganda activity of down-to-earth consequence.)

Washington of the thirties had a whole rash of organizations and mass meetings dedicated to bettering the fate of the Southern sharecropper. Very few of the people who attended these meetings in Washington, D.C., ever had seen a sharecropper on the hoof or ever would see one. But they were genuinely concerned with his problems -- at least enough to go to a meeting -- and were full of a syrupy sympathy for him. The point is that these Northerners represented votes -- enough to swing a close election -- in areas outside the South. Some of them could not only read, but they could write. National journals began to carry a lot of articles about the South. They were an eager audience for a realistic statement on Southern problems, as well as for the fictions which were all they had to go on at first. They were simply a minor indication of a major audience the South could work with.

The farm depression was the most intense aspect of the Great Depression.

The South was an agricultural region, so the South became a major focus of farm program leadership, and -- again and for the same reasons -- the nation approved farm programs benefiting the South. Bureaus and sub-bureaus primarily concerned with one or another Southern problem appeared. TVA focused the attention of public-power organizations on the South.

Southern spokesmen and leaders -- including some well-informed ones -- scrambled to capitalize on the opportunities presented by their ready-made, confused, but attentive audience.

The Southern scholars best prepared to ride the crest of this wave of attention when it came were gathered around the University of North Carolina. Their primary focus of interest was sociological, though like good scholars in any field, they threw off the blinders of academic specialization insofar as they were able. The result of their long years of study was edited and compiled by Howard Odum in his *Southern Regions.* And shortly Washington bureaucracy was full of bright young men who knew the text and tables of *Southern Regions* practically by heart.

The weakness of this group was a result of its initial focus in sociology. Its message, as it reached the North, seemed to point more toward sympathy and welfare-type alleviatory measures than toward basic economic remedies.

The Farm Security Administration -- with its low-interest loans for tenants and small farmers, its case-workers (*sic*) to go over family budgets with farm wives as well as technically trained county-agent type supervisors to advise the farmer, etc. -- was the product of such an approach, and appropriately was headed by Dr. Will Alexander, who was, I believe, a University of North Carolina product.

John "Jack" Fischer was Chief of Farm Security's Information Division. (After World War II he became more widely known as editor of *Harper's.*) I was chief of his editorial and publications section. (Of the working relationship, more later, anent production of the *Report.*)

Coming at the problem from another angle were some people whose focus of interest was more basically economic.

This group was not so highly localized either in its origins or its interests as the North Carolina sociologists. And until *Divided We Stand* [Dr. Webb's book] appeared, it had no textbook to focus its trends of thought with respect to Southern problems, per se. It was wont to think of the South as an aspect of national problems -- it almost never thought of the South out of context in the way the sociologists were wont to do.

Politically, the great service of *Divided We Stand* was to give this group some concepts for fitting the particular problems of the South into their context in a way that clarified the matter for us -- and to give us a sort of standard to rally around. Enthusiasm for *Divided We Stand* got to be a sort of conversational recognition signal by which one of us might know another. ("Us" meant people concerned with Southern problems whose approach was primarily in economic terms, and never out of a national context -- people whose idea was to win the South a better place in the national picture, not to deal with it as if it were a world apart.)

Although the Southern leaders with the economic-national approach were much more varied, much less cohesive and unified, than the sociologist-welfare group, they were, as individuals, much more powerful as a rule.

The political power of the welfare group consisted -- I don't think this is overstating it -- primarily of entree at the White House via Mrs. Roosevelt. On the Hill, their support derived primarily from the consideration -- tangential to their purposes -- that their operations were a method of pouring money into depressed farm areas (therefore heavily into the South).

The leaders of the economics-focused group had much more power, but they were operating on a much broader front. Significantly, I think, my sharpest early memory of New Deal Washington is of sitting and watching Southerner Hugo Black browbeating a Wall Street utilities magnate before a Senate committee. (Profiting: TVA and later, REA.) Sam Rayburn's most conspicuous contribution in the early New Deal was co-authorship of the Wheeler-Rayburn Act setting up the Securities and Exchange Commission. Arnall of Georgia was in the arena fighting about freight rates. Lilienthal of TVA was scrapping on the public power front, though of all the things the New Deal did for the South, probably TVA was the most effective.

(My favorite chapter in *Divided We Stand* is the one on "Modern Feudalism," which is just as good in Maine or Oregon as in the South.)

The point I am trying to make is that the most powerful Southern leaders -- and the best ones -- were not professional Southerners in the same way that the North Carolina group of sociologists were.

Of the four people who actually produced the *Report*, at least three, Fischer, Tex Goldschmidt and myself, certainly were primarily interested in the economic approach. (Note again the title -- *Report on* Economic *Conditions of the South*). All were Texans and all on being challenged as Southerners would have entered a proviso to the effect that Texas is more Western than Southern.

Fischer came to Washington with Tugwell but soon shifted to the Associated Press. My first jobs in Washington involved work on a regulatory act for the bituminous coal industry and an economic study of the automobile industry. We both landed in Farm Security and therefore in a society of professional Southerners by the same sort of fortuitous circumstances that, earlier, had me studying automobiles. As junior draftsmen in the firm of architects who were designing the New Deal, we were in 1938 assigned to sketching in details of the Southern facade of the edifice, but by the merest chance. We had no special training for it aside from the on-the-job training in Farm Security -- our primary interest remained the overall structure. Similarly Tex was busybodying all over the Department of Interior. Concern about the South for him was a job of work as fortuitously encountered as my months pondering the production of automobiles; in fact I remember him with annoyance because he was of the group in the Department of Interior which put the finger on Jimmy Allred's proposal of a state-owned oil-gas pipeline to clear the way for private lines -- which scrap had little compass orientation. (I say "at least three" -- Clark Foreman's orientation may have been economic, but the most I'll give him is the description of "crazy mixed-up kid." He annoyed me from the first time I ever met him, throughout the period we were working on the *Report,* and to date. He was from Georgia and of a prominent family there; his chief claim to status was that preposition "from." He made a dramatic event of being a Georgian -- in the same sense as the copper-skinned scouts who hunted the plains with the U.S. Cavalry were Indians.)

There was a sort of political holding company in which these various interests and approaches to Southern problems were hammered out and welded together -- an arena where the ideas were mulled over and discussed by the people who were using those ideas as tools -- and where all the ideas that went into the *Report* had been kicked around at least once before the *Report* was even thought of.

This was the Southern Policy Committee. It was an organized bull session. It had no dues, no platforms, no printed material, no officers, no staff -- issued no statements (if there was even a letterhead, I don't know about it, and I was acting secretary for a couple of years). It had only a sort of floating membership from completely miscellaneous walks of life -- about fifty-fifty members of Congress and bureaucrats -- some of them eminent, some originally, currently, and ultimately anonymous as far as even the minor public prints were concerned.

The Southern Policy Committee was a sort of mist of human beings which condensed once a week in a room above Hall's restaurant at the end of Ninth Street overlooking the Potomac whenever Congress was in session -- time, about sundown -- and ate 75 cent plates of seafood (dutch) and just talked.

(Perhaps I should make it clear that I am referring to the Washington Southern Policy Committee weekly coffee clatch and not the semi-formal Southern Policy Committee which occasionally, under the same name, held meetings at Chattanooga, Birmingham, Montgomery, Atlanta, and other places, and did issue some booklets setting forth conclusions reached at these meetings. The Washington coffee clatch had a sort of connection with the formal Southern Policy Committee which in turn was loosely connected to the National Policy Committee -- an organization something like the ADA of today.)

The coffee clatch was one of the most successful organizations I ever watched operate.

At one of the more routine meetings, the attendance would be about a dozen congressmen, all Southerners, and a dozen bureaucrats, mostly Southerners. Now and then there would be a big one with somebody like Harry Hopkins or Robert Jackson as guest speaker, and we would go formal and move over to the Continental Hotel, and the number of congressmen would increase to a hundred or more -- most of the Southern delegations plus assorted New Deal congressmen and some other congressmen interested in courting fellow members from the South for various reasons.

I can't think of any category into which the congressional members fit except that all were interested in the South, and none seemed to be evangelists -- that is, I never saw anybody come to the meeting with something to sell the rest; rather they were all full of questions and seemed seriously trying to learn facts and weigh values rather than peddle pat answers. The first couple of times I attended, Maury Maverick and Hugo Black were present -- later, when I was with Farm Security and went to every meeting, more or less in line of duty, Maverick was defeated for re-election and Black was canonized on the Supreme Court and so they weren't present. But the people who rarely missed a meeting at the latter time included Sparkman and Hill of Alabama, McClellan of Arkansas, Chandler ("I'm Boss Crump's man") of Tennessee, and Ellender of Louisiana. The gamut of the liberal-conservative spectrum was covered, but they were a pretty good bunch of men regardless.

The bureaucrats ran heavily to types unable to see clearly the line where politics leaves off and government begins -- that very sharp line seen so clearly by the Civil Service Commission and civics professors. Francis Pickens Miller, a lawyer-scholar from Virginia, was moving spirit of the organization -- come to think of it, I don't believe he was even a bureaucrat, just kibitzing. (He ran against Harry Byrd after World War II and was smeared -- as any liberal would have been.) And other faithfuls included people like Clifford Durr of the Federal Reserve Board, Brooks Hays of Arkansas (I forget what bureau at the time), Bob Montgomery when he was in town, Hugh Bennett of the Soil Conservation Service, Carl Taylor of BAE (who thought what this country needed was a peasant class to till the farms -- but was, thank heaven, a quiet man who seldom spoke and when he wrote ... well, foremost among my claims to the gratitude of my government is that during the period I was with BAE I suppressed more publications by Dr. Taylor than any other living man in an equal period of time). The bureaucrats were miscellaneous, like the congressmen.

The bull sessions covered the horizon of Southern problems -- the ideas advanced by people like yourself and Odum were gone over and digested, with marginal notations and supplementary material tossed in by one and all. Researchers and writers in the bureaucracy like Fischer and myself got promptings for additional efforts along many lines, and some wheels on the Hill were greased -- all without any formal motions or directives. A Quaker meeting sort of thing, but very effective.

II. The Actual Drafting of the *Report*

Out of the ferment I have tried to suggest above, came a lot of work on the subject of the South and Southern problems. Fischer and I were in the middle of it because as "information men" for Farm Security we had the job of wrestling with these particular problems. In the course of a couple of years we had become -- ex officio, as it were -- "experts" on the South.

Perhaps an aside should be injected here about the working relationship between myself and Fischer, to clarify my own role in the drafting of the *Report* and the nature and limitations of my knowledge of how the *Report* came to be.

Fischer was Chief of the Information Division -- his job was handling all contacts, clearing of manuscripts, conferences with intra- and extra-bureau brass, press conferences, etc. -- in short, dealing with people and making policy. My own job was to handle the research and writing to support his work -- research into anything and everything which might support the policies he wanted to advocate and "prove" the points he wanted to make, and writing of anything and everything required to serve his public relations program for the Farm Security Administration, from annual reports of the Administration to paragraphs for the President's State of the Union message, to radio scripts, to definition paragraphs for the annual supplement to the Encyclopedia Britannica and canned editorials for the newspapers and how-to-apply-for-a loan leaflets for semi-literate small farmers.

Fischer, an assistant, and a couple of secretaries were in offices adjoining the Administrator's in the Agriculture Building, and consequently he was dragged into all the conferences and crises which are the grist of the bureaucratic mills. He was a good operator and a very useful man. I had so much distaste for that sort of thing, I would have been a quart-a-day man in three months of it. I, along with four or five young writer hopefuls and a half-dozen stenographers, was in offices in the Barr Building on the other side of town, with Fischer doing a mail-order business with us by messenger service.

I and my motley crew were the shovel brigade. Research and writing. Whatever he ordered he got. When what he ordered seemed especially silly (not blaming Fischer, the ceremonies of bureaucracy require a lot of silly things), I would post the request on the bulletin board, throw darts at a quotation from Sabatini I had posted at the top of the board ("He was born with a gift for laughter and a sense that the world is mad") until I recovered my equable nature, and then buckle in and try my best to produce whatever it was.

In the course of a couple of years of this, I had covered most of the material contained in the *Report* at least once. Farm Security was aimed particularly at the most immediate problem of the South -- its population of poor farmers -- and tangentially we had to study its other problems.

This arrangement suited me perfectly. I like to play with ideas and words far better than I like wrestling with people. My favorite character in modern history is T.E. Lawrence -- and not for the glamour period of the Arabian revolt but for the period when he was a Private Shaw in the tank corps -- a private, that is, except for those occasions, once in a blue moon, when the routine seemed to have come to an outrageous pass and he stepped from the rear rank, announced to the company commander, "I am Colonel T.E. Lawrence," gave the company commander his orders, and then immediately resumed his identity as Private Shaw and returned to ranks. Anyway, the job was to my taste and Fischer was a patient soul who seemed to find the stuff he got worth the riffle.

There was a small, accidental variation from this norm in the writing of the *Report*. Fischer was out of town on an extended field trip, so according to form I left my private domain, crossed town, entrenched myself behind his ante-room and secretaries, and prepared to guard the citadel until his return.

As I sat one day thumbing through a volume of *Agricultural Statistics, 1935,* I got a call from Clark Foreman. Clark alleged that Fischer had agreed to cooperate in production of a report requested by Lowell Mellett of the National Emergency Council on economic conditions of the South. A conference on the matter was called for his office.

I had heard nothing of this and was non-committal but agreed to appear, vice Fischer. Nobody in the office knew anything about it. I grabbed a cab.

Four people gathered in Foreman's office in the Department of the Interior -- aside from Clark and myself there was Tex Goldschmidt, also of Interior, and Louis Bean from the Secretary of Agriculture's office. Clark and Tex, being Interior employees, were apparently in the know. Louis and I listened with growing incredulity.

Clark outlined the situation. It appeared that three months earlier he and Tex and Fischer had agreed that an outline of the South's situation should be produced and given a big publicity buildup -- with the ideas (1) of building public support throughout the nation for bigger appropriations for the South and (2) of unifying Southern elements in Congress behind a rational program for their region. Lowell Mellett, head of the National Emergency Council (an arm of the White House), had okayed the idea. He had agreed to call a conference of Southern leaders -- men of stature and prestige -- to consider and sponsor a brief, coherent summary of the South's situation and, by the weight of their prestige, give the thing a sendoff.

I sighed. This was Edward L. Bernays, kindergarten version,

but staple public relations technique. We would compose a statement, and the brass and bellwethers would dutifully assemble and act as a sounding board for us. The papers would run stories and the free lance writers would come around trying to find a gimmick to individualize their rehash and make it salable to the magazines, etc.

This is precisely analogous to the advertising technique by which, in the name of charity, the advertising company gets the socialite to lend her name and picture to the full page in four colors announcing that Mrs. Gerald Van Astorbilt III smokes Pall Malls. It is, in short, a fraud. And I don't like fraud as a way of life. But it was for a noble purpose, and besides it was the way I made my living, so, though I sighed, I prepared to do my part. I would help manufacture a statement outlining the position of the South in modern America which, after two hours and a couple of cocktails, the conference would solemnly issue -- and the world would just as solemnly receive -- as another daily edition of Magna Carta.

Clark went on. He was afraid, he said, that he had been somewhat tardy in getting started with drafting the statement to be submitted to the conference, and we would have to work pretty hard to get it ready in time for the conference, which had been called for ten days from today. The prospective conferees were good people; chairman would be Frank Graham, president of the University of North Carolina.

Louis Bean's eyebrows crawled up his forehead, over the top of his head, and down the back of his neck. I stared at Clark like he had suddenly sprouted a head of snakes like Medusa.

Three flaming months this thing had been cooking! Invitations had *already* been issued to a set of nationally known leaders in the name of the President of the United States! And we had ten -- count 'em, ten -- days in which to prepare for them a simple, clear, well-rounded summary of everything a generation of scholars, decades of public administration, years of debate in the Southern Policy Committee, Congress, and the world at large had discovered and discussed about the South! (Make that 9-1/2 days -- it was afternoon and the conference was called for 10 A.M. of the tenth day following.)

Louis Bean got to his feet, announced that he had suddenly remembered that he had to see the Secretary about a secretary or vice-versa, and besides his next ten days were full up to the brim with prior, pressing, and unavoidable commitments. And with expressions of goodwill too half-hearted to be accepted as polite except in the broadest frame of reference, he departed, never to return any more.

It was the only sane thing to do. And I would have been right on his heels except that I was tied there by an invisible rope -- I didn't know what Fischer had promised; Fischer was racketing around somewhere in the Western United States and at best it would take a day or so to get hold of him and find out what our commitments were; and yet, whatever Fischer had promised, it was my job to deliver. So I couldn't do the sane thing and skip out.

And besides, as I sat there I felt a sort of pity for those prominent poor bastards that had been summoned to confer. They were pretty good men, mostly. And it didn't seem decent for them to be called in, put under a spotlight, and forced to revise and okay in two hours a statement I shuddered at producing in ten days -- except it be the best possible one that could be produced under the circumstances. And I had a strong premonition that the statement that would be prepared for them if I walked out would be a ridiculous bloody mess.

The egotism this implies is not necessarily egregious. I knew Clark and could cite firsthand experience (besides the immediate one) which made me regard him as a prissy, frat-boy-type incompetent with no sense of proportion at all and no corollary sense of responsibility -- a Georgian who had conspicuously gone far out of his way to get himself a jet-black private secretary didn't impress me as the sort to weigh the nuances of a statement to be issued by prominent leaders from the South. And while it was the first time I had ever met Tex, I figured if he had done much work on Southern problems before that moment, I would have known him or known about him; ergo, the only safe thing to assume was that he was just another bright young man fresh from a viewing of *Tobacco Road.*

So I stood to be harnessed.

Clark read off a list of twenty-two chapter headings -- each calling for a compact 600- or 700-word statement. I noted that they were illogically thrown together -- incoherent like "1. Soil Conservation; 2. Problems of the Middle East; 3. Care and Feeding of Guppies." But I figured that it would be possible to jack these up and trundle a coherent statement underneath.

It was agreed that we would split up the topics among us and draft the related chapters and then simply combine them for submission to the conferees at the forthcoming conference.

Clark read over the list again one at a time and called for a volunteer for each topic. I volunteered like crazy. As I remember it, I took responsibility for sixteen of the twenty-two topics. I understood this played me for a sucker, but that was how I wanted it. What I did was to weigh each topic as it was called out and try to figure out where they would go for information if they had responsibility. Thus, I agreed that Tex should cover the topic of "education"; the Office of Education was in the Department of Interior, and I figured Tex would simply run around to Studebaker's office and get somebody there to draft a statement for him and it would be a pretty good statement. Topics on which I didn't feel sure I knew who it was they could get to do the work for them, I volunteered to do. So that left me with sixteen topics and them with three each.

I went back to Fischer's office and started to put out a call for him but thought better of it. Regardless of how we had crossed the Rubicon, we were on the far bank -- the die was cast; we were committed -- committed, in all decency, to do the best job that could be done. So I gathered together a five-foot shelf of reference books, and in the light of what we had been learning for years past, tried to dish up the best statements I could, full of facts and figures and simply written.

It wasn't a study, it was not an inquiry, it was a preachment in support of some foregone conclusions -- which had been reached in earlier years out of the discussions prompted by *Divided We Stand, Southern Regions,* FSA, and the Southern

Policy Committee, not to mention *Tobacco Road* and the whole complex of ideas accompanying the Great Depression. Witness the way it was occurring -- nobody can do a "study" in that length of time.

Statistics are a fashionable method of bolstering such statements of foregone conclusions, and I used every statistical trick I know. For nine days I worked around the clock and went crazy. At the finish, Fischer returned and pitched in. And on the appointed day we laid before the conferees who were to serve as resonators for our statement, twenty-two mimeographed statements allegedly related to twenty-two set topics.

The conferees swallowed it manfully without a quibble and made extemporaneous affirmative noises and posed for the press photographers. But I will never forget the look of bewilderment on Frank Graham's face as he picked up forty-four pages of mimeographed typing he had never seen before in his life, written by people he had never heard of, much less met, and tried to go through some sort of motions that would appear to constitute consideration and endorsement by the conferees without too conspicuous an exhibition of the hollowness of the process -- like a man with a stuck zipper trying to avoid indecent exposure and yet do so with aplomb, assurance, and flawless dignity.

From that point, Fischer took over entirely. We were back on our normal relationship. My turn for a field trip. I took off on a trip to Amarillo, thence via the University -- where I picked up Creek and Clay for a weekend trip along the Texas coast -- thence across Southern Louisiana, Alabama, and Mississippi, looking at the down-to-earth end of the bureaucracy I worked for in Washington and its functions ... and at the South I had been writing about.

God knows it needed help to climb into the twentieth century. I remember thinking as I drove through Southern and Eastern Alabama and Northern Georgia that the historians had somehow missed an aspect of the Civil War: "What a bitter disillusionment it must have been for Sherman's men when finally they bled their way into that part of the South and for the first time saw with their own eyes what it was they had been fighting to keep in the Union" ... the land so poor, and the people so footless in terms of modern equipment and training in modern technology -- and all frozen in a mold of habit and tradition from which they were helpless to break out except with outside aid.

When I got back, the *Report* had already gone to the printers, and the incredible numbers the modern press can produce were already aimed at the public.

Fischer had done a characteristically beautiful job. In the course of the process politely designated "revision in the light of the conferees' comments," he had shaken down the original twenty-two topics into fifteen, and smoothed it up into the thing that finally appeared -- all with the presence and consent of Clark and Tex (which would have been utterly maddening to me), and then cleared it through Lowell Mellett -- a really competent man -- and thence to the printers in record time.

I had supposed that revision would be a protracted process, permitting me to chip in sources and a final editing. But it was three weeks instead of three months.

And so no real harm done, for Fischer, as usual, had fulfilled his role on our little two-man team to cover whatever derelictions I had been guilty of.

I had not then and have not had since any cavil with any detail of what Fischer made of the manuscript. He tells me there were a lot of figures and statements I had used which he couldn't trace down for checking and so left out. I can understand how that was -- I had dug up and tossed in material and figures I had stumbled across in the course of several years of research, and had manufactured some methods of presenting them which were intended to give them a fresh impact -- so that the clues which might have suggested where they came from were missing. But their absence was not critical.

And in one or two instances, some statistical devices I had intended should mislead the reader had worked on the editors, so the edited version contained some figures which were not merely misleading but technically false. For instance, I had written -- to convey the idea that the South was planting too damn much cotton -- that two-thirds of the Southern farmer's crop income came from cotton and tobacco. I was leaving livestock out of the picture, intentionally. I figured the average reader wouldn't realize this and would think "farm income" instead of "crop income." But the statement was technically accurate and gave increased emphasis to the preconceived idea I wanted to put across. The edited version read, "The farming South depends on cotton and tobacco for two-thirds of its cash income." Reworded to state explicitly what I had intended to convey by an artful omission, the statement was statistically false. But this sort of thing is, to me, inconsequential if the backfire isn't withering -- and it wasn't.

III. Aftermath

The *Report* was a howling success as government documents go.

But to the future historian, it should be emphasized that it came in the dying days of the New Deal. It was, itself, more of historical than prophetic significance at the time it appeared, though none of us was aware of this.

It began rolling off the presses in late summer 1938. World War II was just around the corner, and inevitably the New Deal was to be ground to death under its wheels. In October, Hitler occupied the Sudetenland. A year later he invaded Poland and the following spring, Holland and France.

As an anecdotal illustration associated in point of time with the *Report* ... I remember that a day or so before Clark's call a representative sent over by the Czechoslovak government to study U.S. agricultural programs was sent around to Fischer's office, and the girls sent him on in to me. I spent an afternoon discussing and explaining the nature and relationships of U.S. farm programs. A half-dozen times during the following two months I worked with him further -- helping him find statistics and references, answering his questions. At the end of the two months, he had a pretty good report ready to submit. But he didn't have a government to submit it to any more -- it was post-Munich. He didn't know what to do with his report or with himself ... I never heard of him again.

At any rate, by 1939, Roosevelt, who was so adept at forming his coalitions, saw his destiny presenting him with a new order of problem. In peacetime it was only necessary to have a majority of the people with him, but in war he had to have all the people united in one coalition. So he had to make his peace with the big barons of the realm -- the major corporations -- which are governmental units powerful enough to be comparable in stature with the sovereign itself, the federal government.

Haste was necessary. So he, who understood the need for unity more clearly than they, had to make peace and bring them into the fold on their own terms. The dollar-a-year men appeared, and the old coalition of underprivileged minorities which was the New Deal faded into the background.

The war changed the South -- as the merest inadvertent consequence of its passage -- beyond recognition. The problems we described in 1938 were not the same problems in 1948. The investment of corporate funds on the Texas Gulf Coast alone between 1939 and 1946 make the total appropriations we had hoped to ask for the whole South look like chicken feed. The mold of habit and tradition we had hoped to crack with propaganda was shattered into bits by the impact of the industrialization for war production. In the areas where we had hoped to prime a pump, the war installed a high-pressure water system.

Perhaps a new problem arose to bedevil our children. The war fattened the barons and impoverished the sovereign; without explicit or formal announcement, the centers of power within the country shifted drastically in relative importance.

I am told that in feudal days the lineup was often, in fact usually, the king and the common people (seeking national unity) versus the barons and their retainers. Such an alignment in this country right now makes it folly for the sovereign and the common people to invite a contest. Big (federal) government has to abdicate and hide out. We default the governing of this country into the hands of the barons, and we do whatever is good for General Motors. The sovereign, the nation, may be badly disunited and weakened thereby. But that's a problem for our children. Right now, there is at least peaceful co-existence. And the barons have adopted the South into their realm. And for the South this is a boon -- of sorts. We were hardly a member of the family in 1938.

Meanwhile, we have become again, in the political sphere, a regional criminal class.

Politically, again, the sociologist-type thinkers hold both sides of the stage. And the sociologist approach is essentially mother-female -- aimed at protecting and petting and soothing the little ego in its social environment -- not at training and toughening and teaching purposeful, self-reliant concentration on tangibles with very secondary reference to social symbols and attitudes and status -- which I think of as the economic approach.

A big part of the younger generation of all areas is off chasing rabbits. The bone of contention is whether black people can sit beside white people -- both customers -- at a lunch counter, not who owns the lunch counter and makes a profit. And with this contention occupying the center of the political stage, the Yankee indictment and the Southern defense are at a great distance from reality again, and the economic condition of the South is settled, not on the political stage but in the wings -- in the business world. Economic conditions are hardly mentioned in politics. The sovereign's decision is about martial law in Little Rock, not about resource and industrial development.

Surely, again, re-emphasis on economic issues in the political sphere is needed.

Chapter 10

"How to Read the Wall Street Journal"

In 1980, when Mark was living in Everett, Washington, he wrote a letter to the Everett Herald *about an editorial the* Herald *reprinted from the* Wall Street Journal. *In it he reminisces about his acquaintance with reporters on the* WSJ *when he was in New Deal Washington.*

When the Herald *declined to print Mark's letter, he printed it himself in a booklet with two other letters "rescued from the wastebaskets of newspaper editors" -- one by Franklin Jones, Sr., and the other by Ann Adams. He called the rescued letters "Anti-Pulitzer Prize nominees," and named the booklet* How to Read the Wall Street Journal.

"

7 March 1980

As Our Readers See It
The Everett Herald
Everett, Wash.

I was bemused and dismayed the other day (Tuesday, March 4) to note the *Everett Herald* was featuring a "guest editorial" from the *Wall Street Journal.* The *Herald* usually does better than that.

I was not dismayed that you were quoting from the *Wall Street Journal.* I think it is a splendid newspaper; in fact, it is the only newspaper I read regularly besides the *Herald,* for I find its coverage of the news thorough, competent, realistic, and often more pertinacious and alert than coverage offered by more widely distributed dailies which do not labor under the stigma of the name "Wall Street."

The thing that dismayed me was that given an opportunity to quote from the *Journal,* you were not quoting from its informed news pages but from its editorial page, which, you will observe if you study it carefully, appears to be written by doctrinally orthodox pundits who never read their own news pages or do so only in a doctrinally devout trance-state which insulates them against any and all of the disturbing facts which the news columns present so ably.

The *Journal* has been like that as long as I can remember -- and unfortunately my memory covers an appallingly long span of years. Perhaps I was fortunate in discovering a key in this schizophrenia of the *Journal*'s when I was young. Back in 1935 I landed in Washington, D.C., as an employee of the New Deal government (because it was the only place jobs were opening up for youngsters fresh out of school, I had decided, after researching the matter exhaustively and exhaustingly). The burgeoning bureaucracy was spilling over faster than housing could be built for it, and as chance would have it, my office was stashed in rented space across the hall from the Washington bureau of the *Wall Street Journal.* In time I became friends with the bureau chief and the seven reporters who staffed the *Journal*'s bureau in those days. Better acquaintance speedily convinced me that the staff of the bureau were top-notch reporters, probably better informed and more diligent than the average for the profession. They made a hit with me despite the fact they had two strikes on them when they went to bat wearing that "Wall Street" tag on their uniforms.

At first I couldn't understand how they could be so able and intelligent and still work for the *Wall Street Journal* -- Wall Street! -- with its doggedly and piously conservative, anti-New Deal, anti-Roosevelt, in fact antediluvian editorial clap-trap. But as friendships grew and conversations widened to casual topics like the weather, Sammy Baugh, government gals, politics, and such like, I discovered an odd thing. In the election of 1932, all seven of those reporters had voted for Norman Thomas -- as a protest vote; they weren't socialists, but during the campaign Roosevelt, the Democratic candidate, had been talking about balancing the budget and other nostrums as unrealistic as Hoover's insistence that there wasn't any depression or at least if there was, prosperity was just around the corner. The eighth man in the *Journal* bureau, the chief, had voted for Hoover and was still faulting the people of the United States for faulting Hoover for his non-handling of the depression.

But everybody was happy in his work! There was a division of labor -- the reporters went out and got the facts and wrote their stories, and the bureau chief kept the faith. The news stories were one thing, and the editorial comments were another -- and never the twain should meet, then, now, or *mañana*. Since 1935 I have been a faithful reader of the *Wall Street Journal* -- just skipping the editorial page except when I want a laugh.

So I was dismayed when the *Herald*, when it quoted from the *Wall Street Journal*, picked up an editorial. That's like going to Antoine's and ordering crisped paper pulp sweetened with saccharine and floated in non-dairy coffee creamer, when the menu offers a gourmet's selection of *haute cuisine.*

Ah, well, the *Journal* editorial was *sui generis* -- kind of a religious incantation based on faith, not facts -- purporting to relate to the rapidity of recent price increases (decently covered and obscured by a euphemism, "inflation"). And what does the editor say is causing inflation? Wickedness, that's what. There is a long catalogue of various kinds of wickedness, carefully including "irresponsible federal budget making," each of which types of wickedness, the editorial makes clear, was invented recently and undoubtedly by some demon-inspired Democrat.

And there is a detailed dispensation of forgiveness for the devout, carefully including OPEC and the oil companies, and a special mention for Federal Reserve Board Chairman Volcker, whose doubling of the price of one of our key commodities, credit, is supposed to bring down price levels somehow, though the average reader, without benefit of religious intuitions, may be a little bit hazy as to exactly how. (The average reader, in fact, whose home and business may be covered by one of those sliding-interest-rate mortgages, may think that his cost of living is actually increased by Mr. Volcker's rather frantic performance.)

Of course, as anybody able to read historical statistics knows, inflation (let's not say dirty words like "rising prices") is not a recent dereliction in the U.S. economy. As a constant it dates way, way back to the time when I was a boy. For instance, the price of a bushel of wheat in 1790 was about the same as it was in 1910. There were fluctuations due to supply variables, crop conditions -- but the base price was stable for more than a century. And since the introduction of the Federal Reserve Act in 1916, the price of a bushel of wheat has risen steadily -- fluctuations, still, but steadily rising from one decade to the next, with other prices following the same trend. Inflation is not new any more than I am young.

And of course, as anybody must know who reads the news columns in the *Wall Street Journal* without pious determination to disbelieve what he is reading (thus keeping the faith), in the last few years the prices of oil and credit, two basic ingredients of our economy (*i.e.,* prices which show up as cost ingredients for the whole gamut of other prices) have been raised astronomically, necessitating a wholesale rush of all other prices to keep up. And this, over a matter of the past three or four years, has elevated "inflation" to star billing on the stage of national awareness.

Wherefore the commentators of all stripes, including the editor of the *Journal* (and the *Herald*?) are frantic. Worshippers of the almighty dollar, including the editorial writer of the *Journal*, give free rein to their innate tendency to speak in unknown tongues. They speak louder and longer than ever before, though, unfortunately, their utterances are not made more intelligible by the stepped-up volume. Looking for a historical parallel for the current frenzy, I find myself turning to the Panic of 1896. Panic seems the proper word for our current frame of mind.

When our "leaders" and our "opinion molders" scream themselves out and somebody finally gets around to doing something, I am afraid the action will have to be something like a price freeze -- an awkward device at best, but the only way I know to get the frenzied crowd to settle down and do something rational. It's like playing the National Anthem to quiet a rhubarb in a baseball stadium: It doesn't solve anything, but it gets people to hold still until something useful can be done.

The other day I noticed another item in the news columns of the *Herald* by a *Post-Times* reporter, which considered this possibility of price controls for a few thousand words. The writer seemed to combine a firm intent to be historical with a tendency to cluck like a frightened hen. This, however, did not dismay me; it was a perfect example of the utterances of the time. (Though I do wish you could follow the *Journal*'s policy of keeping such utterances on the editorial page, thus making your paper more convenient to read as a news source.)

"

Chapter 11

The Enemies of My Country

Early in 1940, Mark took leave from his job in Washington, D.C., to return to Texas and work with his father on the Jefferson Jimplecute, *a weekly newspaper in Jefferson, Texas. The following excerpt is from a column Mark wrote for the May 16, 1940, issue of the* Jimplecute:

"

How the War Looks To a Young Man

In making their rounds, the editors run again and again into the question that is on everybody's lips, "What about the war? Will this country get in it?" Senior editor has simply pointed to a head of white hair and replied, "I am not qualified to speak; I would not have to go. At worst it would mean that my sugar would be rationed and I would be inconvenienced. The young men are concerned here."

The junior editor can't disqualify himself on those grounds.

I am well within the army age. Last time the doctor examined me, he looked discouraged, said I suffered from congenital laziness, and suggested that I eat more sauer kraut (or should I say "liberty cabbage" as some very patriotic folks did in the last war?).

I have had some infantry training in college -- of which I remember only a few inapposite details, like, "if your bayonet sticks in a man's chest, you should put your foot between the bayonet and the chest bone to pull it out." I have had a few hours in the air flying solo.

With a wife and daughter, I do not think I would volunteer, but I would be near the top of the draft list. So I suppose I have a right to a few opinions, which are:

I think war is a cruel, stupid, and useless business -- but sometimes a nation must defend itself, and it must be prepared -- 50,000 airplanes a year listens like sense to me.

I do not think we should go to war outside the western hemisphere, but I am not certain I will think so tomorrow -- I have seen too much hysteria around radios right here in Jefferson the past two weeks to predict what I will think twenty-four hours from now; I might decide to go get Hitler myself.

I think Hitler is a skunk, but I think I can find some people just as low as he is much closer to this spot than Berlin. By and large I think reform should begin at home.

I dislike loud-mouthed patriots; I have seen too many half-pint hypocrites with a yellow streak down the back a yard wide out doing a loud job of flag-waving to react very nicely. I don't have to put a very high estimate on myself to think I have done and will do more for my country than 98% of the flag-wavers I meet.

From past experience I draw the egotistical conclusion that I am probably less afraid to die than average, but nevertheless I would walk around the block at least several times to avoid dying. There are several things I want to do first -- write a book and illustrate it, for instance.

I will not on any pretext dodge the draft.

And this unwillingness to dodge the draft is not based on any false assumption that the draft will be universal. I understand that on one pretext or another the rich man's son will not go -- mostly he will get a bureaucratic appointment of some sort to stay home and hound the lives of the loved ones I will leave behind, all in the name of patriotism. ... But most of us poor and middle class fellows who are fit will go. The people -- the sure-nuf down-to-earth people -- will be caught up. And it is in my heart that I had rather share their common fate -- whatsoever it be, however misled, misgoverned or useless -- than to stand aside and claim special place along with the gilded heels and the stuffed shirts. There are a couple of lines from Kipling that have always had a sort of Old Testament prophetic meaning to me:

And Amorite and Eremite or general averagee.
"The people, Lord, thy people are good enough for me."

That's the core of the thing -- I am ready to share whatever fate befalls my sort of folks, along with them -- including the draft.

That's the sum total of my opinions. You notice they're pretty confused personal reactions. I find most other young men of my age in much the same frame of mind. If you ask, "should we join the allies?" all I can answer is, "I don't know and neither do you. History will tell us that fifty years from now." All we can do is guess. I'm guessing that we shouldn't enter the war until invasion of this hemisphere is attempted. I'm also guessing that whether we should or not we will be in it, and that I will go. My next personal statement on the war will be issued when I come back, if I come back.

For what more is there to say? And how useless it would be to say it, anyway! For destiny has arrogated our self-rule, the mob is milling and muttering and storm is king.

”

Mark returned to Washington in March 1941.

The Patents Committee

In New Deal Washington I had led a fairly satisfactory life as a writer (perforce largely a ghost writer) for New Deal outfits and causes, but as war came on, the New Deal was shelved right and left and I did not feel comfortable on my shelf. Tentatively I moved over to the Office of Strategic Services but found its think-tank sections specious, and I was not qualified for work in the K Section, which was fostering resistance movements in German-held Europe.

After Pearl Harbor was bombed, I was borrowed from OSS by the Justice Department and loaned to the Senate Committee on Patents for the duration of hearings on some cartels which were operating under direction of both German and American corporate interests.The prime mover in those Patents Committee hearings was Walton Hamilton, who had been my first boss in Washington. Hammy arranged that I should be borrowed from OSS and Creekmore Fath borrowed from his post as Counsel to the Federal Power Commission, and the two of us then were assigned to the Senate Committee on Patents as the entire Committee staff.

Besides being the man who had taught Dr. Bob and, as head of the Brookings School, had handed him his Ph.D., Hammy was also professor of Constitutional law at Yale and a member of the group who interviewed possible appointees to the Supreme Court for Roosevelt. He was a colleague of Thurman Arnold, who, as the war began, was head of the Anti-trust Division of the Justice Department. Thurman had spent years subpoenaing information to be used in anti-trust prosecutions of American corporate giants.

When the war forced Roosevelt to seek cooperation from the multi-national cartels' American subsidiaries, the cartels' designated ambassadors -- the dollar-a-year men -- demanded that all anti-trust actions against them be dropped "so our executives can turn their attention from these trifling matters and thus be free to tend to problems of war production." With Hitler holding a pistol to the temple of all democracies everywhere, Roosevelt was in no bargaining position. Anti-trust actions were dropped right and left -- with face-saving consent decrees. (I remember that the one with Standard Oil -- which had already been in the courts for seven years -- said in effect that whereas Standard denied that it had ever done anything monopolistic or even thought a monopolistic thought, it consented to promise that it would not do it again.)

The opening day of the hearings marked the pinnacle of my career as a ghostwriter -- with a letter from Roosevelt and statements from Committee Chairman Sen. Bone, and members Senators LaFollette and Pepper, followed by a long statement from Thurman -- all drafted by Creek and myself beforehand. But I have to admit the prize phrase of the day -- in the letter from Roosevelt welcoming the hearings -- was written by Creek, -- to-wit: "Patents are the key to technology; technology is the key to production; production is the key to victory."

Hammy's objective in arranging the Patents Committee hearings was simply to get the mass of information on U.S. corporate organization which Thurman's young lawyers had accumulated into some safe haven where it could be consulted after the war ... before the dollar-a-year men had it declared top secret and then destroyed for security reasons.

And it worked. For months young anti-trust lawyers brought huge corrugated cartons full of photostats marked "Confidential" and "Secret" and even "Top Secret" into the hearing room, then submitted them as exhibits to be printed in reports of the hearings, and gave a brief summary of the industry they had been studying for years past.

Since the American interests included a bluebook of corporate powers -- Standard of New Jersey, General Electric, Dow Chemical, Union Carbide, Rohm and Haas, nearly all the pharmaceutical firms, etc., etc., we figured (correctly) that one of them would have the hearings shut down as soon as our objective became clear. The multi-nationals operated under patent agreements, hence their national and world dominance was threatened by surveillance of patent licensing practices by any democratic government adhering to the doctrines of anti-trust. We all understood this, and since they had just shown us (by getting the anti-trust suits dropped) that they had the power to destroy any threat to them, we anticipated that the hearings would be terminated as soon as the dollar-a-year men realized where we were headed and had time to organize a counterattack through their lobbyists.

But we did have a four-foot shelf of printed committee hearings -- information in the public record -- by the time the lobbyist for a German-controlled pharmaceutical firm was able to blackmail one of the Senators needed to keep the hearings in session, and the hearings were shut down.

Probably of all those actively involved I had been the most pessimistic -- about that era and about the post-war future too.

I thought the war was handing the economic royalists total victory, and the liberal power structure which had sustained the New Deal faced total defeat. I did not think there was any hope that after the war we would be able to salvage any part of the power structure the New Deal had laboriously put in place. Maybe, at 32, I was just old and tired. But I had no hope that after the war the total victory of the multi-nationals could be reversed any more than Rome could have returned to the old days of the Roman Republic after the first Caesar.

So, before the hearings even began, I went down and filed my application for a commission in the Navy. During the hearings, notice that my application was accepted came through. And Senator Bone -- senior member of the Naval Affairs Committee as well as chairman of the Patents Committee -- agreed that the day the hearings were ended he would have me called to active duty. He called Forrestal (handling congressional relations for the Navy at the time), and the afternoon we learned the hearings were ended, my orders to report for active duty the next day came down. That night, in uniform, I dined with Creek and his roommate, Jim Anderson, and made them a speech: "I want to get out to the combat zone where the enemies of my country are shot at rather than bowed to and paid off."

Later that night I drafted an introduction Creek had been asked to write for a book on cartels by a refugee German professor of economics. Forty years later, reading Charles Higham's *Trading With the Enemy,* I was astonished to come across a paragraph from the introduction I wrote that night.

"Since the middle thirties, whenever a German business group wanted to make an agreement with any business concern beyond the borders of Germany, it was required first to submit a full text of the proposed agreement to the Reichsbank. The Reichsbank rejected or rewrote until the agreement met its approval. The Reichsbank approved no agreement which did not fit into the plans of the Nazi State and carry that state another step toward its goal of world domination. In other words, any American firm which reached an agreement or dealt with a

German firm ... was dealing ... with Hitler himself."[1]

The next day I was on the train headed for Navy duty.

I did not intend to come back. I made no announcement to that effect; one friend guessed what I was up to at the time and confronted me with the accusation, but if any others suspected it, they kept it to themselves.

---

[1]Gunther Reimann, *Patents for Hitler* (1942), quoted in Charles Higham, *Trading With the Enemy: An Exposé of the Nazi-American Money Plot 1933-1949*, Delecorte Press, 1983, pp. 21-22.

DATUM IV

World War II and After

Chapter 12

"Me & the King of England"

Mark joined the Navy in July 1942. He was trained at Quonset Point, R.I., and attached to Fighting Squadron 18, Air Group 30. He wrote about his most frustrating experience in World War II in a manuscript he never published titled "Me and the King of England." The Prologue summarizes the experience, and a memo to the captain of the British ship H.M.S. Implacable *gives details.*

"

Prologue

After the operations against Formosa, French Indo-China, Northern Luzon, and the Ryukyus [islands of Japan] in support of the Lingayen Gulf landing, Air Group 30, having experienced 30 percent casualties in four months, was sent back to the states to re-form. Adams, air-group intelligence officer, returned with them as far as Pearl Harbor, where he was detached and assigned as liaison officer to carriers of the British Pacific Fleet, then scheduled to arrive in the Pacific.

He protested, pleading that he was Anglophobe and preferred reassignment to some American squadron returning to the combat zone. Protest overruled. We had promised to put an officer experienced in the operations of the American fast carrier task force aboard each British carrier as it went into action against the Japs in coordination with American fleets. And officers with that experience and available were in short supply.

He accordingly shepherded nearly a ton of maps, reports, etc., to Manus [island in the Admiralty Islands in the North Pacific] by air and reported for duty on *H.M.S. Illustrious.* With *Illustrious* he went through the Okinawa campaign until that ship, having had its plates ruptured dangerously by a Kamikaze bomb, was relieved on station and sent back to Leyte Gulf. Considering the officers of *Illustrious* adequately trained, and believing, correctly, that she would be returned to England for repairs anyway, Adams asked to be transferred back to the American fleet. Refused. Aboard *Illustrious* to Sydney, Australia, where he was detached and assigned to *H.M.S. Implacable,* freshly arrived in the Pacific and scheduled to shove off four days later for training operations in the central Pacific.

Reporting to the headquarters liaison officer in Sydney, Adams was taken to see Admiral Sir Something-hyphen-Something, chief of staff to Admiral Sir Bruce Fraser, Commander-in-Chief, British Pacific Fleet. Admiral Sir Something-hyphen-Something inquired anxiously why British ships seemed to be getting hit so often. Adams replied with a pointed and unprintable analysis of British carrier operations that lasted thirty minutes. To his surprise the admiral was impressed as well as offended. Adams's request for transfer back to the American fleet was again refused and he was asked to submit his analysis in writing for use by the BPF staff. Adams accordingly applied his sober hours in the early morning of the succeeding four days to a 40-page memo, complete with detailed recommendations for reorganization of the Royal Navy. This document was left with the American liaison officer to deliver to the admiral, just before Adams boarded his new ship and sailed north. It is known that this liaison officer had hysterics when he read the memo, and it is believed that he suppressed it. Too bad. It was full of good sense as well as bad diplomacy.

Aboard *Implacable* Adams devoted himself to reorganizing the intelligence department and photo-recce procedures while at sea and to stealing belly tanks[1] while ashore. After the attack on Truk [island in the Caroline Islands of Micronesia in the North Pacific] -- when four British cruisers went in to shell the atoll and one (repeat, one) cruiser actually hit one (repeat, one) island -- Adams considered his teaching efforts successfully concluded

---

[1]Tanks attachable to the belly of an airplane to store extra fuel in. Tanks on the British fighter planes were too small to carry enough fuel to fly long missions.

(the air attack was almost decent by American standards) and back ashore he finished stealing the belly tanks. Accordingly he again requested transfer (memo attached).

(

Memo Requesting Transfer

H.M.S. Implacable
26 June 1945

From: Lieutenant Commander Mark Adams, ACI, USNR, Liaison Officer, *H.M.S. Implacable.*
To: Captain C.H. Hughes-Hallett, *H.M.S. Implacable.*
Subject: Request for Return to American Fleet.
Enclosure: (a) Report of Activities in Support of Effort to Fit Special Auxiliary Belly Tanks to Seafires.

1. Believing that for me to serve longer aboard *H.M.S. Implacable* would be the contrary of helpful to the ship and to relations between the U.S. and British Pacific Fleets, I request that upon our return to port I be put ashore, declared *persona non grata* to the BPF, and turned over to the American Naval authorities -- together with a report of my activities -- for such action, disciplinary or otherwise, as they may see fit. Reasons for believing that I can no longer be helpful are detailed in paragraphs 2, 3, and 4 below.

2. As an ACI officer, my primary mission was to make as many helpful explanations and suggestions as possible on Intelligence procedure in the Pacific. I have participated in the drill of the Intelligence Department of *Implacable* during the Towi exercise and the Truk operation. These drills covered the full gamut of intelligence activities to be experienced in the Pacific. All the suggestions I could think of based on these drills have been made to Commander (O) and to the officers of the Intelligence Department, and have been either accepted, rejected, or ignored on the third repetition. I can usefully contribute nothing further. I believe the basic structure and

functioning of the intelligence units to be sound; the details of administration are not precisely as my own habit and training would have made them, but it is inevitable that this ship should do things differently in some respects; I am not sure but what the differences represent improvement. After discussion and suggestion, the only further effort possible would be to assume executive responsibility; and this would weaken, rather than strengthen, the intelligence unit of the ship, for if I became an integral cog in its machinery, my removal from it following the forthcoming operation would leave it unpracticed in such part of its drill as I had executed. Moreover, my mission was explicitly liaison; it was not intended to supply personnel to do the routine work of the BPF.

As to answering questions on the current operational practice of the American fast carrier task force in the event of joint operations, I can only plead incompetence. I was familiar with its practice as of early last winter, but since that time I have been away -- in the BPF -- the command has changed twice and the tactical and strategical situation, and almost certainly American practice, has altered completely. My advice would be unreliable. Questions addressed by signal to the liaison officer of AAC 1, who has better sources of information, would be more logical and helpful.

3. Without authority or assignment of responsibility, I have participated in an effort to obtain and adapt an auxiliary drop tank for the Seafire [fighter plane]. I felt that the logic of the situation, and a sincere wish to be helpful to the BPF in any way that I could, constituted sufficient authority for action. If I have helped this effort to reach a successful conclusion, and it is helpful to the BPF, I am glad to have had a part in it. It is concluded.

4. The efforts by which I might be helpful to the BPF and *Implacable* having reached conclusion, I find positive reason why I should be discharged from its service, however derogatory to my character and ability the terms of dismissal might be. This reason is that in the course of three months' enforced association with it, I have conceived for the Royal Navy and particularly for

its corps of officers a contempt so nearly complete and so passionate that it amounts almost to hatred. I am happy to find that there are many individual exceptions to this general and typical reaction; many British Naval officers -- including yourself, and including a high proportion of Air Arm flying types -- I have come to regard with the greatest respect and admiration. But at the same time I have come to think the general level of energy, initiative, resourcefulness, and efficiency among officers of the Royal Navy to be the lowest of that of any organization with which I have come in contact in my brief thirty-five years. Hence I find working within the structure of the organization perennially irritating. And in this frame of mind I am not competent to fulfill my duties as liaison officer or to be of real service to the British Pacific Fleet.

5. I am very sorry this frame of mind has developed. I have made sincere efforts to rid myself of it, without success. I understand that this marks me as temperamentally incompetent to carry on my assigned duties, and I expect that U.S. Naval Authority will accordingly take severe disciplinary action against me. Nevertheless, the facts are as stated, and I feel that it would be best for all concerned if the course of action suggested in paragraph 1, above, were taken. With the BPF, I am worse than useless. Returned to the American fleet in which I have served happily and, I think, usefully, even though disciplined and degraded in the course of return, I feel that I might be of some further service to the war effort.

6. In case curiosity should suggest inquiry into the specific sort of situation which has led me into my present incompetent frame of mind, and the way in which I have reacted, I enclose a report of my experiences in connection with the effort to get belly tanks, specifically detailing typical instances which provoked reaction in paragraphs 24 and 25.

7. I understand that no extenuation is possible, and the enclosure is included, not as extenuation, but simply in some small part to explain how my present temperamental incompetence has grown.

Report of Irregular Activities of Adams, M., Lt. Comdr., USNR, Re Belly Tanks for Seafires

1. According to the best information available to me when I reported aboard *Implacable* at Sydney, the position was this: That it would be more than a month before the ship would be engaged in a serious action. That the BPF would take into that action four fleet carriers, of which two would carry Seafire fighters, which would be inadequate for CAP at high altitude (no oxygen) and too limited in range for escorting strikes to the target. That at the end of a little more than a month an action against a target which could put up serious airborne opposition was contemplated. That an adequate supply of long-range [fuel] tanks for Seafires was not at hand. That, as a consequence, the British Pacific Fleet might go into the action essentially crippled for lack of fighter strength over the target.

2. Hence when Wing Leader Campbell-Horsfall indicated a desire to try to adapt some available type of belly tank to the Seafire, I determined to assist him in every way possible -- if it could be done, that would be the most valuable possible contribution to the effectiveness of the BPF; if not, nothing would be lost but the effort.

3. The Wing Leader's effort might be aided by American units in the area. Their assistance might be more readily enlisted if he were accompanied, supported, and vouched for by an American officer. Accordingly, I accompanied and supported him as best I could in his dealings with the various units which might help.

4. Lt. Comdr. C-H enlisted the aid of AROU 1 (Aircraft Repair and Overhaul Unit 1) (USN, Momote) in finding and adapting to the Seafire the best possible long-range tank. The flat P-40 tank (89 imperial gallons) appeared to be the only one with adequate capacity which could be fitted and still provide enough deck clearance. We were assured that it could be found in the area in excess supply (by Lt. Ullman, U.S. Army, Momote, among others) and that fittings for adapting the Seafire bomb rack could also be had.

5. Squadron Leader Franks, RNZAF, offered to assist in obtaining a supply of the tanks. He sent to RNZAF supply headquarters, Guadalcanal, the following signal: "British Fleet urgently requires quantity 200 or more P-40 centerline fuel tanks to carry out modification Seafires. Request you investigate possibility stock held by rear echelon U.S. Army Air Corps your base. If no stock there, request you arrange that activity check by RDO with U.S. Army Air Corps at Biak [island in Indonesia]. Advise urgently." Squadron Leader Franks felt this should produce immediate results, and promised to let us know as soon as he had word through SBNO [Senior British Naval Officer] Manus.

6. AROU 1 undertook to design and construct a prototype modified bomb rack to accommodate the tank and have it ready for flight tests with the only tank available at Momote (given us by the RAAF local commander) by the time we returned from the Towi exercise. I dropped by and explained to Captain Waight [Senior British Naval Officer] what I was doing on my way back to the ship.

7. Getting ashore immediately after our return from the exercise, I contacted AROU 1 and Squadron Leader Franks. (The AROU loaned me a jeep to get about in.) I found that the AROU seemed to be progressing satisfactorily but Squadron Leader Franks had had no word. Lt. Comdr. C-H would be needed at Momote to supervise technical work on the bomb rack and flight tests of the installation on a Seafire. Meanwhile the work of locating and procuring a supply of the tanks should be sped by any means possible. I talked again with Lt. Ullman who thought Biak the most likely spot to get results and told me Capt. Markey, HQ, 4th ASAC, Brokei Airstrip, Biak (with whom Ullman had worked), would know most about the P-40 tank situation of any man in the area. I determined to see Capt. Markey and try to speed delivery of tanks while Lt. Comdr. C-H worked on the problem of adapting the tank to the Seafire. Explaining what I was doing to Lt. Comdr. C-H, I left him at AROU 1 and proceeded independently.

8. I went to Commander, Naval Air Base, Los Negros

(USN), explained why I wanted to get to Biak and return by air, and asked him for aid in getting priority for air travel. He readily offered to assist in getting the priority in any way he could, but suggested that since I was attached to a British unit, I should get some British authority to sign something or other written on a piece of paper so if question ever arose, he could produce something from his files which would serve as evidence that he knew he was not helping me jump ship when he assigned the priority. This seemed reasonable. I wanted to catch a plane that night. I did not have time to get out to the ship and back and still make the plane, so I went to SBNO Manus to get the requisite "piece of paper signed by some British authority."

When I arrived at SBNO's quarters, I found Capt. Waight in a great hurry to change clothes for a ceremony involving CS 4 and Commodore Boake, USN, Commander Naval Base, Manus. I explained hurriedly why I needed a letter from him and that waiting until evening was out of the question. He was very annoyed at my insistence, stating that he had 250 belly tanks in the harbor. I discovered that they were Corsair belly tanks. I explained that this did not meet the emergency, and continued to insist. To get rid of me, he turned to his secretary, directed him to write the required letter and sign it, and hurried off to change clothes. I explained again to his secretary why I needed the letter; the secretary was ready to be helpful but a little puzzled, so to clarify the matter I sat down and drafted a letter. He had no yeoman available (lunchtime) so I also typed it up for him. Since I was conscious that I was bulling the works on sheer impudence anyhow, I thought I might as well go the whole way, so I phrased the letter strongly (but vaguely) as follows:

"Office of S.B.N.O. Manus Island
6.9.1945

"To: Lt. Cdr. Mark Adams, USNR,
Sr. U.S. Naval Liaison Officer,
H.M.S. Implacable

"In accordance with conversations with Commanding Officer,

H.M.S. Implacable which cannot be quoted herein, you are requested to proceed to Biak U.S. Army Air Center upon an inquiry of the utmost urgency concerning the combat potentialities of Seafire aircraft in this theatre of operations. Upon conclusion of your inquiries at Biak you will return immediately to rejoin your ship.

[Waight's signature]
"Captain, R.N."

The secretary signed Capt. Waight's name to this letter, stamped it with SBNO's stamp to make it look more official. With it, I talked myself into a Class 2 priority for air travel and caught the next plane for Biak.

I discovered later that Capt. Waight found this quite upsetting. He wrote a letter to the ship inquiring if I was a spy. He apparently failed completely to remember the visit I had made a week before (see paragraph 6) purely for the purpose of keeping him informed as to what we were doing. Certainly the next time I saw him he denounced me for adding to the many burdens he already bore by this activity in connection with belly tanks. He described his other burdens at considerable, if pointless, length on that occasion.

9. At Biak, Capt. Markey was readily helpful. He told me that two weeks before, he had been embarrassed at having 300 P-40 tanks on hand with no P-40s to use them, that by a feat of persuasion he had finally gotten the Aussies to take them off his hands, and that the last of them had been loaded not an hour before and shipped to the RAAF supply depot at Morotai [island]. He introduced me to Flt. Lt. Billington, RAAF Liaison Officer, Biak Supply Depot. Flt. Lt. Billington was eager to cooperate and immediately sent the following signal to Morotai (with a repeat of the request to Finschaven [in Papua New Guinea] where he thought an additional supply was held by the RAAF; other supplies in Australia):

"Secret. Application has been made by Royal Navy to obtain 200 each belly tanks 109 gallons (US) capacity. Urgently required by *H.M.S. Implacable* for fitment to Seafire aircraft.

Request assurance be given that tanks will be held and made available your area for above mentioned carrier. Suggest supply be made from 109 gallon belly tanks recently shipped from Depot Three. Refer our Q373/u 29th. Advise immediately." Addressee 1st T.A.F., R.A.A.F., info 25 and 29 Air Supply Depots (Morotai).

He felt that this would guarantee supply of the tanks and that the ASP's would test the tanks for us before delivery. He was also hopeful that Finschaven would be able to offer a supply closer to Manus. He would advise us through SBNO Manus as soon as he heard. I told him that when the Seafire squadrons found that they were assured of tanks they would be so happy they would undoubtedly send him a case of scotch so he could join in the general celebration. (This afterthought was intended to keep him working at it while we were at sea, in case his spirit flagged without me there to keep him steamed up. And, of course, as something of a goodwill gesture to a unit which was volunteering aid. When I got back aboard and wrote a report on my activities, I offered, in writing, to pay for the scotch, and asked that the ship should permit the withdrawal of it somehow. I had indicated to the Wing Leader before I left for Biak that if such a gesture seemed indicated, I would make it.)

Meanwhile we went down to the yards of the Army Supply Depot and looked over about thirty tanks which had not been shipped to Morotai because their crates had come off. We found about a dozen of these which appeared in perfect shape, and Flt. Lt. Billington undertook to see that the good ones were flown to Manus for us within the next five days. My idea for this was to permit us to have enough for a demonstration to AC 1 [Admiral Sir Philip Vian] before we went south to meet him -- just in case we should need to have him dispatch a destroyer to Finschaven or Morotai to pick up the remainder (200) tanks on our way north.

10. My plane back to Manus was twelve hours late. It was apparent that if I made the ship it would be very close -- the plane was due to land at Momote at 1130 and the ship to depart at 1200. The NATS pilot radioed ahead for me and a

command car was waiting at the plane to take me to Manus. I paused just long enough to phone SBNO's office my situation and ask that a boat be made available at the pier to take me across the harbor. I was assured that this would be done and I broke all speed limits getting to the Manus pier. When I arrived at the pier I found the R.N. boat office closed and locked and no boat waiting. After all it was lunchtime and I am sure that the bar had opened even earlier. I phoned the port director and he immediately dispatched a speed boat to pick me up. I took advantage of the interval while the boat was getting alongside the pier to phone Capt. Waight, explain what had been done, and request that signals from Biak (I had arranged with the Aussies to signal through him) should be forwarded to us while we were at sea, thus permitting us, with knowledge of allocations and quantities, to begin arranging for shipment immediately we got back into port. Aside from my previous injuries to Capt. Waight, he had been called from lunch to the phone, and he was pretty crisp with me, saying that he would have to consider the position in the light of conditions of radio silence (!!!!!), etc., etc., and that he would arrive at a decision. I had to leave it at that to catch the ship. I could only repeat my request that the signals be forwarded. I climbed a Jacob's ladder to board *Implacable* as it cleared the harbor entrance -- too damn close!

11. I learned that Lt. Comdr. C-H had obtained from the Americans the requisite number of bomb shackles for adapting Seafire bomb racks. I might add that this was done on his own initiative and without my aid -- the wing leader was outstandingly energetic and resourceful -- and effective -- at every point within his reach. His example of initiative and pertinacity won for the British fleet a goodly number of American and Australian friends whose friendship and aid could have been enlisted in no other way.

12. We received no signals concerning the tanks between the time we left for Truk and our return to Manus. Upon our return to Manus I went ashore as speedily as possible and being, as usual, denied transportation or even a courteous refusal of

transportation by SBNO's office at the foot of the pier, I made my way on foot to SBNO's office on the hilltop. (I had already so often borrowed American transport on a plea of British business that I had determined that to do it again except in case of extremity would be to do the British a disservice -- by giving them a bad name for scrounging without reciprocity -- as well as inconveniencing the Americans.) At SBNO's office I again saw Capt. Waight and received my usual verbal excoriations for the manner in which I was adding to his burdens. When pressed, he burrowed into his desk and produced two signals from the Australians at Biak. One notified us of shipment by U.S. Naval Air Transport of the tanks available at Biak. Although these (which arrived just as we left harbor) were plainly addressed to me, Capt. Waight had at once ordered them transferred to Ponam; fortunately, although three days had passed since the order, no action had been taken by his transport organization, so no harm was done. The second signal affirmed that the required number of tanks would be available at Morotai and asked what agency would pick them up. The signal was four days old when I saw it -- we could have been well along with plans for shipment of the tanks when we got back to harbor if SBNO had forwarded the signal as requested. As it was, I hurried back to the ship and presented the signals to Lt. Comdr. C-H who took them to Comdr. Flying.

13. Comdr. Flying informed Capt. Hughes-Hallet, and the captain acted swiftly and efficiently to present to CS-4 [the British battleship and Pacific fleet commander] the question of a destroyer or some other vessel to bring the tanks from Morotai. My information was that the upshot of this conference was agreement that CS-4 would ask Capt. Waight for a minesweeper to retrieve the tanks and that he (CS-4) would forthwith signal the request.

14. Accordingly, Comdr. Flying, Lt. Comdr. C-H, and myself went ashore at nine the following morning to see what arrangements could be made. We were rather stopped in our tracks by Capt. Waight's statement that he had received no signal from CS-4. (I don't know who fumbled in this instance,

either CS-4, CS-4's signalman, SBNO's signalman, or SBNO's office -- it could have been any of the four, or perhaps Capt. Waight had seen the signal and failed to make the association; at any rate when I saw him again, twenty-four hours later, Capt. Waight stated that he had received the signal.) However, we explained the position; Comdr. Flying offered to check on the signal. Capt. Waight said that he could not send a vessel but would check with the Americans. And we left it at that and after hearing another precis of the epic entitled "The Trials and Burdens of Capt. Waight," we departed.

15. Back at the pier we parted to continue our efforts severally. Lt. Comdr. C-H went on to Momote to continue flight tests of the tanks and fittings. I undertook to get the tanks from Momote immediately aboard the ship. Commander Flying agreed to check on CS-4's signal. He agreed to signal SBNO authority for me to draft a reply to the Aussies at Biak -- a receipt for the tanks at Momote and promise of notice of shipment out of Morotai, as an indication that we had not suddenly defaulted. I felt this signal to the Aussies was needed at once, for after all they had acted nearly a week before and had had no word from the BPF since. Comdr. Flying agreed also to speed shipment of our token of appreciation to the Aussies -- *i.e.*, the scotch.

16. Lt. Comdr. C-H accordingly went immediately to Momote to complete flight tests. He devoted that afternoon to technical work. The following morning he took the plane up and kept it in the air more than four hours, completely emptying the belly tank and checking oil consumption. That afternoon he obtained agreement of AROU 1 to make the fuel feed fittings for the requisite number of planes -- as I say, his example and personality enlisted the readiest and most willing cooperation of the Americans; he himself was working, cooperating, and, incidentally, risking his neck with the tests, and the Americans were eager to follow his example of pertinacity. Similarly, he enlisted the aid of the RAFLOs in diverting a plane returning from Leyte to pick up an immediate supply of tanks from Morotai. He brought them aboard for an

evening to show them the carrier, which was a new phenomenon to them. The following morning he dropped a tank to test plane behavior, and after some more work on adaptation of the bomb rack design, it was time to return to Ponam and the ship.

17. I went from the pier to SBNO's office where, on my assurance that a signal granting me authority to do so would be sent from the ship, the SBNO's secretary allowed me to signal Biak as indicated above. I went on over to Momote, obtained a truck from the R.N. liaison office there, borrowed a rearming boat from CNAB (USN) Operations, and had the tanks aboard at tea-time. The American boat crew were unable to comprehend the institution of tea, hence unable to understand why the Officer of the Deck was unable to summon a working party to help them get the tanks up the ladder and aboard ship. The boat was borrowed and I had promised not to delay it, so I pitched in with the boat crew at unloading the tanks. We had only one aboard when two out of 200 observing sailors pitched in to help us as volunteers. Their help was gratefully received.

18. The following morning I spoke a few words to the Royal Air Force officers about air transport of tanks from Morotai, saw some AROU people, watched the Seafire take off for the endurance test, and was in the liaison office writing a note to be handed Lt. Comdr. C-H on his return to the field when I heard my name mentioned by the orderly in the course of a telephone conversation. I introduced myself for the sixth or seventh time and learned that I was wanted by SBNO.

19. At SBNO's office, after the usual denunciation for the way Adams in particular and *Implacable* in general were adding to his burdens, I learned that negotiations for a ship were somewhat bogged down. Capt. Waight phoned Commodore Boake's chief of staff and took me to see the Commodore. I explained the situation briefly to Commodore Boake and with him and his shipping officer, Lt. Loree, made a firm arrangement for FS149 to load tanks at Morotai and return them to Manus. With Loree I saw this confirmed with a signal to Morotai, Biak, the Aussie air supply, and FS149.

20. As to Comdr. Flying's contributions, I do not know what hand he had in getting CS-4's signal forward, but at any rate SBNO had it the following day. As to the other two items (which concerned me immediately because I had persuaded someone else to stick his neck out on my assurance in both instances): The signal authorizing me to draft a reply to Biak had not arrived after what I considered a reasonable interval. However this could have been easily the result of signals difficulty, and the SBNO's secretary trusted me sufficiently to send the signal I drafted at once, waiting for the authorizing signal from *Implacable* which would clear his action of blame after the fact -- if it came some time later, its presence in the files would still be sufficient. When I saw him the following day, however, he said no such signal had arrived. (This was not quite exactly true. What he had received was a signal so ambiguous that he failed to associate it with the event.) At any rate I hurried out to the ship to get a signal which would put his records in order; I never let any man stick his neck out for me without backing him up. I saw Comdr. Flying, and he assured me that such a signal had been sent, directed that a copy be supplied me, and left me to wait for its delivery by the signal department. When it came I found it merely stated that I would be able to furnish information to SBNO; it did not authorize me to draft a signal to Biak -- which is what I had asked. I was a little puzzled at this vague phrasing. Either Comdr. F. was refusing to back me up with this trifling delegation of authority, or it was purposely ambiguous so that if the effort should later come to the attention of authorities and be blamed, he could disclaim knowledge and responsibility -- or he was damned inept at drafting signals. I did not think him inept at drafting signals. I thought and still think that the second stated alternative was the governing one. And I am always a little embarrassed to find myself in company with the moral courage of the little dyspeptic mouse. Either Comdr. Flying knew of the effort and approved it and should have had confidence enough to avow his conviction and openly assist when his assistance was required, or he disapproved it -- and he could have stopped it

with a word at any point in the proceedings. An American prejudice has it that people interested in keeping their skirts clean should keep to such effeminate company as would give point and general acceptance to the art. The matter of the signal was a trifling thing, but I was contemptuous of the spirit of it, whichever of the three possible explanations of the result one might adopt.

As to the third thing requested of Comdr. F, expediting the shipment of the scotch: As I say, I had offered to pay for it myself. I requested that it be packed in a wooden case so that it would not be obviously a case of scotch. (A case of scotch easily identified as such has a bad habit of being lost in transit.) And I asked that it be shipped air freight. I had stated that I wanted it shipped before we got back to port. I repeated the request when I brought the Aussies' signals back to the ship the day we reached port. I repeated it again to Comdr. F the following morning when we went to see Capt. Waight. I repeated it again when I came aboard to check on the signal mentioned above in this paragraph. Nothing happened except delay and evasion. Absolutely nothing. At this point I went over to Momote and plead with Lt. Comdr. C-H to see if he could do anything; I explained that I apparently had on my hands some fastidious "gentlemen" who felt that in having concluded this deal for belly tanks I was proven to be a low-caste scoundrel with whom it was degrading to find themselves associated; I suspected that they regarded the scotch as a bribe rather than a gesture of good will. And they were fastidious about dirtying their hands on the likes of myself and the Aussies, even by remote control. Meanwhile, by their delay and evasion in sending the scotch -- as a gesture I had suggested and more or less led the Aussies to expect -- they were not only giving the British the reputation of being the most snide and graceless scroungers in the Pacific but also holding me up to view as being without even that honor which prevails among thieves. I asked him to either get action or a refusal of action. If action was refused, then I could tend to the matter myself. He, of course, assured me I was misinterpreting the event and promised again to speak to Comdr. F. Comdr. C-H was aboard the following evening, with some AROU officers and the Royal Air Force officers who were arranging air transport for tanks. I also spoke again to Comdr. F. The following morning at breakfast I spoke to him again. He told me to wait in my cabin and the case would be sent down and that when this happened I was to call him and he would request a seaman to help me pack it. I waited in my cabin for two hours and a half. At the end of that period of time a sailor appeared and handed me six bottles of something or other. I asked him if that was all. I was assured it was. The last time I bought a case of scotch, there were twelve bottles, but there was left me little time -- I had to tend to the crating and shipping. So I phoned Comdr. F. His steward answered the phone and told me shortly that Comdr. F. had left word that he was not to be disturbed. I thought this just as well. I would save time getting the thing done ashore. So I went topside at 1030 and asked for a boat ashore. I was told that I might get a boat ashore at 1430. The Captain's motorboat was idle, so I requested his permission to use it in getting ashore. As usual, Capt. Hughes-Hallett's cooperation was instant and courteous. With Snaps, whom I intended to help swap some photo print paper at ASD, I set out for shore. The boat broke down fifty yards from the gangway, immediately astern. Although we lay there forty-five minutes, drifting with wind and current, flashing lights, waving, and hailing passing boats, the quarterdeck did not notice us and we had drifted beyond the *Pioneer* before finally one of the *Pioneer's* boats came alongside and tossed us a rope and towed us back to *Implacable.* We crawled up the Jacob's ladder to the quarterdeck and again began asking for a boat. By making ourselves a confounded nuisance we finally got one about 1240. Ashore, with a trip twenty miles to Air Supply Depot with Snaps scheduled and no transport -- futile to ask SBNO and I refused to ask the Americans lest all welcome be worn out before a special emergency arose necessitating my going to them -- I had little time to get the scotch packed. I turned it over to the Royal Navy Liaison Officer and RAF officers at Momote, who agreed to do the work of packing and getting it to Biak. I continued to ASD.

The RAF officers at Momote also gave me the final word on the air transport they had diverted via Morotai for the tanks; and I thanked them in behalf of the ship.

21. Naturally I enlisted the aid of other Americans in obtaining and sending to the Aussies at Biak the other half case of scotch which the ship failed to supply. For I still entertain the wan hope that the Aussies may, in the end, think well of the ship they had befriended when they were told it was in need.

22. That pretty well concluded the deal on the tanks. In sum, I want to point out that the Aussies had cheerily done the following things: Supplied the tanks, responded instantly and cheerily to the need for signals, arranged transport by air for two batches of tanks, loaned us their only tank at Momote for experimental work, occasionally loaned me a jeep. The Americans had furnished me air transport to and from Biak, made the prototype bomb rack, helped service the plane sent to Momote for flight tests, contributed the bomb shackles needed for adapting the bomb racks, made and contributed the fittings for the tanks, supplied a ship to bring tanks from Morotai, hauled the eight tanks from Biak by air on high priority, supplied me boats and transport whenever my estimate of necessity required. All these things had been done in violation of regulations -- Aussies and Americans alike were cheerily willing to risk personal censure when in their judgment it was helpful to the efficiency of the BPF to do so. And with one exception -- a U.S. Army lieutenant at Biak -- I do not remember a single instance when they were not courteous as well as helpful in their relations.

23. The Royal Air Force officers, when approached, immediately diverted the first possible plane to pick up tanks. Whether their efforts were spurred by my brief recital of what the Aussies and Americans had done and my astringent suggestion that it was about time the British did a little something for themselves, I do not know.

24. In contrast with this, the Royal Navy's effort, aside from

the exceptionally ready initiative and action of Lt. Comdr. Campbell-Horsfall and the courtesy and decision of Capt. Hughes-Hallett, has hardly been substantial, much less pleasant. They were asked to pass some signals, which they did sometimes and belatedly and grudgingly. They were asked to make a couple of courteous gestures -- *i.e.,* to invite the AROU officers and the RAF officers aboard, and to present the Aussies with a case of scotch; the first, being under the personal supervision of the wing leader, was made; in the second instance they failed me in point of time and short-changed the Aussies in point of quantity -- the latter it was possible for Americans, blushing for the ship to which they were attached, however unwillingly, to make good.

25. In all the course of the negotiations I asked two things of *Implacable* -- the signal of authority -- a trifling authority -- and the case of scotch. In both cases it faltered, fumbled, and ultimately failed me.

26. Unfortunately, my experience does not indicate the sample of Royal Navy performance to be exceptional. When I first came aboard *Implacable,* the initiative shown by Lt. Comdr. Campbell-Horsfall had somewhat given me heart; I had hoped to be able to overcome the attitude I had had when I left *Illustrious.* But one man cannot redeem a weakly organized team. At the end of a month aboard the ship, which included the above described effort, I had come to reaffirm the attitude toward the Royal Navy I had felt when I left *Illustrious,* and to join my comrades in interpreting BPF as British Pathetic Fleet. My contempt for the Royal Navy, its precepts, social structure, organization, and efficiency, could not be greater. I credit the officers' corps of the Royal Navy with a stubborn courage, excelled only by the Jap Kamikazes -- but I do not admire courage for its own sake -- only as one element contributing to efficiency. I think that the individual native ability, as distinguished from efficiency, of the average English officer is very high. But for the use which Royal Navy organization is able to make of these rich resources, I have only a contempt which endures and grows.

It is time I got out of it. My character is marked by a poverty of patience, tolerance, and tact, and by an uneven temper. If I stay aboard longer, now that my mission has essentially reached conclusion, I fear that this weakness of temperament will find expression in some incident extremely unfortunate for all concerned; and I am trying to avoid that incident by anticipating it. I found aboard *Illustrious* that for the first three or four weeks, when I was preoccupied with observing and suggesting and working at revision of procedures, and more or less coasting on my initial good will, I got along well enough; after my mission was essentially completed, the sense of general frustration and uselessness raised my natural irritability to levels which were something short of rational. Hence, again, it is time I got out of it; I have done what little I can for *Implacable.* The results of another six weeks aboard would be largely negative.

Through this report I am trying to do what I can to aid your comprehension if not your pardon of my request for return to the American fleet.

’

The request for transfer was granted -- *after* the fleet was already at sea on its way to take part in the final attacks on Japan. When the bomb fell on Hiroshima, the British dropped the war, which had been a secondary mission in the Pacific (primary mission: to make sure they got to Hong Kong and some other places ahead of anybody else for purposes of presenting any possible peace conference with some *faits accomplis*); dropped all Americans at the nearest possible island; and raced for Britain's Jap-occupied colonies.

A year later, still uncertain whether he would have been praised or court-martialed had the war lasted longer, Adams got a small medal from the British indicating that for purposes of cementing relations for World War III at least, he was set on the black side of the ledger.

”

Chapter 13

Assorted Europeans and A Great American

"

December 3, 1987

Mark Adams to Franklin Jones, Sr.
Marshall, Texas

Here comes a sheaf of prose apropos of nothing and headed nowhere. If you wish to avoid squandering time, duck out now.

Of course it's all your fault, anyhow. The fact is that as I set type on your *Pilgrims' Progress,*[1] its perceptions evoke a resonance among the memories of my own anecdotage which affirms, for me, their truth. And I have this impulse to chirp up with equivalents of those "Amens" which erupt from the congregation under the spell of a primitive preacher's sermon.

Amen #1: About the Irish

I agree with Eddie Brown that your letters admirably catch the character of the Irish -- their charm, their strongly emotional, slightly fey, and wholly beautiful imagination, their fascinating and flawed patterns of thought: the consequent colorful and ultimately tragic cast of their past history and present fate. The things your letters set resonating among my own memories:

For me, Yeats' "Second Coming" is the most moving and prophetic poem in modern literature. For all the fey and mystic allusions of its early lines the final lines of both verses hit me with a haunting force:

---

[1]Franklin Jones, Sr., *Pilgrims' Progress*, Packrat Press, 1987. Letters FJ wrote from Europe when he and his wife Huldah visited there in 1957.

The best lack all conviction, while the worst
Are full of passionate intensity.

and

What rough beast, its hour come round at last,
Slouches toward Bethlehem to be born.

And alongside this in my mind is recall of the history of the Eire drainage project which I stumbled across when I was working for the Bureau of Reclamation. They planned to enlarge the arable land of Ireland with rich acreages by draining the peat bogs. The project was huge. They planned a seven-year program which would progressively enrich the entire nation. The government set up and operated an efficient plant to make concrete drain tile, so the bulk of all costs were labor costs -- like our Civilian Conservation Corps it combined economic aid for the individual with nationally enriching results.

Year after year Irishmen had jobs and the nation added *lebensraum.* And then in the sixth year the drain tile installed in the first year began to collapse. Concrete is progressively weakened by organic acids until it is mush, and a peat bog is full of organic acids. The planners had forgotten that one little fact; and though the trouble was speedily diagnosed, at that point there was nothing for it but to spend another six years watching the drain tile progressively collapse and the newly created rich farmlands revert to bogs.

Ireland in microcosm.

Amen #2: About the English

After the Lingayen Gulf landing, Air Group 30 -- Lt. Cmdr. M. Adams, Group Intelligence Officer -- having witnessed the customary thirty percent casualties, was detached from the fast carrier task force *U.S.S. Lexington* and shipped back to the states.

At Pearl Harbor I was detached from Air Group 30 and ordered to report to the British Pacific Fleet as liaison officer.

I protested that I was Anglophobe. Overruled. My Intelligence C.O. explained that the British Fleet, newly arrived in the Pacific, would be operating as a task group (one of five) of the American fast carrier task force and would need help in interpreting the American operation orders from somebody familiar with U.S. operating procedures -- and terms like "The wildcat will be 100 miles from the carrier force on bearing 031." And such experienced officers were in short supply. So, for the next year I had a crash course in the habits and practices of the British -- or at least their Navy.

Again I find your observations resonating images in my memory.

On the omnipresent class structure: A senior officer nursing a drink in the wardroom of *Illustrious* and pontificating about the sad state to which His Majesty's Navy had been brought by the war: " 'Arf the upper decks should be on the lower decks, and 'arf the lower decks should be in jail!"

The senior intelligence officer of *Implacable* stomping around the wardroom after hearing of Churchill's defeat in the elections following VE Day and storming over and over, "I won't be ruled by bloody miners! I won't be ruled by bloody miners!" and a grinning Adams in response repeating the query, "Wanna bet? Wanna bet?"

Rank in the British Navy was truly rank, if you'll pardon the pun.

And the obverse side: A continual stream of youngsters -- including some of their superb "flying types" (*i.e.*, pilots) -- who came to my cabin with the same inquiry: "How can I get to America after the war? At home after the war, I'll find no place for myself except in the niche I was born to."

And about the strength of the social discipline that was consonant with the proprieties rooted in that same cast-iron social structure.

It was wrapped up in the phrase "The suitable thing." Once he understood what "the suitable thing to do" might be, your Englishman of whatever class or rank damn well did it. It was a discipline that was truly awesome. It impressed me as much as the resolve of the Kamikazes.

Sure, Hitler was an oaf, so the suitable thing to do was to

doggedly hang on through Dunkirk and Coventry and the bombing of London until he was put down. No other solution was suitable at all.

And the place names! You, you may lead an impoverished life because you never got to Tooting Broadway. Well, I remember reading in an English journal aboard *Implacable* about a newsworthy event in Nether Wallop, Hants. But in all the years since I, I never heard anything more about Nether Wallop, Hants. I have never found out where, or even what, Hants is. I've had to eke out a provincial existence with a few facts about New Dime Box, Texas.

Amen #3: About the Dutch

Yeah. A sort of sumptuousness of approach -- and centered on food.

In my reaction against the unhealthy scrawniness of Twiggy and her ilk which has been the vogue during much of my life, I have often proclaimed the ascendant charm of Rubens nudes -- all, but *all* of whom needed to go on a diet. But I admit even I had an idea that my posture was a somewhat hypocritical overreaction. Most American girls, thank heaven, have too much sense and too little willpower to starve themselves.

Amen #4: The German Language

Yes, the language seems to consist of a root word followed by modifying syllables until the speaker is out of breath.

I think it stems from a mode of thought which bears some relation to the thoroughness that has been basic to some past advances of German science.

I recall a friend of student days named Clem Linnenberg who was archetypical -- thorough, matter-of-fact, heavily humorous, appallingly industrious. Habitually he would begin with a forthright statement which he would then fence in with dependent clauses leaving no possible opening for misinterpretation of that simple statement before he reached the end of the sentence.

I remember one day Dr. Bob Montgomery, whose grader

Clem was, remarked -- half in annoyance and half in admiration -- "Clem dives into a sentence at the top of page one and surfaces at the top of page three with his verb in his mouth."

Still, sometimes that matter-of-factness and precision result in a certain charm of expression.

I recall my oldest daughter was reading a book of synopses of operas in German. She told me the chapter on "William, the Bagpiper" was headed "Vilhelm, der Dudelsackfifer." Right on! I remembered a bagpipe concert on the quarterdeck of *Implacable* which, dutiful to diplomatic niceties, I sat through for nearly two hours. The pipers would announce their next selection and pipe some more, but if they had not told me different, I would have sworn they piped the same selection fifteen times over. And I have yet to guess whether or not that selection had a melody. (Don't tell Smitty or Ed Ross I said this.) And at least I never hope to hear a better description of the whole performance than "dudelsackfifing."

Amen #5: The Bombing of Cologne

I cannot tell you whether the bombers missed the industrial plants with Allied industrial interests and hit the centers of population of Cologne on purpose or by accident. I wasn't there.

But you will understand that I find the suggestion that the factories in Cologne were spared because Allied interests shared in their ownership no occasion for surprise.

I am convinced that 99.9% of actual combat personnel were without divided loyalties. But in the upper echelons -- I don't know.

I guess all this is preface for a respectful salute to Dog Face Smith. I don't guess I have ever before spoken of my profound, if heretofore tacit, respect and admiration for Dog, or of the wherefores of it. I feared retribution -- visited on him.

But surely after forty years the statute of limitations has run even in the corporate power structure.

The critical incident was on surface completely casual.

Commander Daniel Fletcher Smith was skipper of Air

Group 30 aboard *U.S.S. Lexington* -- the second one, so christened after the first *Lexington* was sunk in early days of the war. He was born in Pittsburgh, Texas, graduated from Annapolis, was a career Naval officer. A daily press reporter asking the conventional questions was told, "My hometown is someplace like N.A.S. Guam. Any other hometown I named would be unreal."

His character was a compound of courage, common sense, and competence. For all the Annapolis background -- and rows of medals (Navy Cross, etc., etc.) -- he was casual of manner, didn't seem to have ever heard of the voice of authority and brace of command commonly thought to mark the effective officer. He was easy-going, with twinkling eye and a quizzical, ingratiatingly self-deprecatory grin. With the initials D.F., he was usually referred to as "Dog Face" and often addressed as "Dog."

And he was the most effective C.O. I saw in action during the war. High and low in the air group regarded him with *both* respect and affection. He did his job well.

But the glimpse of him I remember best was during the hit-and-run attack we made on Hong Kong on our way out of the South China Sea after the Lingayen landings.

As we checked over the operation order, with its slapdash assignment of target priorities, I pointed out the paragraph stating that the oil tank farm at Kowloon was to be protected from attack because the tanks were property of the Texas Company.

Dog Face normally had a tic of the left eye due to some sleepless nights in which he wrestled with nightmares involving little puffs of black smoke from anti-aircraft bursts all around him. (One of those fellows who carry their work home with them.) And I noticed the tic stuttered a bit as he re-read that paragraph.

"Aren't those tanks supplying oil to the Japanese?" he asked.

"Yes," I said. "But they belong to the Texas Company."

He nodded and we continued.

The following day, when I was debriefing him and filling in

the combat report, he gave a detailed and coherent report of the attack, his own observation of points of resistance and points of attack.

Several bombs had done substantial damage to shipping in the Hong Kong harbor.

"And where did you drop your bombs?" I asked.

"Funny thing," he said. "When I let those bombs go, it looked like they might land smack-dab on those Texaco Company tanks."

I nodded. "You can't always tell where those bombs are going to hit."

So I wrote down in the combat report: "Dropped bombs at shipping in the harbor. Missed."

A miss is a miss -- distance is immaterial. If Dog's bombs missed by twenty-eight miles, what matter? I simply recorded the facts for the history books.

When the photo-reconnaissance pictures came up from the labs that night, one of them was a panoramic shot of Hong Kong harbor -- from the island on across the channel to the mainland. And there, across the channel, from the vicinity of Kowloon, an enormous column of black smoke reached up into the heavens as far as the picture reached. Somebody apparently had set those Texas Company tanks afire. I don't know who and neither do you.

But ever since, I have thought of Dog Face Smith as a great American.

Cologne? I wasn't there.

But I suspect the Air Force operation order told the bombardiers where to hit, not where to miss. And I have no doubt they did a good job.

Soupy, I warned you.

cc: Committee of Correspondence

”

Chapter 14

The Accidental Life

During the last year of the war, all of it in combat operations (including a brush with a Kamikaze), I had begun to notice that death-threatening events were not actually all that frequent or inevitable, so I spared a thought now and then to the question of what to do if I got back -- which helped in some respects when I got back. That is, I decided that it was no use going back to rummage in the rubble heap of the New Deal in Washington, D.C., so just as soon as I started to ponder that "What if?" I figured the only (wan) hope was to start over again in the grassroots. When I got back to Washington (the Navy insisted I be mustered out of uniform at the point where I entered), I spent a total of six hours there before grabbing a train to rejoin my wife and child back in Texas. But after that, although my speculations had included some ideas of what to do after I got back home, what actually happened was so twisted by ambiguities and frustrations that even in retrospect I have difficulty finding a pattern in events. Straight-line my life was not.

Back home, the two immediate problems were supporting my family and finding a way to do so which would permit me to get back to a career as liberal propagandist as near as possible continuing in the vein of the pre-war years.

For most of that last year of the war I had been sent to act as liaison aboard carriers of the British Pacific Fleet, which had arrived out there after the landing in France was secured. One of the consequences was that for six months I got no mail from home. And when I finally arrived back in port and got a sackful of mail -- and lined up the letters by postmark date and read through them -- I came upon a letter telling me my daughter had apparently sprained an ankle and was in the hospital ... and other letters telling me it was osteomyelitis, and that she had been moved to a hospital in Shreveport, and of the crises of pain when recurrently she was given injections of penicillin (that was before they figured out how to buffer the doses) and her screams could be heard all over the hospital ... and then of her recovery and return home "with a good chance she will not be permanently crippled."

It was a dispensation of providence that I got all those letters in one mail; if I had gotten half of them and then been sent back to sea not knowing my daughter was recovered, I would have gone mad. As it was, the only dire result of the incident was that all the savings we had ratholed during the previous four years were obliterated completely.

Moneyless, with no place to live and no source of income in sight, I decided to forget the matter of propaganda completely for the time being while I accumulated enough money to support us through any starving period in such a career. And rationally, I still think, I lumped the "place to live" and "income" goals into one project and set up as my own contractor to build us a home.

An old oilfield friend signed my note at the bank for enough money to cover lot, materials, and wages for myself until the house was complete. My father and I did all the work -- design, lot preparation, foundations, carpentry, plumbing, wiring, etc. When construction was complete I sold it to myself on long-term contract, paying off the original loan and assuming monthly payments. This construction game was quite profitable in that post-war period, and initially I intended to go on building and selling houses until I had a nest egg to finance the projected liberal propaganda career. And probably I would have done so, but two things intervened.

Plans for a Propaganda Mill

First thing was that Clay Cochran and Otto Mullinax, like myself freshly out of uniform, stopped by Austin to see me. Otto's suggestion was that the core PDs should all live in the same town, figuring that the bunch of us would be a formidable force -- which is probably true, though as a practical matter it was about as feasible as turning lead into gold. Clay argued that I should not go on with the construction bit after I got my family housed. He cited Dan Moody, who, after a term as governor beholden to the establishment who financed his campaign, vowed to make a million dollars practicing law and then finance his own campaign and govern on his own terms -- except after he got a million in his own bank account, he decided it had to be five million, and after he got five million -- so finally he wound up as the blackest heart of all the black-hearted reactionaries.

Reluctantly I agreed that Clay might have a point, but if I had thought more carefully, I might have realized that the likelihood of my ever being a successful businessman was negligible.

Next thing was that when the house-building gambit was in initial phases, two friends who had heard I was back from the wars -- as they also were -- came out one evening to visit me where I was staying with my parents. Both old friend Bob Eckhardt and new friend Stuart Long were, of course, liberals, and we had a delightful gabfest. I told them of my rather nebulous plans for a propaganda mill anchored in a print shop (to keep propaganda costs within reach of liberal budgets) -- the latter aspect suggested by my earlier experiences as a country editor.

Maybe I made the idea seem more feasible than it was. Anyway, when he got home that night, Stu sat down and wrote Marshall Field, whom he had met in the course of service as an Information Specialist for the Marine Corps. Field, after World War II, was spreading substantial sums of money around to sustain liberal publications countrywide. Stu proposed establishing a liberal print shop in Texas, outlining the idea in the same terms I had used to him and Bob earlier in the evening. Field sent $10,000. And before I finished our house, Stu had Long Publications fleshed out with equipment; so when I finished the house and turned to thoughts of liberal propaganda mills, I discovered the field was overcrowded.

Stu offered me a job reconditioning the equipment and operating it. I accepted gladly. We did a few jobs, and Stu tried to get Badger Reed and Kewpie Young to let us print the *Texas*

Spectator, but they weren't having any. So things rocked along for several months, and the enterprise went into bankruptcy. Stu asked me to manage the firm and its shop through the bankruptcy.

It was a part-time job, and I had nothing better in prospect. Then, going through the files one day, as part of administering the bankruptcy, I found the letter Stu had written to Marshall Field proposing the idea -- and dated the very same day he and Bob Eckhardt had visited. At first I was furious, but my second thought was that maybe the only difference was that now I was managing Stu's bankruptcy, while if he had waited for me to try, he might have been managing my bankruptcy. The idea had been half-baked and needed some refinement.

Meanwhile, I began trying to shape an embryo liberal print shop and propaganda mill of my own, which I named Chaparral Press. It was underequipped and barely -- or almost -- made a living; but on the other hand, it seemed to indicate I was on the right track, because with that shirttail full of equipment, I managed to publish editions of Walter Prescott Webb's *Divided We Stand* and Dr. Bob's *Brimstone Game,* which each sold (and hence put into circulation) three or four times the number marketed by the original national publishers. I thought both books should be textbooks for any liberal resurgence in Texas if one ever occurred. So I credited myself with real progress.

And I kept trying to find a liberal group that my efforts might serve. But this effort, like the print shop effort, seemed to fall immediately into the pattern of ambiguity and frustration characterizing all the years of my post-war accidental life. And as might appear probable when a *pattern* of events appears, I suspect that the persistence of the pattern points to the persistence of certain traits in the character involved, to-wit myself. Let me digress and talk about this for a moment.

It is significant, of course, that I thought my early years leading up to -- and even during -- World War II were a "straight line" of development, and after World War II movement in my life was "largely sidewise" and "full of ambiguity and frustration."

Observe that in association with my father in publishing, although from the age of fourteen I was legally full partner in our newspapers, actually I was happy to be printer and editorial adjutant. I never wished to be big wheel in our outfit, had no secret dreams of ever becoming big wheel in any outfit. And observe that in Washington, D.C., I was happy to be studying and doing research under Montgomery's teacher and sometime mentor, Walton Hamilton, and writing for Farm Security as assistant to John Fischer -- who, when he was a Rhodes scholar still in England, was writing to Montgomery and the PDs in early days -- and even in that final round, as writing assistant to Creek in pursuit of goals articulated by Hammy and Thurman Arnold, I was perfectly happy with my role. I was fretted by no sense of subordination. A feeling that I understood what I was doing and was doing it well was all the ego salve I needed. I guess the brief way to say what I mean is to say I never had any ambition to speak of. And if this is true of my attitude toward hierarchical power, it goes double for my attitude toward money. As long as I had enough to live on in austere but secure style, I never dreamed of wealth in quantities that would equate with power.

Certainly the idea that artists are impractical and starve in garrets while pursuing their introspectively determined goals is a truism -- or at least a cliche widely accepted -- and as I explained earlier, my original goal in life was to be an artist-printer, not a liberal propagandist.

I feel no embarrassment about having no ambition; yet I can recognize it as a weakness. In extenuation of that lack of ambition, I plead the example of Dr. Bob himself: The greatest teacher I ever knew; the model of what a teacher should be -- but he never aspired to be president of the university, or even chairman of the department. He never wanted to be an executive of the New Deal agencies which welcomed his counsel and solicited his support; and he refused to run for congressman from the Austin district when Clay and Creek had rounded up money and New Deal support for him. At the time I thought he was foolish not to run. He said that with Lyndon in the race, it would not do to split the liberal majority and let conservatives win; I blamed him for taking himself out of the race; but later I understood that it would have been a loss to his students and his country if he had tied himself to worrying about postmasters and post offices and perforce given up his classes and his lobbying with all three branches of government.

For an illustration of how this lack of ambition proved a weakness in me, on my return to Texas after the war, I kept trying to find a liberal group that my efforts might serve. It never occurred to me that if I found no liberal group going my way, I should organize one. I just simply never wanted to be a leader; never thought of it. Hence the pattern of "sidewise movement" and "ambiguity and frustration" of the forty years following World War II was more or less inevitable. Certainly I never found a liberal group I could serve or which had a place for me beyond arms-length alliance or limited part-time projects. But I did find many individuals -- some embedded in organizations -- with whom I wanted to work.

First, of course, Dr. Bob. But though that relationship remained cordial to the end of his life, at the close of the war it was restricted by his failing health, which made his friends hesitate to place demands on his time, and by his preoccupation with warning the world against the possibly irreparable consequences of nuclear armaments in the hands of national leaders of uncertain wisdom. So I saw him only sporadically.

Minnie Fisher Cunningham

Another person I had worked with in Washington -- Minnie Fisher Cunningham -- was more accessible. Unlike the rest of us, she was back in Austin and immersed in Texas politics before war's end. Dr. Bob often said that liberal combat cadres were made up of "the young, the ignorant, and the daring." War had siphoned off huge portions of the young and the daring, leaving segments of the ignorant, only, at full strength on the domestic political scene. Minnie Fish and her staff of talented and well-educated aides -- including Lillian Collier, Margaret Redding, and Marion Storm -- fell into the decimated minority liberal groupings during wartime chiefly because of their daring (Marion was young, but the others were not). So Minnie Fish, who had gone back to Texas and continued being herself during the war, found the burden of liberal leadership devolving heavily on her because she was left much alone on the scene.

Before the war, Minnie Fish had been in Washington as an operative on the staff of Wayne Darrow, chief of the Information (propaganda) staff of the Agricultural Adjustment Administration at the same time I was attached to other segments of the Agriculture Department in a similar capacity, and we had become coffee-drinking acquaintances. Then, as we discovered mutual backgrounds in Texas and mutual interest in New Deal politics, she came to rely on me to draft statements, press releases, etc., for Mrs. Collier and other paladins of her personal political operations back in Texas. She regarded these things I had drafted for her as being very effective. So when she heard I was back in Texas, she got in touch. And I cheerfully did whatever I could to back her play. (For free, of course -- she was no more a subsidized politico than I was. We were both incurable liberal dissidents "without portfolio.")

Her play was always of admirable intent, but not always desirable effect. Minnie Fish's operations were quite uniformly compounded of absolute integrity, absolutely dauntless courage -- and frequently dubious judgment. Her role as a young woman in securing the passage of the Women's Suffrage Amendment in Texas is a matter of history. And it seemed to me that she spent the rest of her life trying to prove that women's suffrage *had* lifted politics and government onto a higher plane; always she supported the liberal, the humane, and the intelligent position. Always. Firmly. And without counting the cost. I remember telling her niece, who interviewed me for an intended biography of Minnie Fish, that I always thought of her courage as analogue to that of the famous Texas Ranger, McDonald, of whom it was said that he "would charge Hell with a bucket of water."

Her frequently dubious judgment was simply the obverse

side of her transcendent virtues -- her unswerving integrity and her dauntless courage. Hell has often been observed to survive a bucket of water handily, and hence as a practical matter her tactical and strategic plans were often disasters -- like those of old man Adams and his preposterous son.

Before war's end brought most of us home, Minnie Fish had entered the race for governor of Texas. This was totally unlikely to unseat Coke Stevenson, of course, but it had the practical effect of persuading Coke not to campaign against Democratic presidential electors until after the primaries. That was her goal, and she achieved it. But the next goal was more debatable.

By the time the mob of us got back from the war, a major company (McCarthyite) board of regents had fired Homer Rainey as president of the University of Texas, and Minnie Fish had declared war by maneuvering Rainey into a race for governor. This was, of course, a forlorn hope -- the major oil, conservative, abundantly financed machine was in firm control of the state, and whereas it is possible to beat the establishment sometimes, this takes long advance planning and well-executed campaigning -- and real money (not enough to equal establishment expenditures but enough to build a foundation in public awareness long in advance of the tumult and shouting phase of campaign and enough to counter last-minute blasts of libels, like "the Port Arthur story"). For the Rainey campaign there were no beneficent side effects -- only attrition of forces likely to attend total defeat. When Minnie Fish alerted me, the campaign was already under way, D.B. Hardeman was doing as good a job as anybody could have, I think; certainly at that point I was unable to think of any magic words or incantations that might pull the campaign out of the soup.

But immediately Minnie Fish plunged into her Women's Committee for Educational Freedom and began belatedly to lay the groundwork for such a campaign as had just concluded. And for the outfit I wrote little pamphlets which impressed her for their responses. A last-minute blast at the Veterans Land Amendment got statewide notice and turned out to be prophetic a year or so later when Bascom Giles and cronies got prison sentences. Minnie Fish was pleased. An organizational leaflet in which I advanced the idea that education could replace natural resources as the latter were exhausted astonished Minnie Fish when she discovered it was being used as a text by a prestigious geography prof out at the University (Zimmerman). For such services, I believe she thought well of me until her death; but I don't think she ever forgave me for not having ambition enough to want to run for office or otherwise strive for leadership. We were very much alike except for that.

David's Strategies Against Goliath

Others I had known in Washington -- including Chris Dixie and Creekmore Fath -- I also kept in touch with and worked with as best I knew how. Creek got back from his post-war stint with the Democratic National Committee to run for Congress just as I was trying to get together a print shop after the bankruptcy of Long Publications, and I did the best I could with cards and leaflets -- but it was another assault on the establishment, and he had not had time enough back home to lay a pre-campaign groundwork, so Lyndon's appointed successor beat us handily. Chris tried to help me by sending me a job for Ahepa -- which I owe him an apology for accepting, for I was not equipped to do the kind of job they wanted (they were not looking for originality; they wanted, and deserved, impressive gloss). And he also suggested I submit some leaflets for the Teamsters -- which I never got around to writing for lack of time to turn aside from the sweaty grind of trying to keep the embryo printing venture afloat. In short, Chris did his best, and I flunked out in the end.

Creek, once he had settled into his natural habitat as operator behind the scenes, helped me every way he knew how; for a quarter-century I had a key to his office in the Littlefield Building downtown, collaborated with him on writing -- notably for Yarborough campaigns, which he won. (Yarborough lost that final campaign when, having accepted a non-aggression pact with Lyndon [which I approved as probably the better part of valor], he ditched both Creek and myself and wound up with his throat cut from ear to ear.) In the end, although we drifted apart -- Creek into the wider world of his Washington and Texas contacts and I into a federal writing job which I used to support my family while I drafted a book intended to be foundation for Yarborough's last campaign (which was laid aside by Yarborough as an aspect of the non-aggression pact). I found Creek always a good and generous friend and an intelligent -- sometimes brilliant -- co-worker. And I hope he thinks well of me.

And then there was Herman Wright. Herman had never been one of the dislocated youngsters who had flooded into Washington, D.C., during the jobless hardship days of the Great Depression; he was manning the barricades back in Texas. So his appearance in Austin as candidate for governor on the Henry Wallace ticket found me unable to think of anything useful I could do to help. My attitude toward his effort was compounded of admiration and dismay: admiration because he was true to the ideals of the Progressive Democrats he had served in the thirties. Dismay because during my last days in Washington, I had seen firsthand that dollar-a-year men from GE, Standard Oil, and the financial community of Wall Street could whip the government of the United States to a standstill (had done so!) while the shrewdest political operator of the generation, FDR, headed the government. And I understood that was why Henry Wallace was no longer veep. I grieved because I had no way of retroactively sharing my knowledge with Herman, and Herman's effort was only sacrificial. I found an analogy in the story of William Barrett Travis at the Alamo; I admire his heroism yet nevertheless think his sacrifice a waste because he either never received, or because he ignored, Sam Houston's order to abandon the Alamo and join the retreating main body.

Water over the dam.

I continued the effort to get the print shop going -- and support my family in the process. Herman was back in Houston, so we were out of touch for a while. Meanwhile I continued to try to stay in touch with liberal friends in Austin, dropping by to see people like Minnie Fish and Bob Eckhardt on my printing-sales rounds. Bob Eckhardt had a law office in the Scarborough Building at the time and was lobbyist for the Texas Education Association.

The reign of terror out at the University continued, and a hob-nailed legislature was paring budgets and taxes at the behest of the major oil company and sulphur establishment. Bob and I discussed the power concentration that made such undermining of the commonweal possible. I said that as long as there were single corporations in the state that had more money -- even more employees -- than the democratic government of the state, such things were not just possible, they were probable. We fell to speculating about the possibilities of anti-trust which might whittle corporations like the Standard Oil combines currently dominating the state down to a size the state could hope to handle on some basis better than an eternal David and Goliath confrontation -- in an endless series of rematches, odds were that David wouldn't win them all, and as long as Goliath was backed by national or multi-national corporations, endless rematches were a near-certainty. Alternatively, if the big boys tired of rematches, they could remove production facilities from the state -- leaving the state's workers and their support groups -- merchants and teachers, et al., in limbo.

The Oil Production Tax Bill

All of a sudden at this point an idea hit me. Major oil, our biggest big boy, was not going to remove its production facilities from the state; it was producing oil which had been placed under Texas some hundreds of millions of years ago and could not move its production from the state until it had the last of that oil on the surface and in the pipelines -- big oil was vulnerable to state governmental (popular, democratic) action. I was fascinated by the idea, mesmerized.

Bob agreed that state anti-trust action wouldn't do it. A couple of generations earlier, Texas had won an anti-trust suit against Standard Oil of New Jersey which had barred the company from the state in perpetuity -- and currently the biggest company operating in the state was Humble Oil Company, 50 percent owned and totally controlled by Standard of New Jersey. I suggested the idea of a graduated tax on oil production -- a gross production tax like the one we had, only graduated like the income tax so as to favor small producers.

I figured, from what I had seen of the independent oilmen I had met, that they would eagerly buy up major oil production tracts and that major oil would sell rather than pay a penalty for each barrel it produced; and that once independents owned the properties, they would evade detailed subordination to the powers that had favored them by selling them properties -- there is no honor among thieves -- so David would face small men rather than Goliath and might win consistently. I didn't think such a bill could be passed in the current legislature -- but I thought the idea might catch on with independents (maybe even with local financiers like the Citizens Council of Dallas -- still no honor among thieves). Bob bought the idea.

We set out to draft such a bill and get it in the hopper at once, figuring that if it didn't pass (it almost certainly would not), it might at least distract the attention of the lobbyists a bit -- and once it was in circulation, it would have a chance to grow in the well-fertilized minds of the independent oil fraternity during coming years; so maybe a few years down the road.... We set out to enlist help in drafting the bill, so I went down to Houston to get suggestions from Herman Wright.

In a few weeks we had the bony structure of a pretty good bill drafted for our purposes -- the gradations in tax rate by volume of production were set so only eleven major companies had their severance tax increased, while all other producers got tax reductions, and still the bill would raise more money than the current law. The bill was tossed into the hopper by the tiny handful of liberals in that legislature -- Doug Crouch, Maury Maverick, Jr., Jim Sewell, et al., with Jim Wright as point man.

Subsequent events convinced me once and for all that as a political strategist, I made my father, Minnie Fish, and Herman Wright look like Solomon, Julius Caesar, Cardinal Richelieu, and Jim Farley all rolled into one. I had expected that the bill would be easily defeated in that legislature and could then become a conversation piece for liberals during succeeding years until it gathered enough support to be passed -- as the graduated income tax had. But what actually happened shocked me.

You might say the bill was too good. The lobby understood what it meant as clearly as we did. To begin with, instead of being quietly buried in committee, it was brought up for public hearings at which some very small producers who would have had their severance taxes reduced substantially under the bill were brought in to testify that the bill would bankrupt them. And neither I nor anybody else had prepared any rebuttal testimony, so the bill was buried with a public funeral service that would keep it buried beyond the possibility of resurrection.

But that was only for starters. When the next election rolled around, daily papers in Jim Wright's district carried the story on election day that Jim had been charged with murder in an outlying county of his district. The following day the sheriff who had made the charge announced that it had been dropped, and the same papers carried that story too. But meanwhile Jim, who had been popular in his district as an idealistic young crusader, had lost the election -- and learned a lesson: Don't attack an organization which can and will kill you. And that was a major tragedy.

I remember sitting in a smoke-filled room in the Driskill with Jim present a decade later when some well-heeled liberal fat cats were urging him to run for governor. He wouldn't agree; he urged those who wanted him to run to tell Lyndon of their wishes, but he would not commit without Lyndon's say-so. He had learned his lesson well. (Lyndon tapped John Connally instead.) I feel a bit of personal guilt about The Education of Jim Wright.

Guilt or not, I never learned much. I kept trying to put into practice my original print-shop idea, and I almost got the shop going during the next few years. I made friends with Texas lobby people for AFL and Jeff Hickman at CIO, and their printing patronage had the shop on its feet for a while -- I was granted a union label by the Austin Trades Council, although

I had only two trades represented in my shop. About then a substantial local firm negotiating a new contract demanded that the union see to it that my label -- legally unjustified -- was yanked, and the Trades Council caved. That pushed the shop into bankruptcy, and I slugged up as a linotype operator at the *Austin American-Statesman* (and lived a little higher on the hog) for a while.

Concurrently I continued to keep some liberal contacts and take on writing chores for liberal friends. After the AFL-CIO merger, John McCully threw quite a lot of work my way -- speeches, etc. Finally he urged me to take over the Houston *Labor Messenger* (financed with some money BenJack Cage kicked in to woo state labor), and for a while I commuted weekly from Austin to Houston.

I enjoyed editing the *Messenger* and scripting a labor-ICT radio program, and I might have settled in there except that within a few weeks my wife told me that her doctor agreed that if she moved to Houston, her health would hit the skids and she would be dead within a year. This was credible -- during the war when she came down to join me on the coast of Florida for a few months between my two stints in the combat zone of the Pacific, her health had gone down steadily for no apparent reason except humid climate. There was one point when we walked into the hospital together, and I gave her a pint of blood straight from my veins into hers and then walked out with her; the doctor in Florida thought it was needful, and it seemed to work during the month or so before I was ordered back to the Pacific.

At any rate I continued in Houston at the *Messenger* only long enough for McCully to find a replacement for me. During those years back in Austin, I continued doing piecework for McCully and AFL-CIO between stints at linotype operating -- including writing for a monthly economic *Roundup* which earned them kudos from Washington. I helped Minnie Fish and Franklin Jones launch the *Texas Observer* in 1954 under Ronnie Dugger's editorship -- with me as printer. And finally I got a chance to test my original plan to operate a print shop which would print propaganda for liberal causes.

The J. Edwin Smith campaign brochure

When J. Edwin Smith ran for Associate Justice of the Supreme Court of Texas in 1958, Mark printed a brochure for his campaign, and Russell Lee supplied the photographs.

"

September 1995

Mark Adams to J. Edwin Smith
Houston, Texas

About your candidate-card brochure: I am pleased to believe it was a good bit of work -- even though it didn't gain much yardage on the political field for reasons I will mention later -- and I can even believe that it reflected extraordinarily able performances on the part of each of us, particularly J. Edwin Smith. But I also believe that regardless of the quality of individual performances, we must look beyond the individuals involved -- to the context, to the era and the sphere of interests -- if we would speculate about the possibility of its like appearing again or its becoming a model for other efforts.

I was reassured about its being a good bit of work shortly after the election when Penrose -- your campaign manager in San Antonio -- called me on the phone to report, with some degree of amazement, that when he received only a small shipment of the brochures, he decided that the best he could do was simply to mail them to the poll tax list for the precinct in which he thought you would be weakest -- and that was the only precinct in Bexar County which you carried. With the rest of the county for a control group, that seemed to prove that the brochure had a positive effect.

About the individuals involved: The theme, the thrust of the brochure -- was dictated (literally) by Smitty, the candidate. You may remember that when Creek informed me that I was to produce a mass distribution item for your campaign, I sat down with you in his office and asked you to make me a campaign speech, and you obliged while I sat and took notes. It was a good speech and reflected your thoughts about the proper function of a judiciary in a democracy -- which I presume you had learned at TU law school and in practice with Franklin Jones (Sr.) and others. At least somehow in earlier years you had developed a clear understanding on the matter and could express it clearly. Your understanding reflected the concepts of liberal American thought in the new New Deal era. That speech was the key to the resulting brochure.

Russell Lee had taken pictures of you (at the suggestion of Creek and his AFL-CIO allies, I presume), and Creek handed me a set of them. They were, of course, superb character studies which included a sense of context. Russ was at the time world famous in photographic circles. His presence in Texas was happenstantial to a large degree, but it was the sole reason why his liberal friends could enlist his help in Texas political activities. I don't think love or money could have gotten him here from a distance.

An independently wealthy engineering student from Ohio, Russ had decided upon graduation in the late twenties to study art in Paris. There he fell in with Mann and others who were developing photography into an art form with broader relevance than the conventional portrait photo -- following Daumier and other artists in the earlier media who were including social comment in their works.

Back in this country at the depths of the Great Depression, Russ's interest in photography with a social meaning intensified. Not illogically, Russ wound up as one of the photographers on the staff of Roy Stryker's photo outfit in Rex Tugwell's Resettlement Administration.

Tugwell, an economics professor from Columbia, had a broad view of our society, including the role of the camera in shaping concepts and mores in a democracy. He set Pare Lorentz to making a couple of documentary movies dealing with basic problems of agriculture -- *The Plow That Broke the Plains* dealing with the Dust Bowl, and *The River* dealing with soil erosion -- which paved the way for the numerous documentaries seen nowadays on PBS. And he set up Stryker with a photo section to record in still photos the story of American society -- again with emphasis on rural problems, including poverty. Stryker, although he became a big name in the world of photography, was not a photographer; he was a colleague of Tugwell's in the Economics Department of Columbia, and he refused to pick up a camera for fear that if he started taking pictures, he would be tempted to hire only photographers who were clones of himself. But he trained his photographers to look for and find images significant in terms of our peoples and their ways. Significantly, the Stryker photo section was officially named the Historical Section.

Before he sent a photographer to a given area, Stryker insisted that he first spend a couple of weeks or a month reading all the economic, sociological and historical material he could lay hands on which dealt with that particular area -- and then, after arriving on the scene, leave the camera in its case while he walked and drove around soaking up the local ambience and spotting significant images for at least a week before snapping a picture. The result was sensational. And in a year or so, Luce was starting *Life* magazine, which came at the thing from a different angle -- expanding X-marks-the-spot news photography toward features and documentary reports. Then came Cowles and *Look*. Some of the star performers of both magazines had worked for Stryker. This scene is described in the Aug. 14, 1995, *New Yorker* review of a biography of Walter Evans.

You are aware that Russ has pictures in the classic *Family of Man* exhibit. Actually, I remember when Streichen summoned him to New York while the exhibit was in preparation to help with the final selections for the exhibit. And skimming through the book, I notice half a dozen other Stryker alumni represented -- Dorothea Lange, Carl Mydans, John Collier, Ben Shahn, Jack Delano.

Within the framework of the Historical Section, Russ contributed his own particular creative genius from 1933 until Pearl Harbor signaled the end of the socially conscious aspect of the New Deal in favor of compromise and the needed national unity. After Pearl Harbor, the Historical Section's negatives were transferred to the Library of Congress. (Archibald McLeish was Librarian.) And Russ and Pare Lorentz turned their technical savvy to service in the Air Force photographic branch. After the war, Russ drifted down to Texas (I never understood exactly why) and reverted to life as a photographer somewhat analogous to that of an amateur golfer who can play with the pros on equal footing but does not choose to make the tour in search of prizes. Creek and John McCully and other liberal movers and shakers who had known him in New Deal Washington finagled his aid in some political photographic projects, and thus it happened that Creek handed me some Russ Lee photos along with the brochure project.

Providing a script to go along with -- and exploit -- Russ Lee's photos was by no means a new experience for me. In 1937 when he was working with Roy Stryker and I was chief of the Editorial Section of the same outfit (Resettlement renamed Farm Security), I wrote an article for *Travel* magazine to go with photos Russ had taken in San Augustine, Texas, which happened to be a home town for me. Later, after a trip back to Texas to oppose Pappy O'Daniel (futile because with Germany attacking Holland and France, the electorate was supporting whoever was in power at the time), I was for a time script writer for the Historical Section. My job included writing articles for *U.S. Camera* to go with pictures Russ had made of a community of Dust Bowl refugees who had settled in New Mexico. Etc.

When I got back from the war, I considered my options, dismissed going back to Washington and its new overlords, and returned to Texas, figuring that if there was any hope at all -- which I doubted -- it had to lie in starting back at the grassroots. Decision, not happenstance.

My doubts remained, but I plugged along in alliance with old New Dealers who returned with me -- Creek, Russ, Chris Dixie, Minnie Fish, et al., and any new liberal friends I met. But I never had a plan or sensed alliance with anybody else who had a viable plan. Occasionally a job like the brochure for

Smitty came along, and that was a delight. I enjoyed the campaign biography for Ralph Yarborough (also using Russ Lee photos) and some speeches I wrote for McCully and friends like Tom Moore. But largely I was, and remain, gloomy -- unable to see beyond today's job. Like Russ, I think, I have since World War II been buoyed by no grand visions, yet perhaps for that very reason I have been able to be more attentive to the limited chores at hand.

So there you have the element which was in motion: Smitty with his fresh vision, Russ and Mark with a sense of duty and of craftsmanship, all three shaped by events and circumstances of their times, including the Great Depression, the New Deal, and World War II.

We made up a pretty good showing.

I think of us as being like a scatback (Smitty) and a blocking back (Mark) and a tight end (Russ) put out on the football field with a special team for one play -- that didn't put the ball across the goal line. The moral is that to put a ball across a goal line takes eleven men -- three men can't do it, however effective personally. Their effort is ineffectual until they have a full team -- of planner and managers and distributors (and money, of course) to make even the best effort count. Let us not suppose that it is possible for anyone, however fleet and nimble, to outrun a stampeding herd.

”

Sidetracked Again

In 1958 I sold Jerry Holleman on the idea of buying a half-interest in the print shop where I produced the *Observer*, thus making it possible to extend labor campaign contributions by providing campaign printing at cost.

For a year there I was a happy man working sixteen-hour days. Then after the campaigns were over, Jerry called me over and told me that AFL-CIO was pulling out and demanded its money back. I was astounded. I had not padded the cost figures

I was submitting to AFL-CIO; I had done my dead-level best both as printer and writer. I asked Jerry what the trouble was. Stony-faced silence. At any rate that was that. To repay AFL-CIO's half, I had to sell my own -- during the campaign year I had drawn less money out of the shop than in previous years; I had no savings. It was the end of the road for my liberal writer-printer dreams. The next January when Lyndon took office, I read in the paper that Jerry Holleman was appointed assistant Secretary of Labor, and I thought I understood what had happened to me -- I had been on Lyndon's shit list for a long time -- and he had been on mine ever since he earned his Brown and Root campaign money for his post-war race for the Senate by openly denouncing the Labor Relations Act. The Caro biography of Lyndon[1] documents his habit of destroying hapless people not of sufficient stature to justify the effort, really -- people like myself. The son of a bitch was a certifiable psychopath.

I went to work as a linotype operator again and to supplement those wages, I got Yarborough to help me land a job as a writer for the Bureau of Reclamation Texas Area Planning Office in Austin. For several years there my family lived better than they had since World War II. I wasn't happy, but I wasn't miserable either. I just sort of relaxed.

A Chinese Immigrant in the American Bureaucracy

At the Bureau of Reclamation, I met a Chinese immigrant named Al Chang, and from him I learned nearly all I know about China.

Alfred Z. Chang was the son of one of Sun Yat-sen's lieutenants. He followed his father into service of Sun's nascent Chinese Republic -- as an army officer junior to Chiang Kai-shek, whom he thought well of. Prior to World War II, as Colonel Chang-tse (had you wondered how that Z. got into his Anglicized name?), he was instructor in guerrilla warfare at

---

[1]Robert A. Caro, *The Path to Power*, Knopf, 1982.

Whampoa. During the war as acting Major General Chang- tse, he was assigned as liaison to Mao Tse-tung's headquarters -- shuttling as messenger between the two justifiably distrustful groups, and in passing serving both as observer of the Fourth Army's guerrilla training and as officer in guerrilla combat operations with Maoist guerrillas.

After the war he was included in Chiang's retreat to Formosa when the bulk of Chiang's American-equipped divisions joined Mao. But he was bitter.

The American State Department accepted the refugee Chiang Kai-shek as legitimate head of the government of China, and for a generation ignored the other 750 million Chinese, but Chang-tse scorned the fiction. He felt himself hopelessly exiled from the China he knew and loved. He felt that his life had come to a dead end. He chose to start over.

He arranged to come to the U.S., became a U.S. citizen, and earned an MA degree in economics at Colorado U., then became a nameless junior American civil servant -- in the Texas Area Planning Office of the Bureau of Reclamation, where an effort to develop an inter-agency water plan for Texas rivers was in the works.

That's where I met him in 1960, when I was working as a report writer in the Area Planning Officer of BuRec.

My friendship with Al was slow developing. I first noticed him because I found that when I wandered into the Economics section seeking some report or journal with information I needed, the other economists invariably pointed me to this obviously oriental gentleman who spoke English with an accent (he never did learn to enunciate his *l*'s, though he put in much time and effort with a speech therapist trying) -- and that Al could walk over to the proper filing cabinet and pick out what I wanted without hesitation. He knew the contents of every drawer of that row of filing cabinets -- by topic as well as by title or date. Al suggested this was because learning the 10,000 ideograms of Chinese writing trains the memory of the Chinese student from kindergarten days.

I remembered that Yamamoto explained the fact that he

could at any time tell you the location and status of every vessel in the Japanese fleet with the same statement. Maybe so. At any rate, that was one way this immigrant from China was different from others in my office -- none of the native Americans could do it.

And Al was reticent -- always aware that the brown skin, epicanthic folds, and conspicuous accent set him apart -- and so many humans of any ethnic group more or less consciously equate alien with inferior. (He did not feel inferior. He thought the joke current among compatriots about Jack Kennedy's surprise when he got a telegram which a Chinese-American supporter had phoned in to Western Union which read, "Congraturations on your recent erection" was uproariously funny. And although he felt no inferiority about his accent, he was aware that outside his circles, that accent might be thought contemptible. So he was wary.)

I think the ice-breaker was an inconsequential exchange we had a few weeks after I joined BuRec. Al was in hospital with a minor illness, and I dropped by for a courtesy visit. I had come to depend on him and noticed his absence and dropped by on my way home. Al was pleased. He insisted on brewing me tea, asserting that only a Chinese knew how to brew tea properly. Talk drifted to office tasks -- there our cooperation was increasingly vital to me, so I thought it was only decent to warn him against letting our interdependence in the work become conspicuous because the enabling legislation we were operating under had been put through Congress as a rider by Lyndon and Sam Rayburn, and Lyndon's big-money backer George Brown (whose contracting firm would probably build the dams we would propose) was chairman of the Commission slated to adopt the report, so it would not be beneficial to seem close to me because, although I had a junior senator (Ralph Yarborough) as shield against disfavor from that quarter, he did not, and I was known to think that Lyndon was ... I hesitated, to find a discreet phrase for it ... "He is a crook," Al supplied. Startled, I could only accede: "Yes," and we both laughed. He explained that he didn't give a damn. And soon we talked openly as friends as well as co-workers.

It was after that I learned all the facts about who he was and so sensed the peculiar similarities in the past and current situations of our lives that made it easier to talk openly and enjoy swapping observations and anecdotes. Both of us were refugees of a sort, middle-aged men whose careers had been interrupted at mid-point and shoved aside into alternative spheres from which we looked forward and back with a certain bemused detachment. We could talk more openly about events and people around us because they had an air of unreality for us -- unimportant, of no real concern to us.

Ultimately I understood why Al could "not give a damn" about office politics at BuRec. He was lower on the bureaucratic totem pole -- and pay scale -- than I, but when he invited me over for "a real Chinese meal," I discovered that his home was over on the lakeside in the ritzy part of town -- marketable at about five times the price of my own -- and mine not paid for. It turned out his wife's father and uncle were wealthy and influential enough in the Hong Kong area to have been knighted by the British Crown. To him, the job at BuRec was just another aspect of his new life in exile.

I learned on that occasion -- for the first time -- that what I had always thought was Chinese cooking was only Cantonese -- about as typical of China as chili and tamale are of America. I wonder if what we know of the Chinese in other matters isn't on about the same plane. Al, incidentally, was from the Peking (pardon me, Beijing) area. (The whole of China seems to be appearing under an alias these days.)

Al was bitter, as I have said, but I never got the impression his bitterness was aimed at Mao or communism. And his reminiscences of Chiang Kai-shek were more in terms of sorrow than of anger. "When he was young," Al said, "we would go to him with a plan and say, 'We must do this for China,' and he would say, 'Sounds good. Let's go do it.' And we would." But then, Al indicated, came Mei Ling (Mme. Chiang) and her brothers, the Soongs, with their Harvard-trained management experts and Swiss bank accounts, and "After that, we would go to him with a plan and say, 'We must do this for China,' and he would reply, 'Sounds very interesting. I will refer this to my committee on procedures and operations.' And three weeks later we would get the plan (written in Chinese ideograms) with one word written across it in English: 'No,' and signed (in English script) T.V. Soong." Everything went downhill after that, Al felt.

About Mei Ling, he said, simply, "Even around Chiang's headquarters we always referred to her as 'the Actress.' " After a sideways glance at me, he added, "In Chinese, that is not a nice thing to say." About his exile he was bitter. And he blamed it on Mei Ling and her brothers.

When Al first came to the U.S., he was debriefed at the State Department by Walt Rostow. He thought the net result was a waste of time. "Rostow is a fool," Al said. "He is an expert, so nobody can tell him anything, except maybe some other expert as blind as he is." I didn't argue. I had never heard of Rostow. Later Rostow was in the news as a senior architect of Lyndon's Vietnam policy, and then I understood what Al was talking about. Rostow is one of the pundits who thought the enemy in Vietnam was communism and our troops were saviors of the Holy Grail of Free Enterprise. It was a great crusade like the Crusades of a thousand years ago.

The nearest I ever got to getting Al to talk about ideology was when I tried to sound him out about Chinese philosophers: "Confucius, for example." He shrugged.

"You won't understand the way Chinese people think unless you study Lao-tse, not Confucius," he said. A little more talking and some reading gave me an inkling of what he meant. I have the impression that Confucius was sort of the Dale Carnegie of his day -- interested in how to get ahead in the emperor's bureaucracy; Lao-tse was interested in how to adjust to the facts of life on earth and in the universe -- he was sort of a mystical early-day ecologist. (Al, incidentally, was no Taoist; he was a Chinese Roman Catholic -- which sect had been a presence in China since monastic missionaries followed Marco Polo in the court of Kublai Khan. I seem to remember that the Mongol emperors decreed that all their subjects should believe in one God, but aside from that leaning toward monotheism, they were totally impartial about what god their individual subjects might choose.)

Al attached considerable significance to the fact that Mao's headquarters in World War II was identical to that of the rebel-outlaw band described in the Chinese classic, *Shui Hu Chuan* -- an island in the middle of a crater lake (geologically very like our Crater Lake with its island, but much more extensive). *Shui Hu Chuan* is the Chinese version of the Robin Hood story, and like our stories of Sherwood Forest, a legend grown out of history. Interestingly enough, the Shui Hu band and the Merry Men and Maid Marian of Sherwood Forest were all creating their legends about the same period in history -- on opposite sides of the world. The classic was translated by Pearl Buck many years ago under the title *All Men Are Brothers.* (The title is not a translation.)

Another glimpse which may help understand events in Tiananmen Square and the subsequent repressive measures:

Al's description of the guerrilla training course at Mao's headquarters academy would curl your hair -- not because it expressed some special tenets of communism but because it reflected the grimness of the war as China experienced it. And if a description of that training course would curl your hair, his description of Japanese counter-guerrilla operations which he observed would give you a permanent, frizzy-type. Al hated Japan with a passion I found hard to understand. He wouldn't buy a paperclip made in Japan and bristled at the thought of anyone else doing so. And obviously the Japanese were not communist.

As a final clincher for my insistence that events in China today are to be understood as primarily a reflection of Chinese rather than ideological struggle, let me cite my own inability to recall a protest movement in Russia or anywhere else in Eastern Europe which began with a mass hunger strike.

DATUM V

Retirement and Depression II

Mark Adams,Packrat Press, Oak Harbor, 1983

Chapter 15

"Packrat Peregrinus"

On January 1, 1980, Mark published The Packrat, *a forty-page magazine. Described in the masthead as "our contribution to the continuing conversations of mankind,"* The Packrat *included passages from letters from his family, and a piece which he called "A beautiful reverie about the experience of becoming a registered nurse," by his daughter Kathleen. The longest article, "Packrat Peregrinus," excerpted here, tells the story of his retirement, move to the Pacific Northwest, and second marriage.*

"

Packrat Peregrinus

After my allotted three score and ten years, I am no closer to answering that age-old question of whether or not there is a life after death than I was at birth. Getting closer to the problem clarifies it not a bit.

However, recent years have put me in a position to provide some authentic information on a more immediately significant question, to-wit: "Is there a life after retirement?"

The answer, my own experience affirms, is "Yes ... But Wow!"

In our society, the Social Security Administration has arbitrarily established sixty-five as an appropriate retirement age. I changed from knickers to long pants when I was thirteen and started voting when I was twenty-one, and age sixty-five for retirement is no more arbitrary than those "passage" ages I honored in my youth. So when sixty-five loomed, I began planning for retirement and beyond.

The bugaboo of not knowing what to do with myself when a job no longer filled my days didn't frighten me. In all the fifty years I worked for a living, I can't remember a day when I showed up for work and buckled into it because I could not think of anything better to do.

Truly, I can't think of anything better to do than writing and printing; and those are things I did for a living most of my working life. But whereas I like to write and I like to print, I like to write what I want written and print what I want printed -- which may be (but isn't very often) exactly the same thing as writing or printing what somebody else wants written or printed badly enough to pay me to do it. So not having a job through those "sunset years" looked like an opportunity for freedom to be busier at writing and printing than ever before.

I had a file cabinet full of things I had scribbled at odd times and in circumstances totally unrelated to my work. Moreover, I was convinced that most of the best writing I had ever done was in that cabinet -- unedited, unprinted. And I had friends with similar writing-printing addictions, so there was prospect of comradeship in helping one and another feed their habits in the same permissive atmosphere I would enjoy. In sum, there was enough writing, editing, and/or printing -- in sight! -- to keep me busy for a decade or so.

Thus as age sixty-five and retirement loomed, I was eager enough to start nearly a decade in advance making practice runs in anticipation of that ultimate leap in my sixty-fifth year.

Initially I had thought to rent a shop -- after the manner of a fisherman renting boat and lines at a boat dock. But as it happened, this project fit in with a fancy I had held for a long time, that of a shop in a truck trailer which would be always available when I wanted to print a book or a pamphlet -- like Benjamin Franklin when he traveled over England before the Revolution, trailing press and type in a wagon following behind his coach wherever he went.

I acquired the trailer part of a furniture moving van, thirty-by-eight feet, and installed five tons of printing machinery -- which was ready to roll in two hours ... disconnect the electricity, gas and water pipes, back up the tractor, hitch up and go.

The furniture moving van shop and a successor served limited purposes and metamorphosed again in succeeding pre-retirement years. But for a decade I clung to the idea as a solution, come retirement, and ...

Thus by the time I reached age sixty-five, all questions of what I wanted to do after retirement were settled. The only remaining question was how I was going to work out my detente with the contiguous world, come the day.

The contiguous world with which every retiree has to work out his detente falls roughly into three provinces: money, family, and friends. I suppose each one of us must grope for the terms of his detente according to his own bent and his own particular circumstances.

I don't suppose money was a major problem for Nelson Rockefeller. Nor was money that much of a problem for me, though for a strikingly different reason -- that is, Nelson's family bequeathed him plenty of money, and my family bequeathed me only a scornful impatience with the whole subject -- which can be, as I will explain, nearly as liberating.

I am afraid that, actually, money has never seemed real to me, even before retirement, unless translated into terms of immediate desiderata -- food, clothing, shelter, paper, ink, printing equipment. The really expensive things money can buy -- status and power -- always had and still did provoke me into active avoidance behavior. So at retirement the problem of finding money in the modest amounts necessary to cover the requirements of my chosen life appeared rather easy, since my needs were small.

When I walk into a restaurant with a large sum in my pocket -- say $20 -- I am still likely to ask for a bowl of red because I like chili. My favorite costume is a suit of work clothes, because I like the muted colors, the comfortable cut, and the study fabrics. I live in an eight-by-thirty-one-foot travel trailer; if I were a millionaire, I'd live in a similarly spare life-support capsule -- because it is mobile yet compact and complete (bed, bath, kitchen, table, two chairs, typewriter, filing cabinet, bookshelves, and record player) with no lawn to mow, no acreage of floors to sweep or furniture to dust. Yet if I want to pace, there is a public park adjoining the trailer park which has towering evergreens, sheltered tables overlooking a beautiful lake, miles of paths, and playground equipment. In sum, the necessities of my chosen lifestyle aren't costly.

And even in the equipment required for my chosen occupation I am lucky. Writing? You can get a dictionary with a full supply of words in paperback. Printing? The industry is undergoing technological revolution. Electronic scanners, computers, print-out machines are so much faster (not better -- in fact, not as good -- but much, much faster) that the older printing equipment is obsolete in the whole periodical-commercial printing field. Hence fantastically good, complex, high-precision equipment from the old hot-metal days is simply written off -- given away to old fuds who will haul it off. And since the printing I want to do is good, not fast, printing, I am able to acquire my No. 1 selections for a song.

True, paper and ink go for inflated prices nowadays. But the printing I want to do is not only slow but also small-volume printing; what I have always wanted is sort of a pilot-plant operation -- if something turns out to be commercially valuable, take the established images to a commercial printer and tell him to do his stuff.

Thus, in my experience of retirement, money has been no real problem.

For me, by the time the calendar was signaling retirement, the children were grown and on their own; my parents had died while I was in my early sixties. Most of the grandchildren, even, were entering the world of self-reliance and self-support. Instead of having a family to support, I found society proffering supports to me.

Only my wife remained as family. She had stuck with me forty years through thick and thin -- since I was I, it was mostly thin.

Buckie -- Casey, Willena -- was and is a magnificent woman. Keenly intelligent, courageous, a talented writer, better adjusted to her world than I, with greater acceptance from her peers than I, and with income greater than my own. And she was staunchly loyal, though she found her wayward and disreputable husband increasingly an embarrassment.

In anticipation of retirement, I climaxed forty years of thin support by moving us out to the country and building there Packrat Press, a print shop designed to specifications for my "sunset years." But living twenty-odd miles from her work, in the rattlesnake thickets southeast of Austin, she found finally intolerable. It was too high a price for her to pay for a crazy dream, a bootless and time-money-costly addiction, that was only mine -- not valid for any reasonable person on earth. So I agreed we must move back into town.

I was still employed as a printer at the *Austin American-Statesman*, and I thought to commute to my sunset years print shop. But the commuting was ruinously costly both in time and money.

About this time I stumbled across another writer-printer who had attitudes toward writing and printing remarkably similar to my own. Ann Price had been a fellow member of the *American-Statesman* "black gang" (printing employees) for years, a book editor for the University of Oklahoma Press (including editor for a reissue of Eugene Manlove Rhodes' novel *Copper Streak Trail)*, a union activist, an aspirant fiction writer, etc. I welcomed her into participation in Packrat Press projects.

Buckie might have been resentful of the advent of this crony encouraging me in my deviant behavior if Ann had been male. But Ann was female. So the explosion was of nuclear force, and for all practical purposes the Packrat print shop project was obliterated. Failure of this third in a series of efforts to create a shop in anticipation of my sunset years left me sitting around glumly reciting to myself, "The third time's the charm." For a few months I "just stood around and looked Swedish."

Crossing the Barrier

And at the end of those few months came the appointed day of actual, formal retirement and adoption into the society of Social Security and Medicare.

Once I had cut that umbilical cord attaching me to the workaday world, the freedom of retirement began to be fun like nothing before in my life. In company with Ann, who declared herself a fellow member of the Liberated Order of Tramp Printers, I left Texas going west, driving a pickup which pulled a travel trailer. Who knows? Greeley might have meant "young men and men entering their second childhood."

Life felt right. Events were proving that my fantasizing subconscious mind had been realistic all along about who and what I was -- it was my disciplined, rational (responsible?) conscious mind that had been dealing in fantasies.

In Albuquerque, New Mexico, we paused to investigate a rumor that there was work to be had. We stayed there about a year. Ann went to work at the *Albuquerque Journal.* I worked at whatever odd jobs came handy and continued with writing and design projects in the mobile shop.

I hiked across the West Mesa in Albuquerque to the extinct volcanoes that broke the horizon. We made trips to Santa Fe and Taos, and a pilgrimage to Inscription Rock -- where Juan Oñate carved the *"Paso por Aquí"* that Gene Rhodes immortalized three hundred years later in another language for another culture.

When summer came, we moved the trailer and the camper into the Sandia Mountains, a couple of thousand feet above mile-high Albuquerque, just across a rickety barbed wire fence from Cibola National Forest, and we hiked the trails the rangers had laid out for us. It was so much like hiking the piney woods of East Texas where I spent much of the happiest hours of my childhood that I grew young again in heart and felt the peace of rapport with the great outdoors that had livened my first childhood as it did now my second.

The longest-lived combination of odd jobs for me included afternoons in a minimum wage job at Albuquerque Airport, X-raying luggage and badgering suspicious characters who tried to walk through the metal detectors wearing big metal belt buckles -- and then, after the last flight took off (about 10 P.M.), I went over to a local job shop whose proprietor had a linotype and would let me set type for myself in return for setting odd bits of type for him.

As summer on the Sandia mountainside gave way to bright-leaved autumn and frost, the thought came to us that we'd better get back down off the mountain before winter snows, ice, and venturi-effect winds made the road down Tijeras Canyon into town a little more devilish than we cared to dare.

This thought then began to graze farther and farther afield: If we were going to flee down Tijeras Canyon to escape winter, why stop in Albuquerque? Why not escape winter in lower altitudes yet similar latitudes ... say in Southern California?

And then the grazing thought left that patch of greenery for another farther on. Wintering in Southern California is one thing, but summering there is for the birds and the Muscle Beach buffs (define buff either way, we still didn't want it). So we looked beyond winter to a summer father north -- say in the Puget Sound area.

We got travel books out of the library and studied climate data. The books said yes, the Puget Sound area has a maritime climate. Air masses off the central Pacific, moving in the train of our continent's prevailing westerlies, keep the coastal areas cool in summer -- and only a little colder in winter! Temperatures around the Strait of San Juan de Fuca on the Canadian border are no colder than those in Albuquerque near the Mexican border.

So, when we coasted down Tijeras Canyon in the late September 1978, with the camper and trailer hitched to the pickup and Ann in her Toyota scouting for the caravan, we just kept on rolling for 3,000 miles. And that, my friends, was tasting the very substance of freedom.

In the Puget Sound area we picked right up where we'd left off in Albuquerque, with the added sense of settling into a possible home base locale. Ann went to work at the *Everett Herald* (a subsidiary of the *Washington Post* -- Everett is related to Seattle about like Pasadena to Houston), and I took the first odd jobs that came to hand. About this time Buckie's lawyer arranged a divorce. She married a better man, and Ann agreed to marry me.

Shortly the printing phase of the quest struck pay dirt -- a particularly rich vein. Following grapevine intelligence from one friend to another, I came to Ken Monson.

Ken is a character after my own heart. Reminds me of Bob Barton -- downgraded by a rash of Packrat-like traits.

Ken was photographer and reporter for Washington dailies for years, owned and operated print shops more years, was (and still is) active in behind-the-scenes politics of liberal slant.

He edited the paper of the Boeing Machinists' Local (20,000 members) for a decade. He opposed the Vietnam War actively and remembers with pride attending an anti-war rally in Chicago, speaking for labor and finding himself in the company of Martin Luther King, Jr., Norman Thomas and Harry Bridges. He publishes books at Paine Field in Everett under the name of The Working Press -- history and Americana of various sorts.

All this delights me, but the thing that made him pay-dirt strike for my particular purposes was that a few years ago an old trade typesetting plant in Seattle with a regional reputation for quality found itself facing the wrenching transition to cold type. The secondhand market was glutted with hot-type equipment. Enter wreckers and haulers with sledge hammers. Wham! a model 31 linotype ($35,000 before inflation) was shoveled out the door onto the waiting trucks as $87.50 worth of scrap metal. The hammers pounded and the trucks hauled all day.

For an old-time printer like Ken, it was like witnessing an atrocity, a slaughtering of innocents, the Burghers of Calais. Since then he has been buying (for peanuts) and moving to his Paine Field buildings all sorts of old-time printing equipment -- with a printing professional's sense that the stuff being discarded is not really all that obsolete, plus a touch of humane compassion.

When Ken and I walked through his buildings and talked, I knew I could extract exactly the home-base shop I had in mind from the jumble, and (I think it was important to him) he was convinced I would cherish it, be kind to it, give it a good home.

We struck a deal. I bought a complete shop -- to be paid for by setting type for his printing operation as needed. After five months it is more than half paid for, and by next year it will migrate into some sea-going cargo containers and be installed there, ready to be placed in trucks, spotted wherever we decide to make home base -- and become there operational instantly.

Meanwhile, the shop in its Paine Field quarters keeps me happily puttering ... things like this *Packrat* ... some books are in process ... I have a fulfilling sense of freedom combined with specific hopes.

And there *is* a life after retirement. But wow!

”

Packrat peregrinus traveling the roads of the Pacific Northwest, 1982

Building Packrat Press in Oak Harbor, 1982

Chapter 16

Packrat Press

In February of 1982, Mark moved from Everett to a house in Oak Harbor, on Whidbey Island. On the lot across from his house, he built Packrat Press, his last print shop, and furnished it with the hot metal equipment he had bought from Ken Monson.

"

Oct. 15, 1993

Mark Adams to Colleen Urbanek
Colleen's Books
Houston, Texas

Packrat Press is a purely personal venture established over fifteen years ago when I retired from a motley career (mostly on the fringes of politics) upon reaching Social Security's conventional date of passage. So understanding what Packrat Press does or doesn't do must be rooted in my personal history, not in any analogy to small-publisher norms.

You have already seen a book we have produced in the last few years: Carl Duaine's *With all Arms.*[1] The Duaine-Packrat relationship goes back a long way. It was about a quarter-century ago that Carl approached me -- at the suggestion of mutual friends -- with the manuscript of his *Caverns of Oblivion,* asking if I would print it for him. I was non-committal; I trusted the friends who had sent him, but I had not known Carl before. (In our early maturity we had each been acolytes of Maury Maverick, Sr., Carl in San Antonio and I in Washington, D.C., when Maury was congressman; but although a certain kinship of ideas and attitudes is suggested, we had not known each other at that time.)

---

[1]Printed at Packrat Press in Oak Harbor. Published 1987 by New Santander Press, Edinburg, Texas.

When he brought the *Caverns* manuscript to me, Carl had already self-published two books and managed to sell enough of them to defray expenditures of money, if not time, so his sideline interest in communicating through books was near enough to self-sustaining that he had continued. He knew the territory. (I do not consider the territory of self-publishing an unfortunate habitat except for people who think they're somewhere else, such as the high road to wealth and acclaim.)

At any rate, when Carl approached me with the manuscript of *Caverns,* I was non-committal and read it through carefully. *Caverns* embodied translations of manuscripts by three sixteenth century leaders in the northward expansion of Spanish settlers from the Valley of Mexico -- plus interpretive connecting chapters by Duaine. I found it a solid and fascinating book.

He said the University of New Mexico Press had rejected the manuscript. I could understand why. It was a craggy, rough-hewn book. But I found it a better book for all that. I agreed to print the book, quoted Carl a beer-and-wieners price, and made holiday over editing, designing. Ultimately I produced a champagne-and-pheasant type book.

I was working two thirty-five-hour-a-week jobs at the time to make a living. Printing *Caverns* was a hobby project, so the project stretched out over several months, somewhat to Carl's dismay. But when he got the book into his hands -- and into the hands of friends who expressed great admiration -- he decided the result was worth whatever wait.

Wherefore the episode had a sequel, but of that anon.

That printing of *Caverns* was sold out long ago. Also a "second edition" of a few dozen copies (not a second printing -- after Carl sold out, I just bound up some overrun sheets, experimenting with the binding processes, and sold them to Carl). But if you see it reasonably priced in a used book catalogue, it might be a good thing to lay hands on it. A few years after it was printed, I saw a copy advertised for five times the original price. By this time the appropriate price must be stratospheric.

The sequel to the *Caverns* episode, for us, was *With All Arms*

-- the book you have at hand.

After *Caverns* I didn't hear from Carl for about fifteen years. Then one day in 1986, after our move to Oak Harbor, Carl called me from his home in the Rio Grande Valley, asking if I would put another book into print for him. (How he found me, I can't guess.) I responded with interest, but non-commitally. He sent the 400,000-word manuscript for *With All Arms.*

I sensed, understood, and sympathized with his situation. With advanced emphysema and his eighty-odd years, he felt that he had not long to live and he wanted to see this, his climactic work as historian and writer, in print before he died. Moreover, he wanted to see it in print the way I would print it.

Again, when I read the manuscript, I found it solid -- the sort of thing that gives me a sense of worthy achievement when I put it into print. So again I quoted him a beer-and-wieners price. Toward the end of the project Carl teamed up with Al Ramirez of New Santander Press in Edinburg, Texas, on the publishing. That's how we met Al.

So all is well according to the Shakespearean definition. Carl held the book in his hands a few weeks before he died and seemed pleased with it.

Packrat's favorite author, of course, is Franklin Jones, Sr. We have selected, edited, and published six books filled with his letters. And as with Carl's books, the publishing and marketing situation you would need to understand is strictly *sui generis* -- hardly to be understood in terms of publishing norms.

The relationship between Franklin ("Soupy") and Packrat also goes back a long way -- a very long way. I first met Soupy about sixty years ago at a political rally in Jefferson, Texas. I was there to accompany my father, who was principal speaker at the rally, and Soupy appeared to introduce the speaker to the local audience, and to distribute copies of our Gladewater newspaper.

Throughout the following half-century Soupy and I turned up repeatedly as friendly allies in sundry political and quasi-political campaigns, such as the organization and launching of the *Texas Observer,* in which we both appeared as staunch supporters of an initiative of Minnie Fisher Cunningham. But we didn't stay in touch between campaigns. It was just that for a half-century we seemed always to choose the same candidates and the same causes.

Neither of us was ever a political pro seeking to further a political career as office holder or hired gun in politics. Soupy was a strikingly successful plaintiff's lawyer; his politicking often included campaign contributions -- cash money type -- as well as counseling, speaking, and writing. And whereas I was never able to make a campaign contribution other than by working for peanuts (the phrase is Bernard Rapoport's -- I was never in a position to feel, much less express, the implied disdain for peanuts), I never made as much money as writer-printer in campaign years as I did as writer-printer in non-political years. And certainly if some friend who didn't know me very well ever suggested that I run for office, I always ran for the nearest exit.

Soupy had his own background in publishing. As far as I know, his earliest experience with publishing occurred when the *Marshall News-Messenger* refused to print one of his letters to the editor -- for grossly partisan reasons -- and Young Lawyer Jones simply took the letter to a commercial printer, had it set in type and printed up as a handbill, and strewed the handbills all over town. And after that he remained vocal in journals of his area, and ultimately had pivotal roles in establishing the *East Texas Democrat* and the *Texas Observer.*

After my retirement, when Packrat produced a forty-page letter to our friends titled *The Packrat,* Soupy was among the fifty-eight individuals on the mailing list. He responded and the relationship resumed. Ann and I became members of Soupy's Committee of Correspondence, and shortly thereafter Soupy suggested he would like to finance a reprint of some letters which he had sent back to homefolks during a trip Huldah and he had made behind the Iron Curtain in 1965, which had been widely circulated at the time in the form of carbon copies enthusiastically produced by his secretaries back home.

I seized upon the idea with enthusiasm similar to that of his secretaries. I had just finished printing up 200 copies of a pre-existing manuscript of my own (from 1955) speculating on the psychology of aesthetics and titled *How to Tell If It's Art*, at the urging of an Austin friend, Elmo Hegman, who had seen a newsprint copy of the manuscript.

Franklin's suggestion sounded like a marvelous program for having my cake and eating it too. So away we went with Packrat's first hard-bound book in our new, post-retirement regime, *Operation: Why You Wanna Go THERE?*

I had great fun producing *Why There?* Adapting an idea suggested by Morris' Kelmscott *Chaucer*, in which the type had Medievalist page borders by Burne-Jones, I made page borders from photos Franklin had taken during the trip.

I do not recall how much of Franklin's money went into *Why There?* A letter I came across in my files the other day indicates that some months later Soupy was proposing to put in $15,000 toward an endowment for Packrat (after the manner of Frankie Randolph's endowment of the *Texas Observer*), and that I rejected the idea on grounds my personal venture should not be subsidized -- and thereby committed in advance to projects I might be unable or unwilling to complete. I suggested instead a book-by-book subsidy (repayable in books if so desired), the amount of the subsidy to be reckoned as materials costs plus a minimum wage -- with any Packrat profits (above subsistence) to appear *if* extra copies were sold to others.

How things went in publishing Soupy's other books after *Why There?* is told better than I can tell it by Ann in a recent letter to Bill Dazey. Bill had written a letter to Soupy, with a copy to us, expressing his delight in Soupy's books.

(

[1993]

Ann Adams to Bill Dazey
San Antonio, Texas

Every time I look at one of Franklin's books of letters we published, I am astonished. They are so beautiful. And I'm not bragging on the work we did. I'm bragging on the writing. Your letter to him brought back the time when we were deciding how to publish the *Public and Private Letters* volumes. This must have been in 1983, after we had published his letters from behind the Iron Curtain in 1981.

Mark had known Franklin in person since the thirties or forties. I had known Franklin through his writing since the late fifties. I lived in Houston then, and took the *Texas Observer*. When my copy would come, I would turn first to the Letter from Marshall.

In 1980, when Mark and I put out the first edition of our tiny magazine, *The Packrat,* in Everett, Washington, we sent copies to Mark's friends that he had addresses for, and one of them was Franklin. Franklin wrote back, and that is how Mark and I got into the Committee of Correspondence.

In November 1983, Mark and I visited Franklin and Huldah and went for a boat ride on Caddo Lake. That was the first time I ever saw him. We met John and Nancy Eudy that trip and arranged for them to send us the boxload of letters he had given them to find a publisher for. They had had the letters for some time and had not found a publisher, so they seemed enthusiastic about our taking the project over. Charming young people. We had read some of Nancy's delightful letters to Franklin and some of John's biography of Minnie Fish (Minnie Fisher Cunningham, if you don't know).

What I'm working around to telling you is that I never knew up to then what kind of man Franklin was. His letters in the *Observer* told me what kind of thinker he was, but my interest is in literature. I want to know the person who houses the mind. I would ask Mark, and Mark would say, "He's a Southern gentleman." But it was only when I began to read his personal letters, starting with those he wrote in 1963, that I began to see what that meant. I saw how Franklin dealt with his friends and his family by mail. When I was going through the files, at first I was removing the political letters for publication -- not only the ones to newspapers and public officials, but those he wrote to his friends and family that contained passages about politics.

"Mark, this is frustrating," I said. "How can I separate his political life from his personal life?"

"Don't try," Mark said.

"But this book is going to be 3,000 pages long," I said.

"We'll print it in more than one volume," he said.

Mark is wonderful. It's like having King Kong at your command.

As I read the files, I knew that I could not deprive the reader of what I had so much longed for myself, which was to know what the *man* was like. At first I was setting aside the letters to manufacturers and tradespeople, but some of those were so charming that they went back in. Well, who could do without Franklin's description of a shaver that was working wrong, or his exhortation to a store to send a dress he ordered for Huldah's Christmas present to his office, since "Mrs. Jones not only shakes, but she sometimes unwraps, packages that come to me at the house around Christmas." I did omit one letter to a store, but I couldn't resist putting in a footnote telling history that I was omitting it because it was obscene. In it Franklin offered to cut the manager a new opening in his corpus in which to insert Franklin's credit card.

Naturally we couldn't omit the Stearns letters,[2] although we thought for a time of publishing them as a separate volume.

You give me far too much credit for publication of the letters. I did the editing, but it was Mark's vision that formed and sustained the project, and of course he did the design of the letters from behind the Iron Curtain. Have you seen that volume? While we were working on it, I couldn't guess what it was supposed to look like. I was helping to set the type, and I couldn't guess why we had such a short line length for such a large page. Mark said the pictures would make a border for the type, but I couldn't visualize the page. I was puzzled while pasting up the negatives for the pictures and puzzled throughout

---

[2]Letters FJ wrote on the letterhead of the Stearns Patent Horse Detacher Co.

the first pressruns. It was only during the last pressruns, when we printed the type on the pages that had already been printed with the picture-borders, that I saw what was happening.

Mark is like a good suspense novel. You get glimmerings of what is going on, but it's not until the end that you see the whole picture. His father used to say to him, "I can see perfectly well what you're doing. What I can't figure out is what in hell you *think* you're doing."

It was such fun to read the letters Franklin and Smitty [J. Edwin Smith] wrote to each other in the sixties and seventies when I was going through those files. Smitty's Clipping Service was in operation even then, and there was a lot of Art Buchwald going through the mail. Although I ordinarily didn't include letters Franklin was answering in his published letters, I couldn't resist putting two short letters from Smitty in footnotes -- the one to the I.R.S. regarding James R. Bains, dec'd (which also appeared in the *Houston Post*), and one other, about Elizabeth Rex. King Kong permitted anything that struck my fancy, and he not only permitted it, he made it happen. You ought to see him when he's in his printer's trance.

I regard the Jones letters as particularly felicitous history. Franklin wrote about everything important that was going on in Marshall, Texas, and the nation, and we had the privilege of putting those letters in print. I've edited a lot of books since 1968, when I went to work as an editor at the University of Oklahoma Press, but the Jones letters are the best editing work I ever did and the editing work that has given me the most pleasure. After hours and days and weeks and months and years of working on them, I can still look at one and be conquered again by what a magnificent piece of writing it is, so I know why you retreat to the letters to allow yourself to heal.

A second look at those role models of my youth: Hubbard, Morris, Lawrence, et al., reveals fundamental weaknesses I came to share. All my models were writers whose printing was extension of their writing interests; all had a taste for craftsmanship in antiquarian modes; all were almost grossly inner-directed; and (here is where the pattern has *significance* in the present instance) none of these printers and publishers were motivated or even much influenced by thought of markets; their drive was to get an intended book in print, after which they sort of lost interest. They were communicating with their friends as Smitty is when he writes letters or sends clippings -- no economic consideration involved.

Once a book was in print, those models of my youth were content with small editions. Lawrence printed and distributed twelve copies of *Seven Pillars of Wisdom* and then melted down the type; it became a best seller years later when it was handled by other publishers who thought in terms of marketing.

Lawrence was thus typical of all my group of role models. They all printed and published for their own reasons -- and marketed in unconventional and often odd-ball or ineffective ways. I am no different; Packrat Press has been typical of the group, true to the tradition.

Today, like those role models of our youth, we Packrats are very proud of having had a hand in getting our chosen books into print. But about marketing those books we remain basically ignorant, unskilled, and largely uninterested.

It is true that during my active years in the social-political context between high school and retirement, I managed some publishing successes -- that is, mass production, wide distribution, even prestigious products. But in the political field the object was to give away the product as widely as possible. So my years of experience in writing-printing served only to emphasize my underdeveloped marketing interests and abilities. Thus in the marketplace, also, the octogenarian had metamorphosed little from the high school kid.

”

Chapter 17

The Committee of Correspondence

When Mark got back in touch with Franklin Jones, Sr., in 1980, he became a member of FJ's Committee of Correspondence, a group of people from all over the country who wrote letters about everything, but mostly about politics. In the following letter he describes the Committee to a new member.

"

October 1989

Mark Adams to Bill Dazey
San Antonio, Texas

The processes of aging in our society have recently crept into the forefront of public discussion -- concurrently with the growth in the portion of our population past the commonly accepted retirement age (and the perception of merchants for sundry pharmaceutical and social nostrums that an important new market was developing in this quarter[1]).

The old cliches seem to have a certain validity: "We all live our lives in a circle," the phrase "second childhood." But what interests me at the moment is not so much second childhood as what we might call second adolescence -- the period of marked change in physiological (including neurological) structures and in social function which normally occur during the final years of our lives. We are all of us amateurs in this business of retiring and growing older, just as we were amateurs in the business of maturing in our earlier adolescence.

One element of the changes of second adolescence is a change in the style and function of our correspondence.

In our middle years most of us sat at a desk with an "In"

---

[1]*Mark was amused by a T-shirt that read "Senior Citizen. Gimme my Goddamn discount."*

basket and an "Out" basket. It was our job to do this -- our duty to others, our contribution to the business of the day. The driver of yon truck was waiting for a signal from us before he could transport a cargo of necessities down the road to the point where it was needed.

But with retirement we step out of these lines of function -- and duty. Nobody has to wait for us to do our job so they can do theirs. That truck driver with his cargo of bread -- or rat poison -- gets on down the road without waiting for his signal -- at least from us. Thus the circumstances of our lives change; our previous function is suddenly absent. And thus appears one of the major -- often traumatic -- problems as we enter our second adolescence. For we must change also; we must adjust.

Most of us fumble around trying to understand and adapt to the new parameters defining our lives. But there are no guidelines. Our second adolescence is as troubled as our first.

You and I have seen a lot of retirees who simply failed to find an answer to those questions -- and withered and died a few months or a few years after retirement. Others take flight from the problems posed by those questions by plunging into frenzied vacationing -- fishing, hunting, traveling, collecting bric-a-brac and building storage space for it, etc. -- until they come to feel a need for a vacation from vacationing. Still others simply turn and run -- deny they are seventy, set out to prove not only that they are forty-five but also that they are changeless -- as some early adolescents try to revert to childhood's protected fantasies.

None of these modes of adjustment seems really adequate; so the bulk of us fumble along, trying to adjust to our new circumstances on an *ad hoc* basis. And just so the bulk of us cope with the changes in our correspondence.

I think I find a pattern in our adaptations.

Bereft of any vital role in the world's day-to-day functioning, we sit back and take a wider view of that world and consider longer time frames. As our concern with day-to-day operations dwindles, we turn more and more to thoughts of overall strategies and the long run. With a lifetime's experience as background, we start thinking like "elder statesmen," re-map our wider world with the interests of senior generals, revitalizing -- and touching up -- the map of a wider world we had assembled in more active years.

(That phrase "elder statesman" is embedded in our language as a cliche. So is the image of "old men sitting on a park bench talking politics.")

And slowly our correspondence changes to fit our changed role in society.

For one thing, we write more often to others nearing our own age group who are sharing our enhanced interest in the wider spheres of policy. (The Committee of Correspondence consists mostly of retirees, you may have noticed.)

I do not think I am alone as I fumble and gravitate into this different mode of corresponding. Nor do I feel I am alone if I wonder now and again if any of my activity is of any use beyond its role in helping me kill time while I wait for the mortician. Personally, I have convinced myself -- almost -- that there may be some use -- some function -- in my current habits of living and correspondence.

"It may be useful," I tell myself, "if we old ones can provide Sisyphus Junior with a sketch map of terrain ahead of him. After all, we have been there; we know some things; we can list things that didn't work -- and maybe a few that did, more or less. And if we share with Junior what we know, it might -- it just might -- help him."

Warming to this theme, I continue, "Certainly our own life experiences have convinced us that records -- sketch maps -- left by earlier men have been helpful to us -- have heartened us, have warmed us at least with a sense of companionship and belonging, have assured us that we are not really stepchildren of malign Destiny, have persuaded us that our fragile optimism is not altogether fatuous, have proven to us that even false hopes can strengthen any day's efforts."

Given that we have some words of wisdom to impart to Junior, how do we get the word to him? Can we? This is the really difficult part. And the only sensible answer has to be that we probably can't expect to get the word around enough to make a difference in the short term. That would be like expecting a mosquito to whip a human being in a single savage onslaught. But in the long term, a germ of truth can become an analogue of the malaria microbe a mosquito *can* carry -- it has happened.

A few minutes ago I watched a rerun of the movie *Bad Day at Black Rock,* and I remember how after the movie appeared, finally the nation and its people became aware of and acknowledged the horrors visited on Japanese Americans so cruelly and unjustly during World War II, even apologized and feebly tried to make amends. A germ of truth had been planted in the social bloodstream.

I reach eagerly for the support of others taking this line of argument. I read with satisfaction paragraphs in Isaac Asimov's *Robots and Empire,* in which a human being explains to a robot that "No individual death among human beings is important. Someone who dies leaves his work behind and that does not entirely die -- it never entirely dies as long as humanity persists."

One of the stigmas identifying the correspondence of us old fuds is total readiness to paste in portions of other people's sketch maps to perfect our own -- vide innumerable letters (with enclosures) from Louisa [Hugg], Soupy [Franklin Jones, Sr.], Smitty [J. Edwin Smith], Griff [Lambdin], Ed [Ross], Al [Ramirez], Cole [Smith], Ann [Adams] -- the whole Committee list -- including you. And me. It's not that any of us is particularly inept as a map sketcher -- but as the map expands we turn to borrowing snippets from others because it's labor-saving.

Certainly my own self-assurance about this sketch-map line of thought is nourished by the thought that other well-respected members of the Committee seem to share my rationale. We exchange sketch maps with each other and in doing so seem to sense that Sisyphus Junior peers over our shoulder now and again as we do.

At ninety, the oldest of us -- the irrepressible, the indefatigable, the lambent Louisa -- shares riches of observant writing -- current or still extant, her own or that of others.

Soupy has shared with us a half-dozen books which some notables qualified to judge (Ralph Yarborough for one) have termed the best history of our area and our times -- along with recent letters on which the ink has not had time to dry.

Griff's *Odyssey to Guadalajara*[2] offers a model -- a role model -- for young Sisyphus as he starts on his way.

You and Smitty toy with the idea of autobiography.

Otto Mullinax has published two books of essays and has recently completed a novel about the era of the American Revolution titled *Sam Adams's Freedom Fighters* which reflects some light on our times -- and Sisyphus Junior's. (My own pre-publication thumbnail review: Fair fiction; good history; superb Mullinax -- I couldn't put the manuscript down.)

Even I putter away at a couple of books, rat-holing snippets of manuscript from time to time. One is addressed directly to Sisyphus Junior; the other is a hash of random reminiscences intended to add a few notations for Junior's own accumulating world sketch map.

And among us all the letters go back and forth -- daily or weekly or monthly or yearly as the spirit moves us individually. Heart warming, companionable letters. Maybe useful. Maybe we are still functional.

Welcome to the club. Enjoy it for what it's worth. This is a free-form bull session. Have fun. And please let us keep sharing in your fun.

”

Being liberals, members of the Committee of Correspondence were embattled in the 1980s. Cole Smith of Littleton, Colorado, asked them all for definitions of a liberal.

---

[2]Griffith D. Lambdin, *Odyssey to Guadalajara*, Packrat Press, 1987.

"

Late September 1990

Mark Adams to Cole Smith,
Littleton, Colorado

It is not true that I am the world's worst at answering correspondence; I am only runner-up for the title.

The weakness which precludes my being championship material may be attributed to the fact that once in a while the pressure of unexpressed rejoinders to remarks made in letters I have received (and much enjoyed) from long-suffering friends builds up to a point at which it bursts the bonds of my innate laziness and I break wind with a reply. And there goes my claim to the championship.

Recent letters from you have pushed this pressure of unexpressed rejoinders past the critical point. *En garde!*

At this juncture it is only fair that I should warn you that my lapses into utterance are apt to be daunting to my long-suffering friends, not merely qualitatively but also quantitatively.

Ann, who knows me better than anybody else in the world (including, probably, myself) has remarked that "Mark can't tell you the time of day in less than a thousand words." Ann also, in the course of affectionate household banter, has referred to me as "Heidelberg Man." (Will Cuppy, in his *Short History of Mankind,* refers to Heidelberg Man as arguably learned, but "You ask him a question, he answers some other question.")

This letter, in its rambling length, will demonstrate the scientific accuracy as well as the poetic truth of Ann's perceptions.

Topics mentioned in letters from you which have suggested rejoinders include: (1) The sins of the Bush administration listed in your letter to Soupy [Franklin Jones, Sr.] which Soupy described as an accurate "bill of particulars"; and (2) the characteristics of a liberal.

Decent rejoinders concerning these topics could be brief:

(1) Right on!

(2) For my money a liberal is anyone who feels a sibling sympathy, solicitude, and loyalty to the human family he

belongs to and is aware that these feelings, in any showdown, must override his hunger for fame, fortune, power and other avatars of self. Qualitatively, I think the liberal I have highest regard for was R.H. "Dr. Bob" Montgomery -- of Menard County, Texas, the U.S., and the world. As alternate, I think I would pick Maury Maverick, Sr., of Bexar County, Texas, the U.S., and the Americas. If you want to factor in power to speed change for his siblings -- as a sort of quantitative modifier -- then I think I would plump for Kemal Ataturk.

So here is your third and final chance to avoid the effluvia of a wandering mind by skipping on over to the signature at the end of this letter. Going, Going, Gone!

(1) Was Soupy Jesting?

Your "bill of particulars" on the shortcomings of the Bush administration was rounded and complete. I was all admiration. The thing about it that snagged my mind was your remark to Soupy anent his statement that he approved most of the things that Bush had done early in the presidency: You said, "Surely you jest!" I got to wondering; was Soupy jesting? when is a jest? etc.

I have always been interested in the way the gritty texture and multifarious meanings of events become packaged in the smoother and more easily communicable simplicities of words.

There is the notable incident of Cambronne's finale at Waterloo. Napoleon had ordered his Old Guard to charge the hilltop where the thin (but long) red line of Wellington's forces stood. And so they did, against withering fire, until only one man, Cambronne, remained on his feet -- wounded but still staggering up the slope. Admiring, even awed, by his resolute courage in the face of hopeless disaster, the British officers ordered cease fire and called on Cambronne to surrender. But according to British history books, Cambronne responded: "The Guards die but never surrender" (thus providing a phrase still used in our political discourse), whereupon the British officers ordered fire resumed and at once the flesh that had been Cambronne -- single target of companies of riflemen -- hit the dirt as hamburger meat, and the spirit of Cambronne continued, according to Hoyle, immortal.

However, as any French schoolchild knows, that was not what Cambronne responded at all. He replied to the invitation to surrender with just one word, *"Merde!"* ("Shit!"). To this day French ladies admonish their children that it is wicked (or, worse, uncouth) to use "the word of Cambronne."

And then again there is the anecdote about Admiral Stumpf on the occasion of the naval battle off Leyte.

After the Lingayen Gulf landing, I was with Air Group 30, who, having registered the conventional thirty percent casualties among its pilots, was replaced on the *U.S.S. Lexington* and shipped back to the mainland as casual passengers aboard a jeep (escort) carrier, the *Kwajalein.* A fellow passenger of mine being rotated back to the States turned out to have been navigator on the *White Plains,* Admiral Stumpf's flagship on the occasion of the engagement off Leyte. In conversations we used to kill time between periodic appearances in the chow line to get our rations of Spam sandwiches, he told me about the night of Oct. 24-25 when a task force of Japanese battleships filed through the passage north of Samar.

Admiral Stumpf was in command of one of the three task groups of jeep carriers that were providing close support for the Leyte landing, and his group was cruising off the coast roughly in a line north to south that night.

There were initially three Japanese task forces in the area. One was nearly wiped out when it threaded through the Philippines south of Leyte and was met by the force of slow over-age battleships which had been providing artillery support for the Leyte landings.

A second Japanese battleship force headed toward the passage north of Samar and had been under attack through the previous day by planes of the fast carrier task force. After Air Group 30 sank the *Musashi,* the other ships were observed to turn and head back west. So that night, when submarines reported a third Japanese force, with carriers, coming through the Kuriles toward the Philippines, Admiral Halsey (in command of the fast carrier task force which had been attacking air fields on Luzon) headed north to intercept. The fast carrier task force included a large group of new sixteen-inch gun battleships as screen to protect the carriers from surface attack. And Halsey took those battleships with him -- which left the jeep carrier task groups without protection from surface attack.

Admiral King, following events from Washington via radio reports, spotted the mistake. He radioed "Where, repeat, where is task Group 38.5?" (*i.e.,* the battleships). Halsey, a battleship admiral dreaming, perhaps, of at last sinking a carrier or two with surface fire, did not respond, announcing to his staff that it was necessary to maintain radio silence lest the intended attack on the Japanese lose its element of surprise.

At any rate, that Japanese force headed for the passage north of Samar, double-crossed (or maybe we should say double-turned) American intelligence which had reported it in retreat the previous day, and on the morning of the 25th bore down on the jeep carrier task groups which had nothing heavier than a few destroyers to protect them from the guns of Japanese battlewagons.

On the *White Plains* the watch officer sent below for Admiral Stumpf, who, shaken awake, rushed up to the bridge on the carrier island; there he leaned on the rail watching the gun flashes on the northern horizon, grabbed the dispatch board and riffled through the messages of the previous few minutes, ducked into the wheelhouse to listen to the TBS (short-wave, short-range) radio traffic for a couple of minutes, and then came back out on the bridge, drew himself to attention, and addressed his staff.

Admiral Stumpf was, of course, an Annapolis man and as such had been raised from a pup on a steady diet of historic one-liners: "Don't give up the ship" -- Lawrence; "I have not yet begun to fight" -- John Paul Jones; "When in doubt whether to run or fight, I always fight" -- Lord Nelson; "Damn the torpedoes! Full speed ahead" -- Farragut; and so on. And what he said to his staff was, "Gentlemen, John Paul Jones and Lord Nelson to the contrary notwithstanding, now is the time to haul ass!"

I don't know whether this statement got into the history books or not, but my estimate of the navigator of the *White Plains* is that he was not literary genius enough to have invented the phrasing. So I pay homage to Admiral Stumpf.

And my view is that, whereas you can get the historians' meaning without understanding events, if you understand the event, the statements of Cambronne and Stumpf were more meaningful, more definite, and even more eloquent than the historians have been.

But the question still in my mind is: Were Cambronne and Stumpf jesting?

The situations in which they made their statements were not funny. True, their statements were touched with the sanity -- and mockery of convention -- which is the essence of humor; but nobody laughed. So were they jesting? And to get back to the point, was Soupy jesting?

After Nixon, Johnson, and Reagan -- and the vote of the American people in 1988 -- surely this current situation is not funny. So if Bush has not rushed to push the country into immediate oblivion like those predecessors, it seems like a dispensation from Providence to old (and tiring) warriors like Soupy and myself. And, come to think of it, Jimmy Carter's evaluation of the Bush administration in response to a reporter's question as noted in a recent newspaper clipping was cast in the same vein of damning only with faint praise. (Carter is quoted as saying, "I've been extremely disappointed in President Bush on environmental issues. In almost every case he's come down basically on the same position as James Watt. But on other things, in national affairs, I think Bush is going a great job.") After Reagan (whom Ann has long failed to mention by name, referring to him only as "that idiot"), if Bush refrains from pushing the nuclear button, or doing some of the other things his campaign supporters and contributors demand of him, I find it hard to begrudge him a modified approval rating, based on a list of gruesome things he hasn't done. He has given us a brief respite from utter disaster; his moves to the U.N. are so different from Reagan's refusal of funding and defiance of the World Court that ... well, we have events of the last decade to prove to us things could be worse.

But that leaves still unanswered the question: Was Soupy jesting? For half a century I have known Soupy to be capable of responding to events in the vein of Cambronne's and Stumpf's remarks. But were Cambronne and Stumpf jesting?

(2) The Characteristics of a Liberal

When I was eighteen I understood what made a liberal without stopping to think. A liberal was a person who sympathized -- or, even better, empathized -- with the poor and the powerless and strove to find expression for that sympathy.

I could readily identify a liberal by looking for tell-tale symptoms -- applying "litmus tests." A liberal was one who strove for curbs on the powerful ("tyrants"); one who eschewed aristocracy and believed in democracy; one who loved his fellow man. "Liberty, equality, fraternity," that was the ticket!

Feeling myself to be a liberal, I responded with emotion and resolution to Masefield's "Dedication" in which he proposed to write:

Not of princes and prelates with periwigged charioteers
Riding triumphantly laureled to leap the fate of the years
But rather the scorned, the rejected, the men hemmed in by the spears.

That seemed to me a liberal anthem.

A radical was merely a liberal who was brash about it.

Sixty-odd years later, I find I have lost my facility at identifying liberals and liberalism. I am inclined to think the key phrase in that first sentence of this section was "without stopping to think."

True, with accretion of experience and knowledge, I still adhere to that basic pre-condition for becoming a liberal: sympathy for the poor and the powerless.

But the plethora of litmus tests have gone sour on me. They

seem to have been smothered, almost hidden, under a mass of exceptions, whereases, in-case-ofs, and provisos. "Circumstances alter cases." Killing in self-defense is not murder, etc. The whole gamut of litmus tests includes volumes upon volumes of fine print -- complex, inconsistent, full of internal contradictions, with consequent uncertainty akin to that which keeps the court dockets crowded and makes well-stocked shelves of law books measurable in yards and furlongs.

Liberty is desirable -- until some bastard takes the liberty of driving ninety miles an hour down a two-lane road in hilly country so it would be suicide to brake fast enough to stop before hitting two cars already in a passing situation just over the hill -- even if the driver could stop that fast.

Equality is a fine thing unless one of the equals is a small child intent on playing with matches.

Fraternity is automatic among free and equal persons who have the same interests, concepts, and language. But if there is a conflict of interests, if there are diverse concepts (differences of background), if the parties are not fluent in the same language (any lawyer who has had to serve a client who had no legal background knows such language differences can be substantial), then fraternity becomes a long-odds possibility only -- not a probability.

So out of intellectual laziness, if for no other reason, I long ago set about trying to find something simpler, more coherent (and therefore, hopefully, briefer) that would indicate the liberal stance more accurately and realistically than the standard litmus tests.

I didn't find readings in social science very helpful. Social science, it seems to me, is at a stage in its development closely analogous to that of chemistry back in the days when the alchemists sought a "philosopher's stone" that would turn base metals into gold, and the "elements" were earth, air, fire and water -- a substantial distance from modern chemistry's studies of interrelated matter and energy and a periodic table based on variable atomic structures built with identical particles.

Truly, among the alchemists, the greater the diligence and

learning, the greater the distance from reality they went. And among modern social scientists ....

Adam Smith in *The Wealth of Nations* and Karl Marx in *Das Kapital* each came up with philosophers' stones -- capitalism and socialism respectively -- that are only rhetorically relevant to the real world. (Observation and description of our productive social organizations sans philosophers' stones are found in such books as Walton Hamilton's *Patterns of Industry.)*

I think progress is being made. Freud and his philosopher's stone are being replaced by studies of primate animal behavior. And in the field of cultural anthropology we are beginning to study social organisms (cultures) -- each with its own evolutionary history, just as biological organisms have each their own evolutionary history. And in comparative anthropology we begin to glimpse the development of various cultural mutations, although so far we are mostly in the descriptive stage of observation and measurement of cultural traits.

A real social science -- such as that projected by the science fiction writer Isaac Asimov in his *Foundation* series (he termed it "psycho-history") is far, far in the future.

Meanwhile...

The thought of giving up my litmus tests and starting over to find what a true liberal should do gave my lazy bone a severe attack of arthritis. For if it was circumstances that altered cases, then it was incumbent on a would-be liberal always to know the circumstances -- to a point as little this side of omniscience as possible. Always! Who has storage capacity enough in his brain cell bank to come even close? The best I could hope for was that when faced with a choice of policy, I would at least try to collect a synopsis of facts and concepts impinging on the particular situation. And maybe some day ... At least by trying to prepare to be a liberal I would be no more ill-prepared to choose wisely than somebody who hadn't realized it was necessary to try.

And still in full possession of that over-size lazy bone, I hoped to find some *pattern* in the infinite variety of human cultural-social circumstances that would help me to approach my problems from a position nearer comprehension of reality. Sixty years later I am still trying -- with only fragmentary success, if any.

It occurs to me that at this point I can save myself ten thousand words by simply including here a couple of chapters from the *Texas Testament* which I have recently determined to write -- and probably will never finish. Therein you will find a pretty clear map of where I got to in the past sixty years of trying to find a pattern in human societies.

[Excerpts from *Texas Testament* are in Chapters 1 and 19.]

I think of a liberal as one who understands that in the social organism, just as in the biological organism, functional variations (specializations) are necessary -- and that interdependence is inescapable if the organism is to prosper and survive. Hence a liberal is tolerant of cultural diversity because he understands that humans of other regions, occupations, religions, races, and languages contribute (indeed, are necessary) to his own prosperity and survival. By the same token a liberal is intolerant of ill health in the social organism -- of imbalances which produce dysfunctions in the organism and hence weaken or destroy the organism as a whole.

And if he is to have any practical effect, a liberal must be realist enough to understand -- and to face -- the fact that the processes of evolution shaping both biological and social organisms are merciless -- there are numerous extinctions for each viable species, numerous bankruptcies for each surviving organization. Moreover a liberal must be aware always that the organisms or culture which may be successful in one environment at one point in time may not be adaptable to another environment at another point in time. Environments evolve also. The dinosaurs dominated the earth for many many millennia; and then the environment changed suddenly and all were wiped out.

”

Mark had his ups and downs when pondering the fate of the planet. The following letter is to a member of the Pandorans, a talk group in Oak Harbor Mark helped start in the mid-80s -- sort of an "in-person" Committee of Correspondence.

"

Oct. 27, 1989

Mark Adams to Paul Bixby
Oak Harbor, Washington

Most people don't take me seriously when I announce that the enclosed book (Robert Heinlein's *Friday*) is the best book of interpretive prophecy since Aldous Huxley's *Brave New World* -- and superior to Huxley's book because it is more down to earth, better informed about specifics, less involved with abstract symbols. So if you join the majority, I will not be either surprised or offended.

By way of introduction to the book may I make two points: Heinlein, who makes no pretensions to intellectual elitism, is a writer of best-seller science fiction. He does not cavil at writing straight space-opera fantasy. But also he is very well informed and seriously concerned about the human race in his own way -- a blithely cynical yet sympathetic protagonist of human survival.

And he is not a nut. He was an Annapolis graduate who was invalided out of the service before World War II (he is about my age) and turned to writing science fiction to pay the bills. But he remained in touch with the core of intelligent men who survive in the cracks of the Navy structure. As a civilian he served with some engineering-pioneering units of the Navy in World War II and even delivered the commencement address to the graduates of Annapolis a few years ago.

Read it if you can find the stomach for it, and then we can sit down to discuss if for an hour or two sometime. In advance let me alert you to his portrayal of the interfacing of territorial and corporate states -- a worm's-eye view that by the end of the book has become an overview. Note that his fictional Shipstone complex is modeled on GE -- which is my own favorite *bete noire* for reasons which I will explain sometime if you find the patience to listen.

The final implication is in the terms of the will left by "Boss." That is -- there is no hope for this world; the only hope is to find another world and start over. I have a gut feeling that this is realistic -- but I don't hope to find another world, so pending *Götterdämmerung,* I try to be a decent denizen of the world we've got -- a small positive number among the five billion humans extant.

”

Chapter 18

Letters to the Editor

"

[October 1988]

Mark Adams to Soapbox Editor
Seattle Post-Intelligencer
Seattle, Washington

I'm mad as hell and I'm not going to take it anymore. The Bush-Quayle campaign circus has gone one flag too far.

For months now, this faction of the Republican party -- dominated by a heartless Pentagon Plunderbund and kow-towing to a brainless Fundamentalist Jihad -- has been jamming the TV channels with the charge that anybody who is a Democrat and/or a liberal is unpatriotic, un-American, and a fool into the bargain -- wouldn't know what's good for the country without a Hollywood actor in the White House to tell them.

Of course I have been called dirty names before -- I am older than Ronald Reagan. Joe McCarthy and the John Birch Society called me these dirtiest of all dirty names for years. But then I just considered the source and laughed and let it pass. This time, however, the demagoging badmouth artist wants to be President of the United States and it's not funny anymore. I'm talking back.

The last straw was listening to this ambitious parrot recite his party line the other day and hearing him revising the history of World War II -- Russian style. I don't mean his moving Pearl Harbor Day up to September 7 so he could speechify about it before the election. That was just a silly goof he thought up all by himself. I mean his later derogatory remark about America's part in World War II noting "We were unprepared" -- implying that things would have been a lot better if Saint Ronnie and his Plunderbund cronies had been in charge instead of the Democratic liberal Franklin D. Roosevelt. That time Georgie was reading from his script.

"Unprepared"? Talk about blaming America for everything bad! It's true we were woefully short of ships after -- repeat, after -- Japan's first strike on Pearl Harbor. It may even be true that if Ronnie and his cronies in the Plunderbund had been in charge, they would have spent the years 1929-1939 building a replacement fleet in San Diego while they let the American economy and the American people go hang -- I wouldn't put it past them. But as a matter of fact -- and thank God -- they weren't. So let's take a look at the bottom lines of history, then and now.

As storm clouds gathered over Europe -- long before Pearl Harbor -- FDR began preparing (contrary to what George Bush implies). To do this he brushed aside old antagonisms right and left -- between mill owners and labor, price fixers and consumers, North and South, monopolists and trust busters -- under a regime you might describe as deregulation in reverse. This was hard lines for everybody, but also everybody gritted his teeth and hung in there -- for the team. Dollar-a-year men and career bureaucrats were set to working together. High tech plant superintendents and unskilled laborers, scientists and farmers -- all Americans were organized into a production miracle. If you want to know what real economic growth is like, recall that in four years American production grew 100 percent. That ultimately made all the difference.

This cost money, of course. Over the four years of war, the national debt increased as much as during any two years of Reagan-Bush peacetime. The new debt was financed by selling savings bonds at reasonable rates to plain Americans.

Meanwhile, for years on end there were over ten million of us in uniform. Personally, I was one of those in uniform. I wasn't drafted. In my mid-thirties with dependents, I was also in a draft-exempt job with a defense-related outfit, the OSS. But after Pearl Harbor I thought the best thing I could do for my country was out there in the combat zone, so I finagled accelerated transition into a Navy uniform.

In uniform I was not play-acting in heroic roles on a

Hollywood lot nor yet typing press releases for the Indiana National Guard; I sought and was granted sea duty -- eighteen months (eight campaigns) in combat operations with the fast carrier task force in the Pacific, two citations, return to reserve status when the war was over.

Pardon the personal digression. I am just trying to explain why I believe I have been a good American for 78 years and why I think the Bush-Quayle attempt to brand me as unpatriotic because for half a century I have also been a liberal and gladly supported liberal Presidents -- Roosevelt, Truman, Kennedy -- is not only a boldfaced lie but is also the cheapest sort of political demagoguery.

To get back to this matter of the bottom line. For Roosevelt, the bottom line is that despite Japan's fabulously successful first strike, Japan -- and Germany too -- lost the war. The terms: unconditional surrender.

And the bottom line for Reagan-Bush? It's hard to remember there was ever such a thing as surrender, conditional or otherwise. Huge blocks of American real estate and industrial machinery are in the hands of Japanese owners. Our national debt skyrockets: Two trillion? Somewhere around there; I haven't read today's paper and it's going up so fast yesterday's total is way off. And this new debt is financed in major part by foreign interests -- at loan shark rates set to attract Japanese investors. And that "American-made" car my wife and I bought this year turns out to have a Japanese-built engine -- it was just assembled in the U.S. by workers who had voluntarily taken wage cuts to hold on to those grunt work assembly line jobs. That unconditional surrender by a liberal-led America has slipped into a long-term national disaster, Reagan-Bush greasing the skids all the way with government subsidies for investors shipping American productive capacity overseas -- to Japan, Germany, Taiwan, Korea, Brazil, Mexico, you name it -- wherever cheaper labor can be found.

Of course there has to be a positive side. There is ... There is ... Ah, yes, the glorious conquest of Grenada -- a Caribbean island anybody can find on the map if he's got a real good magnifying glass. They tell me the Pentagon passed out seven thousand medals for service in that one.

And also there is ... Well, we've got to admit our two-trillion-dollar debt has bought our President opportunities to prove himself as a world class flag salutin' wizard. The center piece of his last campaign was that ceremony at Omaha Beach -- a peaceful and picturesque place these last forty years. There were facilities provided for the TV crews and a podium and microphones for the President. And for a backdrop the flags and chiefs of state of the entire Western European community were lined up. The chiefs of state didn't look very happy, but they all kept a straight face -- with the U.S. paying 65 percent of their defense costs for forty years, they damn well knew they better.

It was probably the greatest photo opportunity in history. And nobody can deny our President rose to the challenge.

And in this campaign George Bush is posing in a flag factory and proclaiming that he would have signed a bill to make the Pledge of Allegiance routine and compulsory even if he knew the bill was unconstitutional, thus proving (1) that he is truly eager to step into the old man's shoes; and (2) that when he laid his hand on the Bible and took the oath as Vice-President, swearing to "preserve, protect, and defend the Constitution of the United States," he had his fingers crossed; and (3) that liberals like me who think the one sure way to make the pledge meaningless for our children is to make it routine and compulsory -- in a class with brushing the teeth -- well, he says us liberals are unpatriotic, un-American, fools.

It's too bad, really. I have no more doubt about George Bush being at heart a good American than I have about myself. We served together in World War II; we both did our best. I don't doubt that today George Bush is at heart still the same decent, dedicated, intelligent patriot he was forty years ago when we served together. But in his race for President he's posturing through the faked photo opportunities and he's mouthing phrases put in his mouth by the Pentagon Plunderbund and the Fundamentalist Jihad -- by men who, from the standpoint of real patriotism aren't fit to polish his shoes -- and he's preaching that I and the American leaders I have most admired through a long life -- all of them liberals -- are unpatriotic and un-American.

If ever America should face a crisis under the leadership of a man weak enough to sell his own soul -- his own inner convictions, his integrity -- for the honorifics and perquisites of any office, even the highest office, God help this republic. Happily I cannot believe the American people will risk it happening now.

"

Over the years Mark wrote a number of letters to Western Washington newspapers. In 1991 he had a series of letters about what he called Great Depression II published in the "Voices of the Valley" column in the Skagit Valley Herald, *a daily paper in Mount Vernon, twenty miles from Oak Harbor. Here is one of these letters, featuring his fictitious "young friend Herman."*

"

September 18, 1991

Mark Adams to Voices of the Valley
Skagit Valley Herald
Mount Vernon, Washington

The other day a young friend of mine (he is only in his early fifties) asked if I thought the recession would be over by Christmas. I laughed.

"What's funny?" he demanded.

"Sorry," I said. "All euphemisms seem funny to me. And nowadays when our poobahs try to avoid unpleasant topics by referring to 'the R word,' or 'the recent (past tense) recession,' when the subject is actually our deepening depression, their use of the euphemisms seems funny to me. I was laughing at your use of the fashionable euphemism, certainly not at the somewhat tragic events now unfolding."

"Recession, depression ... What difference does it make? It's just words," he objected.

"It's just words," I agreed, "but it reflects a way of thinking. If you wake up some morning with a bit of fever and chest congestion and you think it's 'just a cold,' you're apt to take a couple of aspirins, go on to work, and wait for it to go away. If, in fact, the right word is 'pneumonia,' going on to work and waiting for it to go away can be a serious mistake. Right now calling our depression a recession and waiting for it to go away seems to me a serious mistake."

My young friend snorted. "You an expert on depressions?"

I hesitated. "I guess I'm sort of an expert on depressions like the old-timer on Fir Island is sort of an expert on floods," I replied. "That Fir Islander recalls some vivid experiences with floods. But on top of that, the odds are that after those experiences he has listened much more carefully than the average man when the specialists -- stream flow analysts, water control engineers, long-range weather forecasters, soil scientists, etc. -- discuss floods. So by now he's sort of a common sense expert on floods without any particular striving to become expert.

"My time of life made me an expert on depressions the same way that Fir Islander became expert on floods.

"I came of age just as the one still called the Great Depression was entering its serious stage. I remember the day in late October 1929, when my college economics prof called our attention to news of a stock market crash the previous day. At the time I shrugged it off. I had no wish to be an economics expert; I hankered to be a journalist.

"But the next few years, as summer jobs -- or any jobs -- got harder to find and hungry people took to the highways, it dawned on me that the professor had been trying to call my attention to something that affected me personally. That put me on the road to a sort of expertise on depressions like a Fir Islander's expertise on floods."

Sixty years of watching and listening later, I don't blush to think of myself as sort of an expert. And I don't hesitate to say we've got a depression on our hands and it would save us a lot of time and waste motion if we faced up to it.

"Expert? Depression? Hah!" my friend snorted. And he walked out, leaving me with the check for the coffees.

"

After the election of Bill Clinton as president in 1992, Mark wrote another "Herman" letter, this time to the Soapbox Editor of the Seattle P-I.

"

February 12, 1993

Mark Adams to Soapbox Editor
Seattle P-I
Seattle, Washington

About a year ago, speaking from the perspective of my 82 years, I wrote a Letter to the Editor of the *P-I* (Jan. 23, 1992) in which I noted analogies between the Great Depression of 1929-41 and the Great Depression of 1989-??. Specifically I noted Herbert Hoover's refusal to recognize that a deep crisis existed in 1932 ("Prosperity is just around the corner," he said) and George Bush's analogous "upturn in the next quarter" in 1992. I suggested Bush, like Hoover, might consequently lose his bid for reelection.

A few days ago, at a coffee clatch with my young friend Herman (he just turned 60 and has no memories of the Great Depression whatever), I took advantage of his euphoria about the inauguration to hand him a copy of that year-ago letter -- thinking to brag about my prowess as a prophet.

As he scanned the letter, Herman seemed inclined to concede me a passing grade in Prophecy 101 until that final paragraph (looking beyond the election) where I said:

"Hoover's successor, Franklin D. Roosevelt, began remedial work at once. And shortly the economy improved to what hospital spokesmen call 'a stable condition.' Effective recovery, however, took another decade, capped by the intense, unified effort accompanying World War II ... I hope this time we may again find a way out within a reasonable time -- say, a decade."

At that point Herman balked. "Ten years!" he protested. "You seem to be saying Clinton can't turn this around in two terms, much less one. Give him a chance!"

"I am not underrating Clinton," I said. "I think Roosevelt did a great job. But the situation he faced was grim. And it was early in his third term before turnaround was effective. Some of the situations facing Clinton are grimmer."

"Grimmer? Like what?" Herman scoffed.

"Like our public and private debt," I suggested. "Events already force Clinton to postpone an attack on that one."

Herman grunted surlily. "I know it's unfair to saddle those debts on our grandchildren in 2010, but what's that got to do with depression in 1993?"

"Everything," I argued. "That record million bankruptcies filed in 1992 were not filed by your grandchildren. Ten years ago 62 percent of the disposable income of Americans went for debt payments, and the 38 percent left was not enough to cover day-to-day expenses with a margin for savings. Our savings rate began shrinking.

"Right now 83 percent of the disposable incomes of Americans is committed in advance to debt payment -- the house payment, the bank loan payment, the car payment, the credit card payment, the charge account payments, the appliance payments, not to mention the tax payments on local, state and national bond issues. And the 17 percent of consumer incomes that's left after debt payments won't even cover groceries, gasoline and clothing.

"So for a dozen years past, we have tided over by borrowing on the credit card or borrowing against our equity in the house, or in some other way going deeper into debt. Uncle Sam and most of his chillun are like a bunch of alcoholics taking one more shot to steady us to another meeting of AA -- or on saner second thought, to the bankruptcy court. In the latter case we're wiped out instanter; and our creditors take a deadly shellacking right along with us. You may have heard about the wholesale collapse of S&Ls and the shaky position of American banks engineered by Reagan-Bush deregulated lenders."

"That was scandalous," Herman conceded. "Those thieving bankers ought to be punished."

"Maybe," I agreed. "But your use of the term 'thieving' is unfair. Those S&Ls didn't collapse because the managers stole money out of the vaults. Most of them failed because people who borrowed despite those horrendous interest rates simply couldn't make the resulting loan payments. The depositors' money was gone just as surely as if the money had been stolen; but the process was largely one of deregulated greed and stupidity, not greed and thievery."

Herman eyed me with an expression akin to horror. "To hear you tell it," he said, "we're already in a crisis -- depression -- over our heads in debt and going deeper by the hour. You see no hope for Clinton and for us?"

"Where there's life, there's hope -- and he and we aren't nearly dead yet," I assured Herman. "This particular problem -- just one of many we face -- is multiplex and enormous, but it is soluble. Of course solutions will require re-regulation of massive economic combines which can -- and probably will -- fight a series of delaying actions that could stretch out over many years.

"Just consider the size of the problem. The federal debt alone is well over $4 trillion, on which we are paying around 7 percent interest, and private debts are $20 trillion-plus on which we are paying over 10 percent ..."

"Wait a minute," Herman objected. "Clinton doesn't have to worry about private debts; he only has to worry about $4 trillion, not $24 trillion."

"Wrong," I countered. "He is taking office in 1993, God help him, as President of the United States, responsible for and answerable to all Americans -- not just CEO of the federal government."

"Actually, the big thing Clinton has going for him is that he seems to know what he's responsible for and who he is answerable to. He talks about revitalizing the economy (not just the government). And he is obviously going that extra mile to stay in touch with the people.

"To do the job at all, he's going to need, somehow, sometime, cooperation among all the diverse groups of Americans -- rural and urban, rich and poor, management and labor, banker and builder -- of the sort Roosevelt organized after Hitler attacked.

"But there is hope. When I say I hope we can pull out in 10 years, I am not using the word 'hope' idly. Let's wish him luck."

At that point I realized I had fallen to orating, because Herman got up and walked off, leaving me with the check for the coffees.

"

Chapter 19

Texas Testament

Beginning in the late 1950s and continuing into the 1990s, Mark worked on a book for his grandchildren which he called Texas Testament. *He never finished it. Here are some excerpts:*

"

Dear Young Ones:

As I sit down to write this *Testament,* I ponder the eternal question: Why should I presume to speak to you?

Am I trying to reach a hand across that much discussed generation gap with intent to grasp you and bend you to my will? To lay an obligation on you to listen to grandpa and do what he says? Am I presuming that because I will shortly do a simple thing no man yet has failed to manage somehow, I merit authority over you?

If I seem to, some demon from my subconscious is sneaking one past me. What I hope I am doing is something else entirely.

What I intend is more like a chat with the oncoming shift at a job that will be the same for you as it has been for me -- and was for our ancestors for a thousand generations back. I certainly intend no version of "down from above," or "master to apprentice," or even "veteran to neophyte" in the *Testament* which is to follow.

A Change of Shifts

I think of you and me as being shift workers with the same job -- just on different shifts. And our shifts overlap enough for us to swap notes and chat a bit before you take over the controls. The job itself has continuity.

You see, I don't buy this "generation gap" idea. Of course the swing shift and the day shift aren't the same people; but there is no "gap" between -- our shifts bring us together for changeovers. And the job will be the same for you as it has been for me -- the same job it's always been.

The job -- long mine and now yours -- is simply that of survival: of living and if possible sustaining a life worth living for ourselves and for the human race -- our kin, our kind.

Some Carryover Problems

Since I worked on the shift that's going off duty, I may be able to warn you about some problems that my shift muffed and then just set aside and left for your shift to sweat over -- it seems only fair that I should.

There are several such problems, and warning No. 1 is that your shift has *got to* do better than mine did. Because problems that were only urgent back when we muffed them have become critical, life-or-death problems for your shift. The pace of history itself is accelerating -- and a whole range of problems is affected by that compression of the time factor.

The nuclear bomb problem is only one of those my shift is leaving for your shift to clean up: we tend to think of it first because it's as noticeable as a 45 automatic pressed into the small of our back. But there are others just as deadly though less easy to identify -- more like a cancer node in the lungs: possible to ignore today, but lethal tomorrow.

There's the problem of a human population explosion. Overall the U.S. population is growing rapidly, both by natural increase and immigration. And in some other areas of the world, like Mexico, next door to Texas, for instance, populations are growing at astounding rates now, year by year and generation after generation. And that means that human demands on earth's environments -- accelerated by rising standards of living -- are growing at dangerous rates.

Just one statistic to suggest the urgency of the problem: From the beginning of time to the date of my birth -- a period of billions and billions of years -- the human population of earth grew to about one billion, seven-fifty million; but *during my lifetime* the human population of earth has reached well over five billion -- it has more than tripled! Meanwhile, this same earth has grown no bigger at all. So now food, materials, energy -- and even breathable air -- approach critical depletion.

Progress in medical and production technologies enabled my shift to win its sustenance from earth throughout this era of mushrooming populations. Medical science helps us survive that first year -- which claimed the lives of awesome numbers of infants in the eras before medicine was revolutionized by science -- and it extends life spans of the elderly. But progress in other technologies compensates somewhat for the added burdens laid on earth's resources by fostering productivity in other spheres: Irrigation can make an acre of desert produce several times as much food as an acre of naturally humid land. After my own children -- your parents -- were born, a "green revolution" was much in the news world-wide. "Green revolution" was a catch phrase for extension of scientific agricultural techniques in hungry regions.

There are limits to our ability to make such expansions of resources by advances in production technology. And your shift, needing so desperately to defend itself against threats of resource poverty, needs to examine some of the restraints on technical progress -- an antiquated patent system, industrial and national secrecy which slow the progress of technology in the interest of corporate and national short-term competitive advantage.

On industrial technology our generation goofed. We let our patent system be used by sub-government groups called corporations for power plays that fenced technologies inside their own domains (which were often multi-national in scope). And when they fenced in a technology, what they fenced out was the rest of the human race, however dire humanity's need. Some system that rewards inventors with something better than monopoly power assignable to businessmen seems logical -- necessary for your crisis-inheriting shift.

And there is a related problem of maldistribution that slows production.

No house is built for a homeless or ill-housed family that simply cannot afford to buy or rent a home because of inadequate income. Every needed house that remains unbuilt means idled loggers, architects, materials suppliers, building tradesmen -- carpenters, plumbers, bricklayers -- and appliance suppliers. And the production potential of an unemployed man cannot be warehoused for future use; every day's useful work lost is gone forever.

Thus all unemployment and pinched wage scales and correlative educational shortages in any segment of the population are brakes on the productive potential of all other segments of our population.

All these problems my shift passes along to yours. No one of these problems is insoluble; but my generation, for whatever reason, muffed them.

The Bomb Crisis in a Shrinking World

My shift knew the answer to the nuclear bomb problem about two minutes after the first one fell on Hiroshima -- before most of you were born -- to-wit: Don't drop it again. Not ever.

And truly, since that second demonstration at Nagasaki a few days later, we haven't dropped another one. But we have just been holding the bomb in our hands and standing first on one foot then the other ... carefully, because we have at least had sense enough to be scared out of our wits ... for sixty years -- sixty long, uneasy, frustrating years ... Carefully -- oh, so very carefully ... but awkwardly ... and getting tired, tired ... Always uneasily wondering when -- not if, just when -- somebody would get agitated enough to slip -- to drop the damn thing.

You see, our answer to the atomic bomb problem has been sort of like the castor-oil cure for a cough. Taking castor oil doesn't do anything about that tickling in the throat, but you know damn well you don't dare cough. And the trouble with this "don't dare" solution to our problem is that sometime, somewhere, somebody's reflexes are going to override his better judgment -- just once, that is all it takes.

You think nobody's that stupid? Remember that story from the Vietnam War -- the one about the commander who explained, "The only way to save that village is to destroy it"? That commander wasn't trying to make a sick joke like Lenny

Bruce. And he was not born stupid or even wicked. He was just trying to do a good job, the way he understood it. His motivation was true-blue loyalty to his craft and his kind. He was honestly convinced the only way to save that village was to destroy it.

And if he has the means and the power to do it, someday, somewhere, some well-meaning, patriotic, true-blue, thoroughly trained bastard is going to see that the only way to keep the human race from going to hell is to drop the bomb and send it there.

For all our well-advised caution, unless we do something about that tickle in our throat, somebody is going to write "finis" to you and the rest of the human race. It gives me cold chills to think about it, much less write it, but I have no doubt that for your shift, "You only go around once" is going to be modified to read, "You only go around half a turn," *unless* the atomic bomb is set back on a shelf out of reach of well-trained, noble, patriotic bastards -- ours as well as everybody else's.

Slapping the nuclear bomb away on a shelf and locking it in there is the only practical answer, of course. And that job is one my shift has fumbled completely -- and is leaving for you.

Of course most of the human race has known all along where that tickle in the throat is centered -- it's in the councils of the major nations of the earth where a sensitive tissue called national consciousness can set aggressiveness in motion on a big enough scale to call for A-bombs.

This is just a technical fact. An atomic bomb is not a practical weapon for a hoodlum wanting to hold up the convenience store on the corner -- or local police seeking to protect that store. The atomic bomb is not a practical way to establish "law and order" of any type -- or of subverting same. It is by its nature a weapon to protect the national sovereignty of a very large nation vis-à-vis another large nation. It has no other possible use.

So national sovereignty must be restricted, superseded to this extent in any world where nuclear weapons exist. And in our world they exist. All over the place. It's too late to think that they don't exist.

And of course ICBMs shrink the distances over which new weapons may be brought to bear.

In World War II the English Channel -- which is less than thirty miles across at several points -- was a critical barrier for opposing forces. The *blitzkrieg* was halted by the Channel. The Wehrmacht gave up trying to cross it, and they lost the war. A few frenzied years later the mass might of our alliance did cross the Channel (at great cost) and won the war.

With ICBMs, the Atlantic and Pacific oceans on either side of America are no barrier at all.

We all live on a shrunken globe. There is no escape.

The answer has to be a United Nations with sole possession of such war-making powers. No man of any nation can live at ease until we have a world federation with operational control of all large-scale armaments -- and enough control of other channels of interaction among nations to keep one of them from trying to advance its national purpose -- a noble or wicked purpose, it doesn't in the slightest matter which -- vis-à-vis some other nation by war.

Relegating the A-bomb to innocuous storage -- or, to state the same problem in positive terms, establishing a viable Union of Nations to limit national sovereignties everywhere -- is one of the biggest problems ever faced. And my shift muffed it.

Knowing Earlier Shifts May Help You Cope

This root problem your shift must solve is not a new problem. It is just on a larger scale and more critical -- by several orders of magnitude -- than it has ever been before.

As a world we face the same problem the American Colonies faced a couple of hundred years ago, when they emerged from the Revolutionary War as sovereign states. The Founders managed to form a Union of Colonies before disastrous wars -- between Virginia and Massachusetts, shall we say? -- erupted. It was not easy for them but they did it.

And herein is a hint for your shift -- too late for mine. You can go back and see how they did it. In the *Federalist Papers* (written by them at that time) you will find some of the best arguments pro and con that guided the Constitutional Convention -- the one that made the thirteen separate Colonies into the United States. The bottom line is that the Founding Fathers solved a problem very much like this one that has been left for you. Your problem is not insoluble.

Your problem is more difficult than theirs. But you have better means of communication for the "Federalist Papers" of your generation, worldwide. And your motivation is stronger, too. If they had failed, the result would only have been tragic for a fragment of humanity in one corner of the world. If you fail, it will be irreversible disaster for all humanity and all the earth.

And so it is, also, about the flow of technology and science in our time -- old problem, new urgency.

It's Your Job Now

Some wiseacre once remarked that "Experience is the best teacher." Then along came a cynic and said, "Experience is the *only* teacher that really teaches." That cynic thinks humanity will never learn how to cope with being wiped out until after it's been wiped out a couple of times. Hopeless.

I don't quite go all the way with that cynic. I agree that experience is the best teacher. Maybe the only good teacher. But I don't arrive at his hopeless conclusion because I remember there is such a thing as vicarious experience.

When I was a barefoot boy, I avoided getting a lot of grassburrs in my feet by noticing when some kid ahead of me came limping out of a patch of grass -- and then just avoiding that particular patch of grass. I was learning from experience -- but his experience, not mine.

And just maybe you can avoid some lethal grassburrs by seeing how my shift goofed, and taking a better route.

"

Epilogue

Thoughts on Death

Mark wrote the following poem aboard H.M.S. Illustrious *during a Kamikaze attack off Sakishima Gunto in 1945. He was thirty-five years old.*

A Pagan's Prayer Before Battle

Lady Luck, once more befriend
A pagan awaiting the empty end ...

THE SITUATION

About me I hear the initial rattle
Of partisan metals joining battle --
Radar sees; a gun mount sings
Response to death on streamered wings
While -- obsolete flesh and blood -- I wait
To learn the random choice of fate.
(Though with this role alone entrusted
I'm occupationally maladjusted,
For I yearn to be, I hold my breath--
An animal needs to run from death.)

THEORY OF JURISDICTION AND PLEADING

Lady Luck, I implore, befriend
This pagan awaiting an empty end ...
(For once the mechanical contact's made
No human strength can lend me aid.
Nor are demons here, nor living gods ...
Just the math of calculated odds --
Wherefore I address my pleas at large
To you as the arbiter left in charge.)
Though odds be ... Well, I know the score,
But leave me living one time more.

ESCALATION INTO INVOCATION AND PRAYER

Goddess of Chance, I pray: Befriend
This pagan awaiting a sudden end ...
(I know you're just an empty game
Crystallized into a name,
But, mindless with need, I'll say a prayer
To a symbol of something that isn't there...
So don you flesh and skirt and bodice,
Ascend a throne and be my goddess;
Beyond this shuddering drum of steel,
Be thou living, be thou real,
Then lend an anthropomorphic ear
To a human hunger ringed with fear...)
Fiction, figment, rock of my belief,
Grant my trembling gut relief;
Blind one, look about the earth
And find in me a special worth;
Indifferent, care! distinguish me
And fend this fate the caring flee;
Above the thunder in sea and air,
Deaf one, hear my silent prayer:
Goddess of Chance, thy law forego
And change for me the odds I know.
Set me ashore so once again
I'll feel the lusts of living men.

SUDDEN MOTION FOR CHANGE OF VENUE

(I say my prayers to deafer than stone
And here it comes ...
I stand alone.
My heart hammers; my feet are cold;
I've a tic in my belly...)
Adrenalin, take hold!
Idiot-lover,
Take over,
Take over!

"

Nov. 24, 1994

Mark Adams to Dr. Ezatolah Rezvani
Anacortes, Washington

I find no convincing proof that an after-life exists, so I do not believe. On the other hand, I am unable to think of any proof that such an after-life does *not* exist -- proving a negative is a near-impossibility. I wind up simply evading the question.

Like all other human beings, of course, I have, since birth, had to find some adjustment to the prospect of inevitable death -- preferably more rational than simply refusing to think about it. In youth I found a particular need for a rationale of adjustment because the circumstances of my life at that time convinced me that I was destined to die young and violently. In the event, that foreboding proved unjustified -- here I am in mid-eighties. However, the rationale I accepted about seventy years ago still serves me adequately. Expressing my rationale more briefly and clearly than I can are these quotes from the English poet, Walter Savage Landor.

1. *Leaf after leaf drops off, flower after flower,*
Some in the chill, some in the warmer hour;
Alive they flourish, and alive they fall,
And Earth who nourished them receives them all.
Should we, her wiser sons, be less content
To sink into her lap when life is spent?

2. [written in his eighties, I believe]
I strove with none; for none was worth my strife.
Nature I loved and, next to Nature, Art!
I warmed both hands before the fire of life;
It sinks, and I am ready to depart.

"

Mark Adams died at the age of 86 on January 18, 1997, at Whidbey General Hospital in Coupeville, Whidbey Island, Washington.

He is survived by his wife, Ann; his first wife, Willena Casey Yane; their two daughters, Saskia Scoggins and Kathleen West; eight grandchildren; four great-grandchildren; and this book.

At Grand Canyon, May 16, 1996

INDEX